To Wrestle Chimpanzee?

Humans Wrestle Apes At Fair In Warrenton

Ape Show Highlights Fair Opening

Gorilla Act Featured at County Fair

NEWS-MESSENGER HAMLET, N.C. 10-2-59

One of the feature attractions at the Richmond County Agricultural Fair this week is an animal act featuring the only touring gorillas in the United States.

Mr. and Mrs. Robert Noell, owners and trainers of these animals, have on hand also a chimpanzees, one mandril, two constrictor type a variety of birds

The coupl' business f and bot' hit th traj'

Show Features Gorilla At VFW Lot This Week

In sters, years o. Noells the three-year-old. The pair cost $6,000 and were African animal imp are natives of Span Topsy and Tommy are cial exhibit every night fair.

• • • •

IN ANOTHER UNIT, fairgoers will have a chance to test their physical skill against the apes. They can box with Joe, wrestle with Butch or Kongo, or run with Bamboo.

Mrs. Noell reports that illas — the prese our other

Noell's Ark Gorilla Show which is appearing this week at the VFW lot in Troy, boasts three species of Anthropoid Apes of Folly Beach, which is the largest animal in the collection, is a Gorilla (shown above in November. He was purchased at a cost of $5,000. At that time the animal weigh- Admission ed a tiny 13 pounds and was said night is raised in the Noell trailer — hav. 5 and to be eight months of age. He was a ' a Le a special cage, instead of a play pen. "As he grew," he continued sit- Mrs. Noell ting on our laps" he is in th says, "and now that he proba- 300-pound class, he thinks we are shrinking! inks Noell also carry rare Borneo also pets old

Bob Noell and his Noell's Ark Ape Show will pack them in at the Roanoke Fair this week, if Noell's experience in North Carolina this summer is duplicated in Roanoke.

The fair opens at Victory Stadium at 6 p.m. today.

The Ape Show is one of the attractions traveling with Green's Fun Fair works this way:

At the end of a trailer truck that doubles as a transport and fighting arena there's a big sign, "Gorilla Show."

Under that is a smaller notice:

"Wanted: Athletic men to earn $5 per second ($20 limit) by holding ape's shoulders on the floor. If you don't throw him, you get $5 to try."

Noell, so far has had no trouble in finding young men willing to step into the ring with his "ape," which is neither a gorilla nor an orangutan, but a chimpanzee.

The human challenger is outfitted in an old-style leather football helmet, and can either wrestle or box the chimp.

Noell says no challengers have ever been hurt badly — scratches, bruise its is all —. nan

Ape Show In King This Week

Noell's Ark Gorilla Show is in King this week. The show is located on the Tobaccoville Road at Jefferson Church Road, near new 52. The show carries eleven great apes which are publicly displayed from time to time, according to the manager of the show. A small carnival is also connected with the show.

Gorillas in the collection are 600 lb. "Tommy", an adult male, bought in Nov. of 1957 - a 250 lb. female, "Tarpie", bought in Sept. of 1965, and 55 lb. "Otto" a young male acquired in April of 1971. Gorillas are on the endangered species list, and number fewer than 10,000 individuals left on earth. When any wild animal numbers so few, they are very close to extinction. Recently, zoos have been having remarkably good success with captive-breeding.

Even more serious is the plight of the Orangutan. There are (according to the U.S. Customs inspector at Atlanta, Ga.) fewer than two thousand individuals now extant. Breeding of Orangs in captivity has been so successful that all but about 200 Orangs are in captivity.

Noell's Ark is quite proud of the Adult pair who have presented the Noells with a lovely little "Girlorang" who was named "Jewel," (age 3).

Chimpanzees are the clowns of the Ape Realm, and the Noells have a lovely pair of four year old Fraternal twins, "Pete" and "Donna" for display.

The "working animals" are chimps, also. And they star in orthodox Boxing or wrestling matches with people who volunteer out of Audience.

This show has been at the King Fair several times.

The male Gorilla is still me and still likes to play ith his trainer, but due to his reat weight, these games nave been discontinued, for fear of damage to the trainer. However, he will be on display from time to time.

She Can Understand The Apes' Language

By RALPH SUMNER
Tribune Staff Writer

TARPON SPRINGS — Mrs. Mae Noell says she has learned the "call of the wild."

Owner of more than $50,000 worth of apes, she is trying to understand their "language." And she carries on conversation with them.

"All my life I've admired and envied people who could speak several languages," she said. "But I'd never thought of my talking to the apes in the same light."

"I didn't realize until now that it would interest anyone that I can speak the languages of my animal friends."

and even a baby orangutan

Mrs. Mae Noell

TAMPA TRIBUNE

1960

...eumonia when cooperate. a single sour years Finally, S an display from time to time.

From one performer to
another:

To Ron Dentinger

Sincere best wishes

From

Mae Noell

Gorilla Show

Book and Jacket designed by the Author.
Frontispiece and Jacket Drawing
By Jay H. Matternes

Edited By
DAVID K. HIMBER

Printed in the United States of America
BY DANIELS PUBLISHING CO., INC.
1209 29th Street
Orlando, Florida 32805

Published By "Mae" Noell-D.B.A.
NOELL'S ARK PUBLISHER
Tarpon Springs, Fla.

1979

Dedicated

To My Entire Family

both

Human and Animal

"All we needed was a cow pasture big enough for the crowds," Bob Noell

The History Of

NOELL'S ARK
GORILLA SHOW

The Funniest Show on Earth
Which Featured
THE "WORLDS ONLY ATHLETIC APES"

Written By
ANNA MAE NOELL

Edited By
DAVID K. HIMBER

"From Cow Pastures to Big Cities," Joe Deddo

JAY MATTERNES

It is a distinct honor to have been the happy recipient of the exquisite work of art that is the frontispiece. facing this page. This beautiful drawing was done especially for the readers of this book. It shows Kongo in a wrestling match with a contestant.

The artist who did this fantastically life-like drawing has been classed by authorities as "the foremost muralist at work today," and as "The Audubon of the prehistoric animal." We are humbly grateful to be numbered among his friends. His name is Jay H. Matternes.

Thanks Jay!

Sincerely
Mae Noell

MATTERNES ©

To Bob & Mae, with many happy
memories. Jay & Del

The Monkey's Viewpoint
on Evolution

Three monkeys sat in a coconut tree
Discussing things as they're said to be.
Said one to the others, "Now listen, you
   two,
There's a certain rumor that can't be
   true;
That man descended from our noble
   race!
Why, the very idea is a dire disgrace!
No monkey ever deserted his wife
Starved his babies and ruined their life!
And you've never known a mother monk
To leave her babies with others to bunk
Or to shove them around from one to
   another
Till they scarcely know who IS their
   mother!
Another thing, you'll never see
A monk build a fence' round a coconut
   tree
Forbidding all other monks a taste
And letting the coconuts go to waste.
Why, if I built a fence around this tree
Starvation would force you to steal from
   me!
Another thing a monk won't do
Is go out at night and hang on a
   "stew,"
Or use a gun, or club, or knife
To take some other monkey's life.
Yes -- Man descended, the ornery cuss
But, brothers, he never descended from
   US!"

Anon Y. Mous '

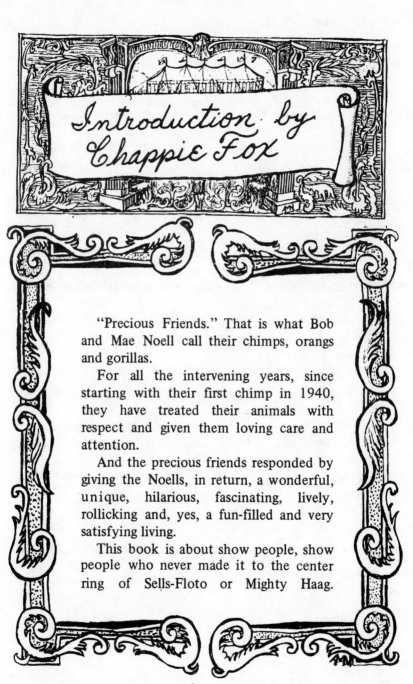

Introduction by Chappie Fox

"Precious Friends." That is what Bob and Mae Noell call their chimps, orangs and gorillas.

For all the intervening years, since starting with their first chimp in 1940, they have treated their animals with respect and given them loving care and attention.

And the precious friends responded by giving the Noells, in return, a wonderful, unique, hilarious, fascinating, lively, rollicking and, yes, a fun-filled and very satisfying living.

This book is about show people, show people who never made it to the center ring of Sells-Floto or Mighty Haag.

Strobridge in Cincinnati never lithographed any three sheets of their act. They never had an advance brigade. They never carried baggage stock.

In spite of these apparent drawbacks they made it big in towns like Gum Neck, North Carolina and Sign Rock, Virginia.

Where Bob and Mae played they did not need Madison Square Garden for a spring opening – the townspeople welcomed them with open arms – they were expected and enjoyed annually.

This book is the story of "Noell's Ark" and "the World's Only Athletic Apes."

It is typical of the many varieties of small, intriguing shows that played country fairs and travelled the back roads to the small towns. These shows were loved by the towners and were looked for each year.

For the first time, Mae Noell tells the story of one of the most unique, astonishing and wondrous shows that ever hit the road.

Many are the books published on the Circus, Rep Shows, Minstrel Shows, Chatauquas. You have read about Wild West Shows, Stereoptican Shows, Magic Shows and Medicine Shows. There were numerous Dog and Pony Shows written up. However, the one and only "Noell's Ark" with their "World's Only Athletic Apes" made its own mark in the show world – and Mae Noell records all of its aspects here in a heart-warming, lively and poignant story.

C. P. "Chappie" Fox
Winter Haven, Florida
(Circus Historian)

To my dear friends,

Thanks!

It is wonderful to have good friends, and I realize I have been abundantly blessed with friends when I hold a copy of this book in my hands. Without the help and prodding of friends, this book would never have been written. Take, for instance, my very good friend and teacher, Prof. David K. Himber. I studied English under him at the Tarpon Springs Campus of the St. Petersburg Junior College, at the time I explained that I wanted to write this book.

I thoroughly enjoyed working under Prof. Himber and got good marks. However, I procrastinated for several years after and the book fell by the wayside. Recently Prof. Himber came to our zoo and asked how I was doing with my book. When I admitted I had done nothing he "hit the ceiling." After a few minutes of persuasion he said, "If you will write the book, I will edit it for you!" How could I pass up such a wonderful offer? See what I mean about **friends**?

Then I called our local Tarpon Springs Library to let my friends there know that I needed a typist. They put me in touch with my new friend, Margo Lagemann--whom I feel I've known for a lifetime. She has been my **prod**. When I get slack she "pushes me on" -- something I really needed to get this job done! And what a patient lady she is! She has typed this manuscript several times, from scraps of paper, notebooks and file cards. She has organized and reorganized, and made priceless suggestions until it was a temptation to say "By Mae Noell and Margo Lagemann" on the title page!

To name some others to whom I am indebted, I must mention:

Our circus historian friend, Chappie Fox, who wrote the introduction to this book, and circus fan Jack Slagle, who has helped in other ways, as well as authors Joe McKennon and Brooks McNamara who gave valuable advice about publishing a book;

Our newspaper reporter friends, Lorayne Carlson, Bob Talbert, Roy Thompson, Fran Fry, Jr., Bayne Freeland, Malcolm MacPherson and Fran Brush among others;

Our very special friend -- the artist Jay Matternes who did the fantabulous frontispiece especially for this book;

Our good friend, the prolific author, Ms. Emily Hahn;

Our radio-announcer friend Charlie Moore, and T.V. friend Don Riggs;

The photographer friends Norman Zeisloft, Flash Jarocki, Bob Weiskopf and Dave Underwood -- among others;

The Editors of **Argosy** and **Newsweek** magazines and Editors of the **Atlanta Journal-Constitution**, Atlanta, Georgia; **The State** in Columbia, South Carolina, all of whom gave their gracious permission to use the stories in chapter four.

And of course, sincere appreciation simply must be expressed for the priceless help we have received (in caring for our animal friends) from Dr. Orrin L. Ebersold, Dr. Norm J. Pinfold, Dr. U.S. Seal, and Dr. Lee Simmons as well as our friend Frank M. Thompson who was so concerned for Otto's welfare.

And "just plain friends" like Miss Lillie Holdren, Alice Lambert, and the many many male "ape-fighters" who showed good sportsmanship -- and of course, my special friends, Margo Lagemann and Dave Himber. And I know there are others I can't think of now who have contributed their expertise to make this book worthwhile to my readers. (I hope they will forgive me for not naming them all here.)

How **do** you say "Thank you!" to such wonderful human beings? God bless them every one.

Mae Noell

Preface

I love the great apes as a doting mother loves her children, so it is gratifying to me to see the progress science has made, and is making, in understanding the mental abilities of these, our distant "cousins." Many things just being discovered about apes are things we were fully aware of back in the early forties. Our chimps did some remarkably intelligent things, and we had to stop telling friends and relatives about them because we were ridiculed and were afraid they might send the "man in the white coat" to get us. There were not many chimps around at that time and the few people who had chimps told us that they, too, found it impossible to convince people that they were telling the truth about the things their chimps contrived to do.

Recent scientific studies have vindicated us to a great extent, because it has been proved that the mental and physical make-up of the great apes is more closely related to that of man than had been believed in the recent past. Human blood and the blood of some of the apes is so very similar that it is extremely difficult to distinguish one from the other. The great ape has exactly the same number and kind of bones in his skeleton as does the skeleton of a human, and there seem to be no communicable diseases that cannot be transferred from one to the other -- in either direction!

Some of the stories I have related in this book will serve to offer some very strong proof that the great apes can and do think in much the same way as we, the "highest of the order of primates", think and solve problems and definitely **do** dream as we do, among the many other things that we think of as being strictly humanoid.

Another thing that pleases me is the debunking of the myths and horror tales perpetuated by Paul du Chaillu in his book, **"In Darkest Africa."** He was the one who retold the imaginative fables told to him by the natives. An eager and ignorant world was waiting for anything sensational they could retell about the explorers' experiences in Africa. So the gorilla and chimp were maligned with such atrocious stories as the ones in which they were supposed to sit on tree limbs over paths to grab the unwary native passing beneath and strangle him with their finger-like toes. Or the one about the big bull gorillas kidnapping the native women for ulterior motives. Some of these goofy stories persist even until today, as told by some ignorant people!

About the worst that could have been said -- **truthfully** -- would have been something about the apes' great love of bananas and the terrible destruction they can and do cause on a banana plantation. Many a gorilla family has been slaughtered and eaten for their part in such a foray. For eons gorillas and chimps (as well as orangutans) have been fair game for hunters in search of food and if the apes could tell **their** side of it, the horror stories would not have to be fabrications of anyone's imagination. The bare-faced facts of the cruelty of the slaughter should (and often does) make modern man cry, "for shame" upon the human race.

The late Phil Carroll (who brought gorillas from Africa in partnership with the late Henry Trefflich) gave me photographs of gorilla skulls he had collected from the "barbecue piles" in the woods. He was an angry man. He photographed the skulls along with a sign that berated the French law that prevented exportation to zoos, but which did nothing to stop the wanton slaughter of the animals by natives who ate them, or killed them "for fun." He told us he found twenty-five skulls in ninety-eight kilometers of travel through the forest! (See photo album section - this book).

What a horrible thought! At the rate they are going in that place, gorillas will be extinct in almost no time. I believe Robert M. Yerkes may have overestimated when he said they would be extinct in another hundred years. Sadly, it could be much sooner. (**Gorilla Census and Study** by R. M. Yerkes--1950).

We are fortunate to have had gutsy, dedicated young people like George Schaller, Dian Fossey, Jane Goodall, and Barbara Harrison who have lived in the woods to study and make reports on the behavior of the gorilla, chimp and orangutan. A wonderful book was done by Schaller, titled **The Year of the Gorilla**. I have lived in close contact with captive gorillas since 1950 and found Schaller's book to be one of the best things I've ever read about any animals. Jane Goodall's books on the chimps, **My Friends the Wild Chimpanzees**, and **In the Shadow of Man** are fact-packed and interesting. I have drawn a few comparisons from these people in this book. They are studying the animals scientifically in their native habitat, while we have lived with captive animals and watched as fascinated laymen when they demonstrated their mental prowess to us. The comparisons should prove interesting and of some value to people concerned with this type of study.

When people ask me -- as so very many of them do -- "What's the difference between an ape and a monkey?" or worse -- "What's the difference between an ape and a gorilla?" -- I answer with a question: "What's the difference between a dog and a Great Dane?" Then I go on to explain that the word ape covers a large family, the same way the word dog does; the Chihuahua and the Great Dane are both members of the dog family, and the gorilla, orangutan and chimp are members of the anthropoid ape family, and any monkey without a tail is an ape. Well-read people already know these things, but I am repeatedly surprised at how many people still ask this kind of question.

Still more ludicrous was the way people in the forties who had never heard of a chimp -- much less seen one -- would garble the word "chimpanzee." They were "chimpaneze," "chipmonks," and "varmints" to most people. A lot of people even refused to try to say "chimpanzee" and opted for "gorilla," which seemed easier for them to say. So we finally yielded, in exasperation, and called our little aggregation, "The Gorilla Show," as early as the late forties, (not to mislead anyone -- but only because it was easier to say). It's interesting to note that today the word "chimpanzee" is used easily and properly, even by first-graders who have seen so many chimps on television.

Because ours was a popular outdoor show that played the same territory for thirty-one years, it became a legend in its day. After we are gone there will -- no doubt -- be a lot of wild stories about the show concocted by over-fertile imaginations. It is mostly for the purpose of forestalling just such outlandish make-believe that has already been written by careless or unscrupulous "authors" that I have written this, the history of Noell's Ark Gorilla Show. After all, we were pretty proud of our reputation and the best way to "tell it like it was" turns out to be to tell it ourselves.

TABLE OF CONTENTS

Chapter One

Mardi Gras in New Orleans! We had looked forward to this day and now it had finally arrived! It dawned clear and cold, but this didn't hold us back. We were going to spend the entire day – maybe 'way into the night, in the city. Our two children -- Bobby, six, and "Sister," not quite two years old – my husband, Bob and I, all put on warm clothing and off we went. Little did we dream that this was to be one of the last trips the family would ever make, as a group. If anyone had told us this we'd never have believed it.

We didn't go in costume – it was enough fun to watch the merrymakers. And there were so very many of them! And a memorable day it turned out to be. We watched REX "come in" and then went to see King Zulu come in on his magnificent barge. We joined the throngs on the sidewalk and heard the kids yelling, happily, "Hey, Mister! Throw me a coconut." We were amused to see that some of the men actually did pass out coconuts to the kids, who eagerly grabbed them, punched holes to drink the milk and then cracked them open to munch on the meat.

We wandered from one end of this lovely old city to the

1

other, mingling with the side street crowds and daring to cross Canal Street with its hopeless crush of frivolous humanity only a couple of times, at the North end. We dared not take our two little tykes through the crush of the crowd at the "lower" end of the street. Anyway, the side streets were more interesting with their truckloads of merry makers, stopping here and there to dance in the streets in all manner of costume and makeup, as the hired pianos carried on the trucks tinkled out happy rag ime music!

As we walked along St. Charles Street that night, we noticed one of the last "Store Shows" we were ever to see. A "store show" (or "dime museum"), in case you dont' know, is an empty store building which has been rented by a group of show people who then decorate it lavishly "out front," put a ticket box at the front door, and charge an admission. Inside, the patron finds a tremendous selection of good clean amusement, if it's a good store show. Usually a series of platforms is arranged inside (as was the case in this one) to make what is usually known in show jargon as a "Ten in One" — meaning, of course, there are ten acts (or attractions) under one roof. A lecturer (or now-a-days an M.C.) walked from "stage" to "stage" to enlighten you on what you were about to witness, to introduce the performer or act on the stage, and later to sell postcards of these attractions to all who wanted one.

We went in to see what they had, and right away Bob fell in love with a little forty-nine pound chimpanzee dressed in striped "T" shirt and overalls. He had a little human buddy, about four years old, who played with him. Both rode the tricycle, pulled or rode in a little wagon, and seemed devoted to each other. When we were told the animal was worth three hundred dollars, we were 'flabbergasted.' This was in February, 1940, and times were still pretty slack for small-time outdoor showfolk. But Bob was very determined to own a chimp. Many times, when we would go to a zoo — no matter where — we always ended up in front of the chimp cages. And, always, Bob would say, "I'm going to own one of

2

those things one of these days!" I always argued, "Oh, no you're not! That thing might kill my kids!"

We didn't make a practice of leaving our equipment unattended, but because it was Mardi Gras day, and we thought we'd be heading North the next day, we parked our little animal show on the levee, across the river from the city. We had been medicine show people until 1938 when we changed our format to that of a free show -- as before -- but instead of medicines, we sold tickets of admission to see our animal exhibit. We had a collection of about thirty small animals, ranging from white rats to a pair of African green monkeys. They were housed in a specially built cage-truck which was known in show business as a "wild-life exhibit." Parked beside the animal truck was our nice new trailer. Bob harrassed the owner, trying to get him to sell us the chimp, whose name was "Snookie," but the man refused.

We had planned to head North, because Mardi Gras means "Fat Tuesday," a religious holiday, and the next day, being Ash Wednesday, signals the beginning of Lent. During Lent, small shows never make any money in Catholic territory, so it was just common sense to move North as soon as Mardi Gras was over. However, Bob wanted that chimp, and instead of going north, we went down on the delta and put the show in two or three small settlements along the river, so he could run into town every day and harrass the man to sell him the chimp.

We needed to replace our car since it was almost ready to give up the ghost. So we had sent a telegram to Roanoke to a loan company to let us have money to get a used car. The maximum that we could borrow at that time was $300.00. The money had arrived several days before Mardi Gras. As soon as Bob saw the chimp I said good-bye to the chance to get a decent car to pull my trailer.

At long last the man relented and Bob took "Frisco," a young fellow we had as a helper, and ran up to New Orleans to get the chimp. Like so many people who see a cute little chimp and think they can handle it, Bob and Frisco were in

3

OUR THIRD TRAILER - 1934. PLATFORM WAS CARRIED ON THE BACK END OF THE TRAILER.

THE HAYES TRAILER WAS OUR FIRST FACTORY-BUILT TRAILER (1937) FOLD-DOWN PLATFORM WAS ADDED TO THE BACK END. (SKETCHES FROM PHOTOGRAPHS)

PROBABLY THE BEST TRAILER WE EVER OWNED WAS THE FABULOUSLY LIGHT WEIGHT "HOWARD HUGHES" TRAILER - THE 1946 SPARTAN MANOR. WE LIVED IN THAT LITTLE 8 X 25 FOR ELEVEN YEARS. THEN IN 1958 WE BOUGHT THE 35 FOOT SPARTAN. ANOTHER 11 YEAR HOME ON WHEELS.

4

The first card using "Noell's Ark" title 7x13
ca. 1939

COMING

The Twentieth Century Show

NOELS ARK

ON WHEELS

DAM NECK, VA.
AT
BARNES' STORE

Strangest Animals Ever Captured Alive

Besides a full evening's entertainment, including:

VAUDEVILLE - TALKING PICTURES
MAGIC, KNIFE THROWING
BLACK FACE ACTS
VENTRILOQUISM

Admission; CHILDREN, 10¢   ADULTS 20¢

BIG FREE ACT

OUTSIDE AT 8 O'CLOCK

BEFORE MAIN SHOW STARTS

5

for the surprise of their lives.

The wife cried as she dressed Snookie in his little striped "T" shirt and overalls. The man handed the lead chain to Bob, and also a short piece of rubber hose, which was to be used to whip the chimp if he didn't behave. The woman came out and gave them Snookie's chamber pot and told the men that Snookie would not soil his clothes but should have the pot nearby at all times, to use when he needed it. (He really was "broken" to that "pottie.")

They put the chimp's cage in the trunk of the coupe, then decided it was too cold for him to ride in back. Frisco sat by the door, Bob drove, and "cute little forty-nine pound" Snookie rode between them. I have an idea the man thought these two greenhorns would be back in a couple of hours begging for a refund. But if he did, he reckoned without Bob's "bull-headed" determination to own a chimp.

The way the two men looked when they arrived at our show lot was testimonial enough as to the ordeal through which they had survived. Shirts torn, skin scratched, physical exhaustion written in every premature wrinkle showed, clearly, that bringing the belligerent little rascal home had been anything but a picnic. Bob told me that because he felt sorry for the little fellow, he threw the rubber hose to the shelf behind the seat. His mistaken attitude at that time was one we were to see many thousands of times in the years that followed; i.e. "he's so little, I don't need that hose. I can control him without it." What a misconception!

Before they had gone five blocks they discovered how wrong it was to think that both of them -- grown men -- could control a forty-nine pound chimp! Snookie got the hose, and jumping up and down gleefully, he beat both men black and blue -- snarling traffic along Canal Street for blocks. This behavior was repeated every four or five miles -- and we were parked about eighty miles south of the city! It had started to rain and was very cold so they had to tough it out with the little monster inside with them. It must have been a veritable nightmare of a trip.

I laughed at the way the men looked and at the tiny ape between them, who looked as if he was ready for another go at them. But I was soon to change my tune. It was too cold to put him out in the truck with the other animals, so my husband decided the chimp had to move in with us! I protested, but in vain. He argued that the $300.00 investment was too much to risk — and I had to admit, I didn't want it on my conscience if the chimp got sick. But we were too late with the care; the little fellow already had a pretty bad cold.

Because we knew so little about chimps, we didn't realize how sick he was when we got him. Respiratory problems are one of the worst threats possible to all simians, and Snookie had a bad "deep" cold. We kept him in the trailer those first frigid nights on the delta. Then, because we could see he was getting no better, we checked with a local M.D. and he advised us to make an egg nog with sugar, milk and brandy. Since we never use alcoholic beverages, we had to go out and buy some brandy. Not long after Snookie drank it (with noticeable relish) he showed definite signs of intoxication. He acted silly, laughed, and deliberately flopped off the top of his cage with reckless abandonment. We put him to bed in his cage for his own protection, and he seemed much better the next day.

But the first night we had him we cleared out a closet in the front end of our nice new trailer, and tied him to the door knob. That closet was beside the couch that folded down and made our bed.

The family lined up along the couch to be "introduced" to the chimp. When I think about this now, the "hackles" rise on my neck. How stupid we were! Our two little defenseless kids sat on the couch and a forty-nine pound chimp walked along sniffing each of us! Wonder of wonders, is that he only nipped our daughter's big toe! He could have maimed her for life or even killed her. He fell in with Bobby almost immediately, but it was a constant trauma for me to have to keep the daughter away from him. She was the baby and I've always thought he was merely jealous of the attention she got.

The first night was one I will never forget for another reason. I had put the bed down and usually slept on the "outside" – near that closet door – so I could get up in the night if the children needed me. But this night I insisted on sleeping on the "inside." When I awoke the next morning I was afraid to move. Snookie had opened the door, and had backed into the bed as far as his chain would allow, and was under the covers with Bob. What really surprised me was the fact that Bob had his arm around Snookie, exactly the way his arm was usually around me! When he woke up, Bob was startled, at least as much as I had been, because, he said, he had thought it was me on that side of the bed!

After we got well acquainted with Snookie, Bob enjoyed taking him out for walks on a lead chain. He walked him around the show lot every day, just to give him an outing. He usually tried to do this when no one was around. However, the chimp was like a magnet and people seemed to materialize out of thin air when he took his walks. This happened one day in Georgia. Two men walked by and one of them was wearing white shoes. We have never really been able to know, for sure, why white shoes hold such an overpowering fascination for a chimp. I think it suggests the "full bloom"of a female chimp in oestrus, or it may resemble something chimps go after in the wilds, and is something like an "instinctive memory" – if such a thing exists. At any rate, Snookie decided to follow those white shoes. The men had no desire to get near the chimp nor to let him get near them, so they ran. However, when it comes to running, the chimp is no slouch, and Snookie had no intention of being left behind. Bob tried to hold him back, but Snookie was too strong. To antagonize the animal while he wore no muzzle would have been suicidal. Bob called to the men and told them to circle around and go back to the show lot so he could get my help. I was not even aware that the chimp was out of his cage. It took a lot of persuasion on Bob's part to get the men to cooperate. They finally circled a building and came back to the lot. Bob came screaming, "Mae! Mae! Help me!" I jumped out of the trailer just as the two men went by, diverted Snookie's attention to a "goodie" I had for him, and the emergency was over.

When we had our show at Gum Neck, North Carolina, Bob would take Snookie each night in the back door of the store when the show was over and after everyone had left. Snookie would sit on a drink crate, eat some cookies and drink a soft drink, and then go back home to bed. Since chimps are afraid of the dark, we often let him run at night for a short while, under close supervision, because he would never go beyond the circle of light, if it was dark everwhere else.

One night two men came on the lot in a pick-up truck. When the driver got out Bob heard him say, "You wait right here. I'm gonna take a peek at that varmint." Always the 'practical joker,' Bob waited till the man was nearly on the platform, then he opened the door. Snookie ran out between Bob's legs. The man had put his hand on the door and in his fright he thought he had set the animal free. Panic-stricken he ran toward his truck screaming, "Open the door!" Instead of opening the door, his friend locked the door and closed the window. Thinking it was a game of "tag" and he was "it," Snookie took up the chase. The poor man ran past his truck and into the darkness, whereupon Snookie gave up the chase, not daring to venture into the dark.

About an hour later, Bob took Snookie, on the lead chain, in the back door of the store, as had become his habit. As he went ahead of Bob, Snookie's chain was not visible and it looked as if he were loose. Bob got almost all the way into the store when pandemonium broke loose. He had not noticed that the same man was in the store trying on a pair of shoes. When he saw Snookie he bolted for the door. The night was warm and the outer screen door was all that was latched. That poor fellow hit the door with such force that he ripped the latch free. I asked him, after, if he hadn't hurt himself. "No'm," he answered, "only skinned my knee a little."

Snookie used to enjoy riding in Bob's little "Crosley" automobile. He always wore clothes for these trips. And, to guard against "accidents" - he carried his own little personal pottie with him. He never soiled his clothing, always demanding we stop when nature called. He removed his own trousers for the job at hand, and when finished, waited patiently, 'til he was "put together" again. He enjoyed frightening people – and would stand up in the front seat – looking over the windshield, waving one arm in a threatening attitude while he held on for dear life with the other – and people would dive under porches and over fences when they saw this weird outfit coming down the road.

Another time, at Sedalia, Virginia, the store man (Mr. Dick Mason) thought he would have some fun with Snookie after the show one night. Knowing about his fear of the dark, he wanted to see if Snookie would be afraid of a ghost. He wrapped up in a sheet and ran after the scared little chimp, who climbed the first pole he came to. When the ghost started to climb the pole too, it was just too much, so Snookie decided to attack in self defense. Dick had to run around the store three times, with Snookie hot on his heels, before he could get untangled from his sheet enough to square himself with Snookie. These escapades always scared me speechless and delighted Bob into near hysteria.

Bob and I were seldom able to go off together, for fear of something happening to the animals while we were gone, but one time I especially remember we did trust them to a helper while we went somewhere for a few hours. We had two men working for us from Bob's home county at that time. These two had known each other for a number of years. When we went away, we made it plain that no one was to go near the animals and certainly never into the truck. Any stranger who came up was to be warned away. When we got home later that afternoon we were puzzled by the laborious manner in which one of them carried out his duties. Finally I called to him and asked if he was sick. He denied anything was wrong.

Next day the store man told us that a bunch of drunks came up and told the older boy that they would give him $5.00 if he would go in and referee the "fight" and "let the little guy fight the ape." Both boys agreed, because, when Bob was around, the animal played with both of them. But what they didn't know was that with Bob gone, Snookie was "Boss."

So -- they went into the cage with the unmuzzled animal. How they ever got in and then out without the animal escaping will forever remain a mystery! And instead of the big boy being the referee, Snookie whaled them both, "to a fare you well."

I never did learn whether the drunks gave them the $5.00 or not. But this little episode decided something for us -- for the rest of our lives, with animals. And that is, that never are the animals left alone. One or the other of the two of us is "on hand" around the clock. When Bob goes somewhere, I stay, and vice-versa. Of all people, we thought we could trust that fellow, but he proved to be more fool-hardy than we thought.

Later, another young fellow came on the show, and --even with one of us on the lot -- he opened the cage door to feed or play with Snookie, unbeknown to us. It was only recently that we found this out when he confessed to us, in a letter, that he had done this! It makes me all the more certain that some of the "escapes" we had to live through were probably really "releases."

Chimps are tough. A fall that would almost certainly kill (or at least cripple) a man is of no concern to a chimp. This was noted by Dr. Robert M. Yerkes in 1925 when he mentioned his observation of a chimp who fell "from the roof...to the cement floor of the cage HEAD FIRST, but without harm." Many, many times have I witnessed our captive friends' antics while playing in trees. My first experience with this was when we were camped at Sedalia,

Virginia, about 1940. Our chimp, "Snookie" was an escape artist, and always made his "jailbreaks" while Bob was away. On this particular day, Snookie decided to do a few acrobatics in a tremendous, and beautiful elm tree on the campsite. He climbed, rapidly, to the very top of the tree, then leaped with seemingly wild abandonment as if intent on suicide. I held my breath and feared the worst, for that tree was more than thirty-five feet tall! But as he fell he grabbed limbs that snapped off as he went. He landed, with a sickening thud, "on all four," and, laughing hysterically, he ran to the top of the tree to do it again, and again. Each time he fell he snapped off from two to five limbs, and he didn't stop this wild game until some thirty or forty minutes later when the tree was almost completely stripped of its limbs! Dick Mason, who owned the campsite watched him destroy that lovely tree and laughed at the chimp till the tears came, as if he were vicariously enjoying those perilous leaps. Then, too, his laughter was encouragement for show-off Snookie to keep at it. Then Snookie decided to go into the man's store but I'm going to let Roy Thompson of the Winston-Salem Journal and Sentinel, North Carolina, tell of this escapade. He does it so much better than I could:

"Snookie found a new way to escape. They couldn't have held Snookie on Devil's Island. He got out once while they were in Virginia. He didn't wreck things that time...just went shopping.

Snookie walked into Dick Mason's grocery store there, at Sedalia. Dick had some stools at the counter, and he had some customers loafing on the stools. Then Snookie walked in and it was just like when the Bad Guy comes into the saloon in Western movies. The people took one look at Snookie and made room for him at the counter. Snookie took this courtesy without so much as nodding his head. He flipped himself up onto a stool and pointed at something he wanted. Dick Mason brought it. Great! He pointed again. Dick Mason brought it. Snookie sat and ate and drank. The people who had fled began to drift back in to watch Dick wait on an ape. Snookie paid them no attention. He was busy.

One thing Snookie didn't notice -- not that it would have made any difference to him -- was the fact that Dick was making a little note of everything that Snookie was ordering. He wouldn't have cared. He had no more sense about credit than most of us have. He just kept sitting and ordering and stuffing.

When he finally had enough he ordered some chewing gum, put the whole pack in his mouth, and out he went.

Popping the gum, of course.

Dick sat down and added up the bill. It was a dilly. He hated to think what Bob was going to say when he saw it. Bob has quite a temper, particularly when it comes to spending his money foolishly.

Bob took one look at the bill, turned a little pale and then started laughing. If one of his other children had done it, it would have been too bad. But this was Snookie, and Snookie -- well, Snookie was different.

Bob paid Snookie's bill -- still laughing. Now he looks back on the incident and is grateful for one thing:

Snookie never got his hands on a credit card."

Snookie soon became a star attraction on our little show. People back in the country in the 1940's liked to see great apes, as it was very seldom that they got the chance to view one without travelling to some zoo, or in theaters, often many miles away. As his value as an exhibit animal increased, we gradually disposed of our other animals and eventually remodelled our entire show. Instead of the seven cages which we had previously used to rotate the animals in from night to night, we had one super cage built so Snookie would have plenty of room to play and amuse the people who soon became his fans in every town we played. We even changed the name of the show to "NOELL'S ARK GORILLA

13

We Are Laughing At
The FUNNIEST SHOW ON EARTH
Noell's Ark
GORILLA SHOW INC.
EACH NIGHT, AFTER THE BIG
FREE SHOW
YOU WILL LAUGH, TOO, WHEN YOU SEE
SEVERAL LOCAL MEN
WRESTLE ONE OF THESE
BIG ANIMALS AT ONE TIME

FREE
SEE THE LIGHTNING CARTOONIST
NOELL'S
SYE
SEE SAMBO THE TALKING DOLL!
FREE

WANTED to
Athletic young
men to earn $1.00
a minute, boxing
JOE

Name of Town and
date plus hour
goes here.

HANDBILL
DRAWN
BY
AUTHOR
CA. 1955

14

SHOW," not because we wished to misguide anyone, but because so many people insisted upon calling him a gorilla. Some of them had a notoriously hard time saying "chimpanzee", and we got so many variations of mispronunciation from "chimpanese" to "Japanese" that just plain gorilla came to sound better even if it was incorrect.

Even though a great majority of the people watched him with amusement, it was also interesting to notice the other reactions of some of the folks who saw him. I have seen ladies who considered themselves delicate look at the animal and be so repulsed by him, as to be actually sickened. And right next to such a person might be another woman cooing to him and telling him how cute he was! An outstanding case of admiration was a woman who came in to see Snookie one day while no show was in progress. She was intoxicated and insisted that something should be done about us locking up a poor old man like that. She was actually angry. Before she left, she gave him a half dollar and warned him not to give it to anybody until they brought him what he wanted, and she further warned him to make us give him back his change! As a parting gesture she kissed him goodbye, through the bars.

It was not unusual for me to overhear chance remarks, without the intention of eavesdropping. Such was the case one day when I accidentally overhead a man ask his friend, jokingly, "Reckon that thing is any kin to you, Rufe?" And Rufe replied that he "couldn't recollect seein' ennybody in his family like him," so he " 'sposed not."

During the first month that we had Snookie we learned a lot from him. We found that he was very clever at getting out of cages -- a regular Houdini, in fact. One day Bob went to New Orleans on business and while he was gone, Snookie pulled his first escape act. We still had a few of our small animals, one of which was a young Coati Mundi we had named Snookie long before we bought the chimp of the same name. Then when Snookie joined our ranks, we redubbed the little pet "Swinkie" after the little animal in a comic strip that was popular about that time, called Wash Tubbs. The working boy backed into the trailer, which was most unusual for he had always knocked before. I asked him what was wrong and he said in a strange voice, "Snookie's loose." I, not thinking of the chimp, thought the boy had lost his mind. I said, "What of it? He won't hurt anything, let him run awhile." The boy was actually pale as he said, "I'm not so sure about that." Then I realized something really was wrong! I asked, "Do you mean big or little Snookie?" He looked at me like he was sick and said, "BIG Snookie." I felt limp all over. I was more afraid of the animal than the boy was. Bob had only been gone a very short while, which meant that it might be hours before he returned. Even as I was wondering what to do, I could hear people calling to each other from house to house to, "Close the windows, the BEAR's aloose." I realized some man might get panicky and shoot our prize exhibit, so decided that even if it meant getting a bite out of the experience, I had to catch that animal! I went out and saw him running round and round the truck. I was encouraged when I saw that he had a dog chain dangling behind him. When I got out there he must have been running quite awhile, for he was panting and sweating. It was no trouble to get close enough to step on his chain and after this was done I cautiously lifted it from the ground, wheedling him all the while. He followed me like a good little boy and I took him into the house, and fed him some goodies. That event set a precedent. Every time one of the animals made an escape since then, I made it a point to have him come into the trailer, and fed him well. That way, when they got loose, they came straight to the trailer, knowing they were going to a party. None of this running all over the neighborhood trying to catch them and begging the police not to shoot. So far this plan worked like a charm. I treated them like honored guests that I was delighted to see and cleaned out my ice box and cabinets to make them happy until Bob could come to the rescue.

That was one of the most hectic afternoons of my entire

lifetime, I guess. I was afraid of the little fellow, and he seemed to know it, taking the fullest possible advantage of his opportunity. Lacking something more substantial, I fastened his chain to the light fixture. The trailer was a commercially-built job in which a very lightweight plywood had been used for the interior, and after only a few minutes the light fixture was ripped from the wall. After a super-effort, I got him fastened again, this time to the cabinet-type handle of the wardrobe door. This proved a little more substantial, but it put him too close to all the places he had always wanted to investigate and made life most miserable for the next hour or so. Seeing that Bob was likely to stay longer than I had anticipated, I finally decided, in self defense, to try to get him into the truck where he belonged, at all costs. Calling to the boy I said, "Get me another lead chain, and come over here; I'm going to try to put him up." As soon as the chain arrived, I fastened it to the collar. Handing one of the chains to the boy, I said, "you keep him off of me, and I'll keep him off of you, and between us maybe we can get him into his cage." The boy was afraid at first that one of us would be hurt, but after a bit of coaxing, he agreed to help me out. Snookie was fascinated at first, and willing to go along with what he seemed to think was a harmless experiment. As soon as the light dawned on him that he was going back into his cage, he objected strenuously, but it was already too late. We slammed the door shut and left the two chains on his collar, glad to be rid of him. (Here was the first clue that two people talking and reasoning with a chimp will often get desired results that would be impossible for one person to achieve).

I went back to the sad task of re-doing all the housework that had been interrupted, and repairing the damage he had done, as best I could. And when Bob got home that afternoon, he found it hard to believe until he went into the truck to see for himself that Snookie did indeed have two chains on his collar. To this day it is a mystery to Bob how he got out of that cage in the first place, but I've always

17

thought that 'Frisco took him out and then lost control.

As soon as we were able to, we took a brief vacation during early Spring in New Orleans. During our stay there, it got terribly cold again, and the two boys we had with us decided to sleep in one end of Snookie's cage, so as to be able to keep an eye on the heater, which was one of those primitive kerosene arrangements. They figured they could put their neat little bedrolls across one end of the cage, opposite the end Snookie preferred for his nestlike bed. In spite of our warnings, the boys were eager to try the idea out. One of them thought the piece of rubber hose would be enough to keep the little fellow off of them if he should get any wild ideas in the night. Bob put them to bed, after they won out over my protests, and locked the door behind them. I went to sleep only after worrying for a couple of hours.

About five next morning, Bob jumped out of bed and ran out to the truck in his shorts to rescue the boys. A veritable bedlam had broken loose in the truck. When the boys went to bed the night before, they had carefully tucked the rubber hose under their pillow, and confidently went to sleep. Snookie had merely waited until he was sure of himself; then he sneaked the hose from under the pillow and had a Roman Holiday beating those two boys up.

During this first year with Snookie we learned a great deal, the hard way, about the peculiarities of the chimpanzee. I guess, in experienced hands, Snookie would have been a prize chimp. But as it was, he was learning about people as we were learning about chimps -- each from the other, instead of him learning from us.

For instance, I think it worth mentioning that Snookie performed a heroic deed for someone he loved, in those first weeks with us. As I mentioned earlier, Snookie loved Bobby. Well, one nice warm day we were parked up on the levee of the Mississippi River, about a mile from the big bridge at New Orleans. Bob decided the air would be good for Snookie and took him for a stroll along the top of the levee. Bobby followed, (even though he'd been told not to go to the top of

18

The car that pulled the Hayes trailer.

BOB'S LIGHT PLANT 1935

A lot of the places where we showed had no electricity in the thirties, so Bob carried a tiny light plant on the front bumper.

the levee) unnoticed by his Dad. Snookie had what seemed to us an unreasonable fear of the water, which caused Bob a great deal of amusement, because the little fellow would scream in terror every time Bob walked towards the water. Along the edge of the levee at that particular spot, there was a retaining wall of black tar, which was sloped at such an acute angle as to be impossible to stand upon. Somehow Bobby had walked unnoticed to the brink of the wall and lost his footing. Too terrified to scream, he held his weight out of the water by a mere clump of grass. Snookie saw Bobby's plight and ran to the water's edge and pulled the child in by offering Bobby his foot, almost before Bob could grasp why Snookie had suddenly abandoned his fear of the drink.

I feel now as I felt then -- if Snookie hadn't done just what he did, we probably would have had no little boy, next day. Bobby was only six years old at the time. After this experience it was harder than ever to get Snookie up on that levee!

Once, weeks later, while we were camped beside a bayou, we tricked him into a flat boat hoping to cure him of what we felt was an unreasonable fear of water. He sat so still that he looked like a statue throughout the entire ride. Then when the boat got close enough to the shore, the little fellow got ashore before the others could even get organized to land. In this he showed more intelligence than his humans who could not swim, either. Even later, when the truck in which he rode went over a bridge, Snookie barked until the truck landed on terra firma again. He was very skeptical of ferry rides too.

In his book **"Men and Apes,"** Desmond Morris mentions that Madame Abreu (the wealthy Cuban woman who had many animals in the 'twenties) had to contend with people who ridiculed her and wanted to know why she did not adopt a child rather than to raise apes. We have experienced some of this attitude, too. However, when we explain that we do have a son and a daughter, six grandchildren and two great-grandchildren, and that the animals are a part of our

EARL WOLTZ DESIGNED AND BUILT THIS VERY
ATTRACTIVE PROSCENIUM FOR OUR SHOW, ABOUT 1945

ONE OF OUR VERY EARLIEST OUTFITS (1934) HOME-MADE
TRAILER AND MODEL A FORD. NOTICE STAGE ON BACK
END.

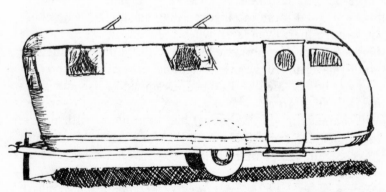

OUR LITTLE 25 FOOT SPARTAN MANOR - (1946) IN
WHICH WE LIVED FOR MORE THAN ELEVEN YEARS.

business, people are usually satisfied. However, there is no denying that the animals automatically became precious "friends," or pseudo-family members and we do get emotionally involved with them. They are our "ape-children," as Dr. Robert M. Yerkes called them in the 'fifties.

As I write this I have a mental picture of cute little Snookie as he was in those days. Often our friends would kid us because Snookie would curl up like a baby in my arms and go to sleep. But he would never relax that much around Bob. His reason for this was clear to me. I was his pal, but Bob was his boss. I learned early in the game that chimps are ticklish and do definitely laugh. And what I liked best was that chimps love to romp and giggle. So an alliance was formed. Snookie and I would have romps as often as was practical. Never let it be said that I ever had even the remotest resemblance of control over him. I was not his superior; I was only his equal, or maybe less. But he loved me, and would often humor me when I made requests. It was not the least unusual for him to start on one of his typical chimp bursts of noisy enthusiasm over what seemed to us to be absolutely nothing, only to stop when I would say in a cajoling tone of voice, "Sit down, Snookie, sit down." Shouting at him only intensified the burst. Later, when he was a mature fellow, his "spurts" were more dignified and restrained, and I doubt very much that I could have made him laugh for me as of old. He still liked me, I am sure, for every time I got close enough to the cage he reassured me in all the little ways a chimp has of "talking" to those he trusts.

We had never been around chimps -- more than to look at them in the zoos we had visited -- and in 1938 had seen the famous chimp man, Reuben Castang, at the Fair in New York City where he presented such a marvelous act that we were awed at the wonderful intelligence of the chimps. Having never had an association with any animal people whatever, we had to start from scratch. At first Snookie was not even asked to work. Having him there on the show to look at was enough. The people went away satisfied with just having seen him. Often the same people would go in our truck to see him night after night. Then Bob had an inspiration. Snookie had played with so many people during the daytime that Bob figured the crowd would like to watch him play with a human playmate. At first it was Bobby who would go in and romp with him. The people liked that so well, soon some of them were requesting to be allowed to play with him. Being ignorant of the potential danger of the animal, we were willing to let folks go in and visit Snookie if they so desired. Eventually someone suggested to one of Snookie's visitors that he try to get the animal's shoulders on the floor. Snookie resisted so nimbly that it was really very funny, and the best part of the deal was that Snookie never lost sight of the fact it was a game. He liked to play so well that we found it hard to carry on the rest of the show, as people were content to stand right there the rest of the night watching him, thus throttling our routine and cutting off some of our income.

Our little animal show started out as a seven-cage exhibit, built on a "straight-job" 8' x 16' truck-bed. Six cages were about 2' wide x 3' long x 3' high, and the "big" cage at the end was 7' long x 4' high x about 4' wide. When Snookie arrived we had to put him in the "big" cage and put the two monkeys who had lived there before, out on leashes. Then, later, we had to rebuild the entire truck into one big cage that became the wrestling arena. All the other animals were given to Bob's foster-father who built an exhibit like ours had been.

The format of our program was a hold-over from the old medicine show days, when we would give a lot of free entertainment, interspersed with sales. Only now, instead of selling medicine we would charge an admission to come to see the animals. Our livlihood depended on a pretty fast turnover since we were charging only 10¢ for children and 25¢ for adults. So when Snookie came on the show, the turnover slowed to a near standstill. So few chimps were

24

around that people wanted to watch him for hours. At last Bob hit on the idea of putting a box in his cage. After a proper viewing period, Bob would go into the big cage and put Snookie in the box. With nothing to look at, the people would then go outside. Then Snookie was let out of the box for a new group to come in and see him.

This was how our wrestling show came to be originated. One night Snookie refused to go into the box. Bob struggled and wrestled and grunted to the vast amusement of the spectators. As is usually the case, a "kibitzer" started heckling Bob by saying, "Aw, man! I could put that little blankety-blank in the box with one arm tied behind my back!"

Bob -- exhausted and angry -- said, "I'll give you $5.00 if you can get him in the box!" The heckler said, "Lemme at him!"

So Bob told the people to go out and come back at 50¢ each and he would let the guy try to put Snookie in the box. The people eagerly cooperated. After about ten or twelve minutes of strenuous effort on the part of the man, and almost hysterical laughter on the part of the crowd, the man had to give up, and the "athletic ape show" was born.

This encouraged the more daring men in the crowd to match wits and brawn against the little fellow. Snookie took it all in the spirit of good clean fun and just deftly eluded them, just as he had always eluded Bob when he saw he was about to be put up for the night. If Snookie had been resentful of these goings on, I shudder to think of what the outcome might have been.

We never lacked contenders -- it seemed that everyone wanted to get into the act, and all went well until one night when Snookie playfully ran in and out of the box, thirty dollars worth! It almost wrecked our bankroll. So Bob came up with the idea to hold his shoulders on the floor. This worked well for several months until one night when Snookie laid down about fifteen dollars' worth. At this Bob changed the rules again. Now they had to try to sit on the ape's tummy. That was the clincher -- no way could anyone ever sit on his tummy and from there on the show was a success in that we were making a little money with it. Between 1940 and 1971 when we finally retired, we estimate that between 35,000 and 40,000 men, women, and children have played with our chimps in races, or boxing or wrestling matches.

Mrs. Lillie Holdren, a lady who lives in Bedford, was the first lady to go in the cage with Snookie. It almost became a ritual for her to go in the cage with Snookie, and later, with Butch, every time we appeared within a huge radius of Bedford, Va.

Several times she came so far that we put her up for the night in our trailer. And she was only the first of many ladies who entered the cage with Snookie or Butch over the years.

Snookie wrestled for almost two years before we realized the potential danger and built a muzzle for him. By the time he was wearing the muzzle, he was a seventy-five or eighty-pound adult, fully capable of biting a finger or hand off. We were lucky greenhorns to have survived so long with an adventure so dangerous! The saving factor was that Snookie was not a vicious animal and was actually playing, no matter how serious the men were while "wrestling."

However, Snookie was gradually becoming more and more his own boss -- and more and more the boss of the whole roost. Life was getting to be a miserable burden. It was really tough trying to get the people out of the truck, because he made them want to stay to watch his clowning. Finally in exasperation Bob started giving Snookie what I thought was pretty severe chastisement. He would take a leather strap to him, only to have it taken away from him, and turning the tables on Bob, Snookie would flail him with it. It had gotten to the point that Bob was no longer Snookie's boss and was threatened each time he went into the cage. That was why he started trying to punish the animal, hoping to dominate and subdue him. Just as well a Lilliputian should try to beat up the Cyclops. No single human is a fair match for the smallest chimp, when that chimp really intends to get you. And

Snookie had come into his so-called "dangerous age" with a suddenness that alarmed us. He fought Bob every time he tried to handle him at all. Finally Bob started going into the cage only after wrapping his hands in dog chains, as protection against Snookie's ever-ready teeth. The chains were often snatched and swung with a viciousness that made a speedy exit imperative. Once in the heat of battle Snookie ripped the entire shirt from Bob's back and beat him with the fragments. When Bob came into the trailer that night, he was "polka-dotted" with the print of the buttons. Realizing the danger of his teeth at last, we had a muzzle made to fit his oddly shaped head. We felt much better now that we were able to cover his teeth. More than once some careless drunk had stuck a finger in the cage and had yanked it back, bleeding.

At first he resented the muzzle and we had many dangerous episodes over putting it on him. However, in time, he came to realize that the muzzle went on just before he got to play with the men, so it got to be less of a hassle as time went on. We worked Snookie as a wrestler for two years before we made a muzzle for him because we had no idea that we could build a muzzle for a chimp. And we'd had no real knowledge of the terrible potential of an angry chimp. Everything that we had ever done with Snookie had always been in fun so we didn't even think of putting a muzzle on such a precious pseudo-human.

However, we found out it was not only his teeth that we needed to cover. In one spot in Texas, a big, burly bully decided to make a hero of himself. He had the misconception that he was strong enough to go in and kill that ape. He was vicious and tried everything he could think of, above my protests, but he was no match for little seventy-five pound Snookie, and Snookie was too good a sport to bite. However, Snookie was not above using a few manual dirty tricks of his own. He put a stop to the fight by suddenly ramming his two tiny thumbs up the man's nostrils and stretching them apart till both sides tore. This episode – and the fact that we had

Noell's Ark

Ape Fighter's Certificate

Awarded To
John W. Doe

Who, having entered into a

Boxing match with *Joe*

on the *First* day of *September* 1960 at *Podunk, Fla*

and having shown good sportsmanship in said match, has hereby

been elected a member in good standing of the

Exclusive Order Of Ape Fighters

By Authority Of Noell's Ark Gorilla Show

SPECIAL RATED A-1 Sport AWARD

Purposeful heart award- only for the ones who emerge from the match without a scratch

JOE the BOXER

BAMBOO the RUNNER

BUTCH the WRESTLER

KONGO WRESTLER

Joe the Boxer

THIS MEMBERSHIP IS SUBJECT TO REVOCATION IF CONTESTANT EVER RE-ENTERS ARENA
AND VIOLATES THE RULES

COPYRIGHT 1960 BY MAE NOELL

FIRST EDITION SECOND PRINTING

already had quite a few scratches -- was what decided us to make leather mittens for the chimp.

At Big Island, Virginia, there was a shoemaker named Richard Wood who agreed to try to make the muzzle. Snookie sat willingly throughout each fitting until, at last, we had a safety device against too serious mayhem.

But even the muzzle was not always a guarantee against bites. One man -- even after our forceful warnings not to touch the muzzle -- put his fingers in the muzzle in an attempt to control the animal, and suffered a severe bite on a finger. He was a serviceman who had been sent to deliver a message and to wait for a reply. He figured he could sneak over to the show and fight the ape and never be missed, because he anticipated a long wait. His buddies rushed him to the base hospital and one of them told us he was likely to be court marshalled over the escapade, for two reasons: one, he was supposed to wait for the message and rush back; and two, he was to be reprimanded for damaging government property -- himself!

These were the most serious mishaps we had with Snookie, and were the reason I wrote up the rules of the "game" and tried to enforce them. Often as not, however, the contestants gave me a hard time about the rules because they thought the rules were to protect the animal. Finally in 1960 I came up with a solution. I designed and copyrighted a Sportsmanship Certificate and would give it only to men who were smart enough to follow the rules, and, as a result "to emerge from the match without a scratch." There are thousands of those certificates in Pennsylvania, Maryland, Virginia, West Virginia, North and South Carolina, Georgia and Florida. I was adamant; when a man broke the rules and got himself messed up in any way, I would not let him have a certificate. Many times the men would say, "I don't want to do it for the money; I'm doing it for one of those certificates."

The rules were simple enough:

1. "Don't hit or kick at the animal. This only infuriates

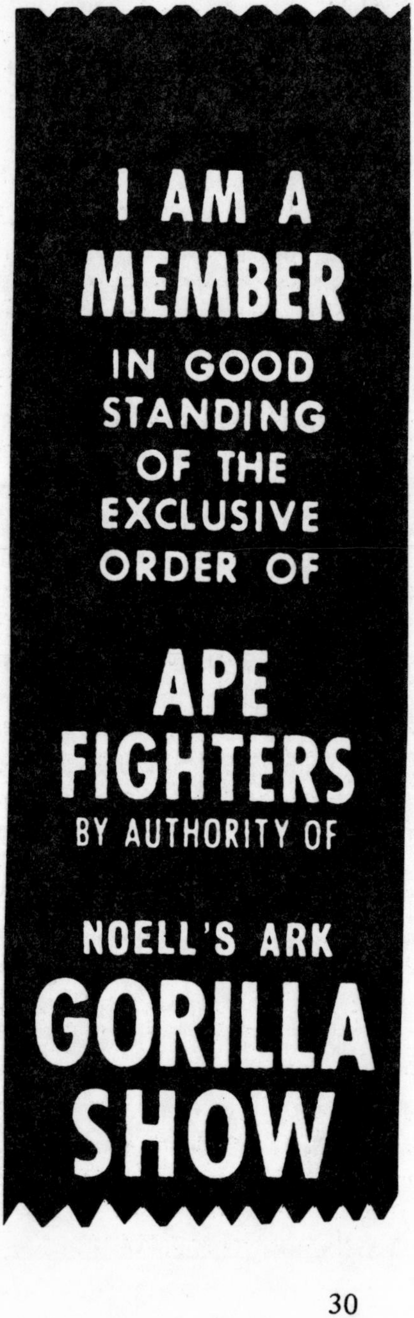

I AM A
MEMBER
IN GOOD
STANDING
OF THE
EXCLUSIVE
ORDER OF

APE
FIGHTERS
BY AUTHORITY OF

NOELL'S ARK
GORILLA
SHOW

GOOD SPORTS WENT HOME WITH A CERTIFICATE AND A PURPLE RIBBON AFTER THEY BOXED OR WRESTLED AND FOLLOWED THE RULES. MANY MEN "WENT INTO BATTLE" ONLY TO GET THESE TROPHIES!

him and makes him dangerous."
2. "Don't pull on the muzzle. He has teeth under it."
3. "If the helmet comes off – put it back on. Everything inside is made of iron and your head ain't that hard," etc., etc.

I put the helmet on the men and tied it in such a way that it would come off under severe stress. My method was to cut halfway through the string so it would break when pulled too hard. It was often quite difficult to make the decision between cutting deeper or less. If it came off too quickly, the man stood a very real risk of a fractured skull if he bumped his head on any part of the cage. But if the string did not break soon enough, the chimp could drag the man around the cage, choking him mercilessly with the horrible risk of breaking the guy's neck. Is it any wonder I developed ulcers, diverticulosis and a hyatal hernia and finally angina pectoris -- all symptoms of nervous stress? Thank God, we never had any really serious injuries in all the long run of thirty-one years' operation.

Bob never wears neckties around the animals for a very good reason. One time Bob was trying to put the muzzle on Snookie. He foresaw a struggle, so he put the chain (from Snookie's collar) up over a "rafter" in the cage. This enabled him to hold the chimp off himself, if the chimp decided to attack. The chimp did decide to attack, and Bob found the chain was shorter than he realized (he has a knack for getting himself into jams like this, and then yelling for Mae to come rescue him). The chimp was swatting at Bob with his long arms. Bob was holding the chain with both hands, and was praying or swearing (or probably both). One sweep of Snookie's arm gave him the end of Bob's necktie. It "slipped" and was choking Bob as Snookie pulled harder and harder and Bob hung desperately to the chain. About the fourth or fifth yank the tie parted; Snookie chewed it up in his rage and, the "vengeance fit" over, sat down.

It was a close call and could have been disastrous. There

was nothing I could do when I got there but talk soothingly to the chimp and try to calm him down. This always enraged Bob; he seemed to think I was sympathizing with the animal too much. But it was always done to get the "fight" settled, and almost always worked.

It's funny, but I could singsong, "Sit down Snookie, sit down;" and, no matter how angry he was, he would sit down! This was very handy and gave us a chance to change tactics and bring the situation under control. However, when Bob was angry it always showed in his voice.

During a conversation with lion trainer, the late Captain Eddie Kuhn, I mentioned "baby talking" to animals. He said, "Baby talk conveys neither fear nor anger, so is, therefore, the best way to talk to an animal." It seems always to have worked for me.

Snookie's great strength was shown to us when we tried to keep a collar on him. We used to tie a cow chain around his neck as a collar because he had broken every leather collar we ever put on him. Fastened with a small padlock, we figured this collar was one that would stay. However, one day when Bob went to feed him, he found Snookie's collar on the floor. Broken! He figured this must have been a faulty piece of chain, so fashioned an identical one. Next time around, ditto. Broken! The third time Bob decided to watch through a peephole (where Snookie could not see him) to see how the cow chain collars were being broken.

After waiting -- patiently -- for twenty or thirty minutes, Snookie "listened" for a few seconds to be sure he was alone; then, sitting on the floor, he balanced himself with his hands and put both great toes in the collar and pulled till it snapped!

One of our most unique experiences involved a group of convicts. We were showing beside a little country store in Virginia, beside a highway. All morning we had been aware of a road gang of convicts working toward the show. When lunchtime came around, all the men sat in a shady spot to eat their sandwiches. During the lunch hour one of the guards came over and asked Bob if we would put on a show for the whole gang. When Bob protested that we had no "fighter" to wrestle with Snookie, the guard said there was a big, strong fellow on the gang who wanted to try. So Bob relented. When they finished eating, the guard handed me a huge rifle and said, "You stand here and my other man will stand over there and you can put the show on safely, then." I took the thing and left the butt on the ground and balanced it. I never picked it up. Their man went in and it must have been a good show by the way they all screamed and laughed. When it was over, they continued working on the road away from us the rest of the day. Someone once said, "I guess that was the first time you ever held a gun on an audience, huh?" About two weeks later someone came to us (I've forgotten who) and said both guards had lost their jobs over the incident, and there was a story about it in a magazine. We never knew whether or not this was true and could never get hold of a copy of the magazine.

One year we had a bear. We had bought it from a woman at Gum Neck, N.C., who had hand-raised it. At the time we got it, it must have weighed between twenty-five and forty pounds. It was collar and chain "broke." Bob decided to give the bear to Snookie as a pet. They were great buddies. Often at night, we could hear Snookie "laughing" and the bear grunting, as they romped and played into the wee hours of the morning.

The bear was tied out to a pear tree one day where it could run in circles for exercise and eat some of the pears on the ground. The next morning we heard weird noises coming from the cage and ran out to see what it was. The poor bear was having some sort of a frenzied fit, trying its best to bite poor Snookie. The chimp seemed to know that this was no game, and was doing his best to stay out of the way. At last the bear fell down and became rigid. Bob rushed in the cage and took Snookie out. And none too soon. The bear revived and ran around the cage -- again -- wildly snapping and biting at everying in sight. It was the most horrible thing I've ever witnessed. Finally, the poor thing died.

I've thought -- since -- we just might have witnessed a death due to rabies! But we all decided that the pears must have given him cramps. Until that day he had been healthy and happy with bread, milk and water as his diet, and the "leavings" from Snookie's meals. We buried him right on the show lot where he died -- so, now will never know what really did kill him. At the time of his death he must have weighed something like 100 to 110 lbs.

We had a tiny black spider monkey. He was real cute, so long as he remained in his cage. However, as soon as Bob got home from the Navy Yard, he would turn the little pest loose. If I had my table set, ready for supper (this happened at least a dozen times that I can remember) the little stinker would come into the trailer and land right in the middle of my table! If I happened to have already put the food on the table, it meant discarding a hot meal and resorting to sandwiches. If I had only the dishes and silver on the table, it meant clearing the table and "doing dishes" before we could eat. I liked the monkey alright, but not having him loose. Bob thought it was "funny" and laughed at my anger.

I knew the little thing would get in trouble if he kept letting him out, and warned Bob not to do it. But it was so tame and cute that Bob could not resist, and it ran free almost as much as it was caged. One day Bob let the little fellow out and then, a half hour later, decided to take Snookie for a walk. Always, when we put Snookie up after a walk, we would put some tid-bit near the door for him to take into the cage with him. As Bob led him back that day, the monkey was eating out of Snookie's can of pork and beans. Before anything could be done to prevent it, Snookie grabbed the little fellow and with one sudden move, he crushed its little head between his teeth! Which would seem to be proof that pets should not be allowed **absolute** freedom -- for their own safety.

Because he wanted to train Snookie, Bob bought a pair of roller-skates with the intention of teaching him to skate.

Snookie wore clothes willingly when we got him. Even wore shoes. Therefore Bob thought it would be pretty easy to teach Snookie to skate. Bob went in the cage without saying anything to anyone about it. The first I knew about it was when I heard a terrible commotion in the cage -- Snookie screaming and then Bob laughing. I ran out and said, "What happened?" Bob stood outside the cage laughing, and the screaming and banging continued. I ran and looked in the cage and Snookie was hanging by his hands from the top of the cage and kicking frantically. "What happened!" I insisted. Between guffaws Bob told me he had put the shoes and skates on Snookie, and when the skates rolled under his feet it tickled or scared him and he jumped to the top of the cage kicking and screaming. It was only by sheer good luck that Bob got out of the cage undamaged. The skates finally flew off his feet into pieces. We never tried skates on him again.

One of the funniest and cutest shows we offered each week was a foot race between Snookie and some kids. He loved kids, and we had a game for little boys or little girls. We would let them run away from Snookie in pretense of playing "tag." Only Snookie was always "It." A safety pin held the greatest possible fascination for him. When we let strange children play with him, we would always pick a likely "victim" and fasten a big pin near the seat of the child's trousers, without letting the child know we had done it. In trying to get the pin, it would create hilarity because neither the audience nor the child would know what he was after, and at an ever-increasing momentum, the animal and child would run in what looked like a "scared to death" game of "tag." When at last, he did get the pin, he lost all interest in the (relieved) child and concentrated on opening and closing the pin. It was especially hilarious when Snookie ran after a kid who wore white shoes. It took us quite awhile to realize that white shoes excite male chimps unduly. It got so serious that I had to refuse admittance to see the show to some of our patrons if they wore white shoes. If Snookie spied a pair in the audience, he stopped whatever he was doing and stared as he whimpered. Thus the show was abruptly over when he spied a pair of white shoes. Maybe this will explain the sign we had out front that read, "We reserve the right to refuse fighters or admittance to show, with or without reason." Sometimes we would be "hard put" to explain why we had to refuse to let certain people near the animals, either in or outside of the cage. After working so many years with the apes it is not hard to know what to expect most of the time. Of course, there are many times when new situations arise and we learn still more about them.

Snookie could also show a gentle side to his nature when the occasion demanded. One night he was puzzled by one man who left his crutches outside the cage. He hopped into the cage on his one leg. He had his pant leg, on the amputated side, folded up and Snookie walked around and around him trying to figure out where the other leg was. Then he played very gently with the man. He seemed to realize something was wrong with the man and felt sorry for him.

Although chimps are among the most intelligent and most lovable animals in the world, they often throw fits or extremely dangerous temper-tantrums. In her book, "My Friends the Wild Chimpanzees," Jane Goodall describes what she calls a "rain dance," in which the male chimp puts on a hooting, screaming, and stomping display of aggressive and threatening activity. All male (and most female) chimps do the same thing, even the ones in captivity -- with or without reason. I think they are just releasing a "pressure valve" and "letting off a little steam."

Snookie would often sway from side to side and "sing" his little "woo-woo-woo" song in rythmic time to his movements. Then, building up tension, he would get louder and louder and finally stomp, scream and then throw things or beat on the wall or the ground. If anything or anybody was too close when he started his "fit," it was too bad. This "song and dance routine" always preceded the chimp's wild flailing attacks on the contestants in the boxing or wrestling matches.

For many years our chimps proved themselves unbeatable in unorthodox boxing and wrestling matches. How could we explain the Marquis of Queensbury rules to a chimp! They used their own tactics, and the only training we gave them was to stop when told to. But if the man had riled the animal enough it was often hard to get the animal to obey as quickly as we wanted.

I remember one hair-raising incident in Sign Rock, a small community only a short distance out of Bedford, Virginia. We had a huge crowd on the lot one night because I had been making movies of people walking on the street and we were showing them from night to night. We advertised, "Come and see yourself in the movies; Free Show tonight." At that time (the mid-forties) home movies were just coming into their own.

A man who was drinking went into the cage with Snookie. When he saw the ape he fainted dead away. I didn't see what had happened, so really thought he was hurt. Frantically I called over the P.A. set, "Is there a doctor in the crowd? We need a doctor right away!" The grocery store was right beside the lot and was run by an old friend of Bob's. He heard me, so quickly called the life-saving crew.

They arrived almost in a flash. The crowd opened up to let the stretcher through and two of the men ran into the cage. By this time we had put Snookie up and the man was sitting on a chair. One of the crew examined him, then came to me and said, "Mrs. Noell! Don't you know when a man is dead drunk? That's all that's wrong with him." I apologized, but he held up his hand and said, "It's all right! You did the right thing! Don't worry about him, he's OK," and he left. The next morning Bobby (our son) went into Bedford and heard a rumor that the man who had fainted was in the hospital with a broken neck. "You'd better go see about that, Mama," he said. "Everyone thinks it happened in the cage."

I ran to the 'phone and called the hospital.

"Do you have a Mr. X in the hospital?" I asked.

"Yes we do," was the reply.

"Could you tell me what's wrong with him?" I wanted to know.

"He has a broken neck," the nurse replied matter-of-factly.

After a shocked pause I asked, "Can you tell me how it happened?"

"Yes ma'am. At about five o'clock this morning he was in an automobile wreck."

With a deep sigh of relief, I thanked her and hung up. But the rumor was hard to live down. It was just too coincidental.

Because I had always been taught to show respect for the aged, I tried to talk an older gray-haired man out of going into the cage with Snookie. He was the typical "big bad man" and had been drinking. I told him what not to do in the cage when I saw I could not persuade him to stay out. It was Saturday night, and while he was not exactly drunk, there was no question but that he'd been imbibing a little too freely. These were always the ones who "got it in the end" and he turned out to be no exception. Just as I had expected Snookie mopped the floor with him. He was bruises from stem to stern. Bob felt sorry for him and stopped the fight, whereupon the man angrily demanded the prize money "Because," he argued, "I'd have whipped him if you hadn't a stopped me!" Bob said, "O.K. – go ahead and finish the job, then. I won't stop you." Second go 'round Snookie really worked him over, and swinging wildly on his belt from behind, Snookie slid the man's pants down in the back as the man held the front up. All the while he was screaming, "Stop him! Get him off of me! Stop him!" When he finally came out of the cage he was sporting a beautiful black eye. Little ninety-five pound Snookie had brought a two hundred-forty pounder low.

The next day we camped at Wallace, N.C., near a stockyard, to lay off for a couple of days. Our son opened Suzy, the little chimp's door to feed her. Suzy weighed all of twelve to eighteen pounds at that time. She bit the child on the hand and broke for freedom. There was a lot of tall grass around the truck and she ran into it, hiding successfully. We surrounded the field, but she had already made her way out of it and up the highway some five or six blocks away. I heard her scream and told Bob to get into the car and go after her. He did and when he got where she was, there was this big gray-haired man with the black eye.

"Don't get too close to him, fellows," he was telling his friends. "He looks small but he beat the hell outa me last night!" He thought it was Snookie. When Bob got there Suzy was delighted to get in the car and go home.

A highway patrolman told Bob this story on himself:

He said he and his buddy went into the cage and wrestled with Snookie. During the match his buddy got a couple of long scratches on his chest. Two days later they went to answer the call to the draft. As they were going through the medical examination one of the medics asked, "How did you get the scratches on your chest?" He answered, "Fighting a gorilla." The medic said, "Sit over there by that table." A few minutes later this policeman came along. The medic looked up from his papers and said, "You're from the same place that fellow's from. Do you know him?" When he replied that he had known him all his life, the medic asked, again, "How'd he get those scratches on his chest?" He too was sent to sit at the table. He laughed when he said a psychiatrist asked them lots of silly questions for about three hours before they finally decided they were sane, and signed them into the service.

One of the "bright lights" of intelligence displayed by Snookie, was something he figured out on his own. He saved "samples" from favorite foods. For instance, he would eat a banana and save a strip of the peel, eat the bread and save a piece of the wrapper. He had, among other things, chewing-gum paper, orange peel and apple peel. The stuff was carefully stored in one corner of the cage. He would attract the attention of some member of the family who understood him and who he knew would respond favorably – (usually me) – and wave a bit of peeling and whimper plaintively

(Snookie's "menu"). When cages were cleaned that corner had to be left untouched. I actually saw him carry this treasure with him when he was being transferred to a clean cage. If he asked for one thing and you gave him something else, he would stand on his head and scream because you were so stupid and could not understand plain chimpanzee. If the craving was strong enough for the particular food for which he asked, there would be no peace on the outfit until he got it.

He seemed to know that we had to keep the animals quiet in most of the places where we set up. He played this fact for all it was worth to us for him to be quiet. He caused us to have to get into the car and drive until we found what it was he "ordered", and because he retained his "samples" there was no way to kid him into thinking we did not understand. The whole thing was entirely his own idea, and this was back in the 'forties, before anyone had taught a chimp sign language. We even kept episodes of things like this quiet. Too often we had been ridiculed for telling unbelievers things of this nature. The usual response had been, "Who do ya think yer kidding? Animals don't do things like that! You must think I'm nuts!"

Snookie (like all great apes) was terrified of a large body of water, but loved nothing better than a basin or tubful and either a rag or a cup with which to dribble the water back into the tub. I've often wondered if he was merely admiring the cascade, or was some inventive idea locked away in his mind because of our language barrier?

With these simple "toys" he could amuse himself for hours on end. He would use the rag to wash his face as he had so often seen us do. But his favorite way to handle it was to wring the rag out, over and over. First he would dip the rag into the water, hold it aloft watching the water run off into the tub, and then wring it carefully, looking at it as if this was a great mystery he alone was called upon to solve. He would do this literally hundreds of times. Sometimes he would vary the procedure by rubbing the soap on the wet rag and making billowy suds in the tub. He would even try to eat the suds. Then back to the rag wringing bit. We never figured out why this amused him so much, and if we wanted to remove the tub, he would throw a temper tantrum. It was such a consuming pastime to him he would refuse to let the tub out of his sight. Even when we took him into our trailer (rarely) the first place he went for was the wash basin in our bedroom, where I turned on a sink full of warm water, gave him a rag and a piece of soap and then we could all relax for at least an hour.

It has always been a mystery to me why people like to start rumors into circulation. We travelled a regular route, yearly, and were welcomed with opened arms every place we went. But once, in the 40's, up and down the whole territory through which we travelled in the Eastern Seaboard states, a rumor went like wildfire that Snookie had killed Bob and that I'd had to shoot Snookie in order to get Bob's body out of the cage. It was tragi-comic when we pulled into our old locations, unannounced (as was often our habit) and friends would rush out and embrace Bob in a frenzy of joy, because it was not true. This was the beginning of a long, long list of damaging and even dangerous rumors that went around, from time to time. It was demoralizing too, because it often "gave us the willies" to hear some of the things that were supposed to have happened. I got a letter from my father, once, in which he told me some Carnie had a big chimp and was passing it off as a gorilla. On the front of his show was a picture of me with Tommy -- our gorilla, and the carnie was ballying, "See the gorilla that killed the lady."

We even had a worse one pulled on us in 1968 by a smutty little sex sheet, in which pictures (for which the photographer was not paid)were "lifted" from a legitimate news story in Grit, turned a quarter turn and used completely out of context. The big two-page spread ("Double truck" is their parlance) had in big black headlines that the gorilla had killed Bob! This just shows how careful a person should be about believing everything he reads. And we were distressed to learn how very gullible some people are when confronted with a printed page. Once we called up a show manager-owner to try to book our unit with him. He said, "Hell, no! I wouldn't have a gorilla on my lot! I saw an article where one of those things killed a guy in Florida!" No amount of explaining that it was a lie could convince him of his gullibility. **Don't believe everything you read. It isn't always the truth.**

One time, while we were parked at Bob's brother's place, I didn't even know the animals were out, and Bob turned Snookie and Suzy loose! He said he knew they wouldn't go far, and it was more than a mile in any direction (from Bob's brother's place where we were staying in the Blue Ridge Mountains of Virginia) to a house. He was curious to see what might happen if they got out somewhere else. He saw! It was almost dusk -- and two hours after their release -- before they came home! After they had been gone more than half an hour, Bob came to the trailer and said, "Mae, maybe you'd better come and help me try to find Snookie and Suzy. I turned them loose about a half hour ago and haven't seen them since." I practically screamed with shock. "What!!!!??" as I dashed out of the trailer. "Do you know what you've done?" I shouted, "Suppose they are seen by a hunter?"

"I didn't think they'd go more than a few feet away."

I rushed out towards where they'd last been seen. At that moment I knew I'd never "heard" such complete silence! Not a breath of air was stirring -- not a bird chirping -- not an insect! All was as quiet as a tomb! My pounding heart was all I could hear. I wondered if they could find their way back. I knew they would come back, but feared someone might take a shot at them before they could. I began calling them -- frantically giving the danger signal and calling their names. I would stop and let silence prevail for long minutes, then start calling again. I figured if they were lost they could "beam in" on my voice. After what seemed an eternity, I heard a cow, down in a valley, bellowing urgently. I called to Bob and said, "They'll be home pretty quick now, they're down in that

42

valley and just scared a cow."

Realizing they are afraid of cows and horses (or anything bigger than themselves) I knew they had spooked the cow and were, in turn, scared witless. Now we all kept calling and giving the danger signal. The cow must have been more than a mile away, from the way she sounded, so we knew it would take a few minutes, through all the undergrowth, for them to get back. About half way between where the cow had been heard and where I stood, a flock of crows wheeled, noisily, into the air. This helped our cause even more, and also told me about where our beloved pets were, and that they were actually headed home.

In a few minutes Snookie came rushing home, panting and perspiring. We took him to his cage and impressed it on him that he was lucky to make it home. It was fully five minutes before poor little Suzy was able to catch up with him. Every bit as hot and out of breath. This was never tried again and I had been frightfully apprehensive for their safety.

From the very first, Snookie took a definite liking to me and to Bobby. Although he liked Bob alright, Bob was the Boss and we were his playmates, more his equals. Velda Mae was so small that we had to be especially careful with her because he was jealous of the attention she got. I was always careful to keep her away from him; and, of course, this prevented their getting acquainted, too.

One day, Bob tied Snookie to a wire clothesline in a friend's yard so the chimp could get some exercise while Bob went uptown. He told me to watch the animal, even though I had pleaded with him not to leave Snookie outside. I could not convince Bob that as soon as he was out of sight Snookie acted as if he were the Boss, and all kinds of weird things happened. I stood guard so no one would get too close – a job I detested because people simply will not listen when you tell them an animal is dangerous, especially when the animal in question happens to to be tied out. On more than one occasion I have been forced, in the past, to be really nasty with people to prevent having them go up to him and get maimed. So it was with this kind of fear in my heart that I went on "guard duty."

The baby was asleep somewhere. In the house-car, I guessed. Anyway, when I saw Snookie make a sudden dash towards the other end of the line, I looked up and saw my two-year-old daughter coming "in range" and Snookie making straight for her! There were at least a dozen people around, but none of them realized the danger. Our six-year-old son was standing nearby with a toy baseball bat in his hand. I ran past him, grabbed the bat as I went, and got to Snookie just as he grabbed the baby and threw her to the gound. I didn't wait to see what he planned to do to her. I knew, all too well, that he was going to bite her. I came down across his back with the little stick and he turned on me. I ran backwards along the clothesline, to draw him away from her, swinging the bat, and frantically trying to keep him off of me at the same time. As I ran I screamed, "Move the baby! Somebody move the baby out of range!" Near the other end of the clothesline was a tangled mass of weeds, and beneath this mess was an old piece of wire fencing. I tripped and found myself sitting on my left foot with my right leg stretched before me. A perfect target for Snookie's teeth. He grabbed my knee with his right hand, my ankle with his left and started chewing up and down my leg like a hungry neolithic man might have chewed on a dinosaur bone!

When he was "finished" he walked away and sat and looked at me as if to say, "Now! What are you gonna do about it?" I tried to whip him with the toy bat and did get a few licks in -- but he was too fast for me. When Bob came home, Snookie pretended innocence so convincingly that Bob actually blamed me for the whole incident. When Bob unsnapped his chain later that day, he found the chain was broken, and only a small piece of one of the links was holding it together! In another lunge or two, he'd have chewed me up again!

As it was, I nearly lost the leg. When I looked at it, there was only one tiny spot where the skin had been broken. The rest of the leg, from knee to ankle, was one solid, black bruise. Gangrene set in, and it was many weeks before I could walk again. Because this was before antibiotics, Dr. E.L. Johnson of Bedford, Virginia, saved my leg by prescribing constant bathing in hot epsom salts water. After this, I refused even to speak to Snookie, and this was the worst punishment I could have wished on him. Because I was one of his beloved playmates, it was hard for him to take my ignoring him. Bob said, pleadingly, "Mae, he's so pitiful; speak to him!"

"No," I insisted, "never again! He did not have to do what he did. I realize he's an animal but he's not that stupid!"

Then Snookie would come over and hold his hand out to me and whimper. I almost melted several times, but I would say, angrily, "No! You're a BAD BOY! Look what you did to me!" and I'd point to the bandage, whereupon he would come over and kiss it. How could I hold out against him? After a short time we were back on good terms. Snookie never again tried to bite me, although he did bite Bob, more than once, during his lifetime. Once, almost a year after this incident, our daughter, Velda Mae, poked her finger in his cage and he bit the end of it off. Yet, years later they formed a friendship that was almost as firm as the one between Snookie and Bobby.

We tried putting on a school show, a few times, with Snookie. Bob did the ventriloquism act, juggling and balancing, and I would do the lectures and my "lightning cartoon" act. Then Bob would bring Snookie on stage and let him ride his tricycle around a little bit, dressed in his striped T shirt and bib overalls. Then I would have a question and answer forum while he put Snookie in his cage, One day Bob got in too big a hurry to get back in the auditorium to help me pack the props, and when he put Snookie up, he forgot to snap the lock shut. The Janitor came into the auditorium and said, "Better get the little boy, he's running loose in the hall." Snookie had escaped into the school still dressed in his overalls and T shirt. It was hard (in those early days) for some people to accept the fact that he was not human.

People enjoyed looking at Snookie so much that we often had some strange requests. A store man in Louisiana asked Bob to take Snookie over to show him to some of his customers who were in the back room playing pool. Bob complied with the request. As Snookie walked in, several of the men dived head first out of the windows into the bayou, over which the back windows were facing. Then Snookie started throwing the stove wood and several others left, too. After this experience, it will probably be a long time before the owner will want another chimp in his store!

While we were at Bob's brother's place, Bob took a trip away for the day. I was recuperating from the serious bite Snookie had inflicted only a week or so before. Several people were in the store, and someone yelled over to the house, "Hey! Snookie's loose!" I didn't want a repeat performance on the leg, so I told my sister-in-law, Velda, to lock the house up. She saw him in the hall, so the only thing we got locked was the door to the room where we were. Snookie went to the pantry and got into the honey crock. When he came out on the porch where we could see him through the window and curtains (and he could not see us), we saw he had reached in deep and was running all over the place with a big hunk of honeycomb, dripping as he went. His belligerent behavior indicated that someone was going to "get it." Bob finally came home and saved the day, but not before Snookie had "gummed up" the whole house from kitchen to front porch. Velda was nearly in tears, because she is known to be a fastidious housekeeper. Snookie, as usual, put on his sneaky "innocence" act, but this time Bob could not defend him -- covered as he was with the sticky mess.

Often as not, Bob would tie Snookie out in the hay in the barn at Sweetie's place. One night a neighbor who had been imbibing a little too freely, bet Sweetie he could put Snookie's shoulders on the floor. Sweetie was only a little bit more sober than the neighbor. They decided they didn't need to wake Bob up to referee the fight, and they went out to the barn at about 11:30 or 12:00 P.M. to "fight the ape." That was foolhardly enough, but what made it worse was the fact that power lines had not yet reached that area and it was "pitch dark" in that barn and everywhere else. They didn't even carry a flashlight!

We were awakened by the screams. When we got out there the neighbor was holding his wrist and letting the end of one of his fingers bleed. Sweetie was "laughing his head off." He had won his bet. Bob said wearily, "Get in the car. I'll take you to the Doctor."

On the fifteen mile ride over dirt roads, Bob asked him, "What in the hell were you trying to do?"

"I was gonna put his shoulders on the ground," he said.

"You didn't have any light out there. Do you mean to tell me that you went out there, groping around in the dark, and grabbed that sleeping chimp and didn't think he would bite you?" Bob couldn't believe it.

Bob continued, "Is that what you are going to tell the Doctor? You know what the Doctor is going to think? He's going to want to ship you out to the funny farm. You'd better think about it, man."

"Yeah," P.C. said sheepishly, "that's right. Don't you tell him! I'm gonna tell him it got mashed off when I jacked up my car. Don't tell him what really happened." They had to wake Dr. Johnson up in the middle of the night. The nearest hospital was twenty-eight miles away. Every time we met him after that, P. C. would hold the hand with the finger stub up and wink. We never told on him, but I think he told it on himself years later, because everyone in Bedford County knows about it.

Snookie was especially fond of children and loved to play games with them when he was tied out or on the leash. When I look back and remember that he weighed a hefty forty-nine pounds when we got him, I marvel at how good he was! How gentle and kind with kids! He played his own version of "Blind Man's Bluff" that was especially cute. He (apparently) remembered the ghost incident when he was smaller, and

47

figured to play the same trick on the kids. We would give him a man's handkerchief and he would drape it over his head and pretend he was not able to see through it. He would then pursue anyone who would ran away from him.

Once Bob scared him with a little rubber snake. He ran away from it. Then when he found it was not real, he tossed it aside. Some twenty or thirty minutes later, when Bob wanted to put him up, he pulled Bob over to where the rubber snake had been discarded and took it with him into the cage, where he proceeded to frighten poor Suzy with it, precisely as Bob had frightened him!

I had a fox terrier and she had a litter of four-week-old puppies that we let run loose, while we were camped at Bob's brother's little "Jot Em Down" store in Bedford County, Virginia. While we were there, Bob always tied Snookie out in the woods, across the road, where he could climb and play all day. He let Suzy run loose because she would not leave Snookie. Usually when one animal was tied, the other would not leave, but Suzy worked a trick on us that caused her to be tied thereafter. She stold groceries from people's wagons and cars. They would go into the store and bring the bags out, put them in the vehicle, and go back in the store to talk or to pay the bill. When they got home, several of the items would be missing. They'd come back and fuss at "Sweetie," Bob's brother, who would be flabbergasted. He was such a teaser that everyone thought this was one of his bad jokes. Upon careful investigation, it was found that Suzy had been stealing the stuff and piling it up in a special hiding place. She had quite a collection, so it had been going on for some time.

While she was free to come and go as she pleased, she did some cute things. Once she found where Bob had stored a hundred-pound bag of pecans. She got as many as she could hold in her hands and feet and waddled to where Bob was sitting on the grass. She dumped them in a pile and handed one to Bob. He took the hint and put it on a nearby rock and hit it with another one and handed it back to her. She grinned and chirped her "thank you" and sat and ate most of them then went back to the bag for another "load". This was repeated until she had her fill.

With Suzy on the loose every day nearly everyone in the area was, more or less, on the alert.

We had a little pet monkey, and he got loose one Sunday morning. He went galloping down to the black folks' church in the valley. When they realized he was in the church, he was drinking out of their water bucket. Someone yelled, "There's the Go-riller!!" Since the water bucket was at the door, several of the men lept through the opened windows. The monkey was quickly caught and brought home, and the interrupted services took up where they had left off.

Suzy had a little kitten which she had "adopted," and which she carried almost everywhere with her. There was a dead pine tree in the yard, some thirty or thirty-five feet tall. On top of this Suzy built a nest, and she carried that little kitten to that tree-top nest, then sat there grooming it, for hours. The first time she went up, everyone was terribly concerned for the safety of the little cat. But when Suzy decided to come down, she brought kitty along with her, safely to the ground. The cat must have enjoyed it, because it became almost a ritual; every day that Suzy was loose, she spent a couple of hours in her tree-top nest, "Playing house." I told curious spectators, "That's her play house and kitty is her doll." Kitty never tried to avoid her so he must have liked it too.

Many years later, "a lady chimp," Cheeta Meluzzi came to the Chimp Farm, and had several chimp children. One of her babies went to Mr. and Mrs. Keith White in Pinellas County, Florida. They named the little fellow Pepsi.

We thought it would be nice for them to take the baby over to Tampa to show it to Cheeta's former owners. They did. When they came back and reported the Meluzzi's reactions to us they had this story to tell about Cheeta; it seems someone in the family had a baby who was just toddling. Cheeta loved the baby and was allowed to play with it. Her maternal instincts worked overtime, one day, and she carried the beloved infant to the top of a tall tree. There she sat, happily grooming the baby for quite some time, with the frantic parents standing helplessly beneath the tree -- wringing their hands and pleading with Cheeta to come down. This was the reason she was "retired" to the Chimp Farm. If our Suzy had not been a "cat stealer" in the early days even **we** might have found that story hard to believe. But Cheeta brought the little "victim" down, unharmed, just as Suzy had brought the kitten safely to the ground.

In his fascinating little book **My Friends the Baboons**, Eugene N. Marais tells of a similar experience a Dutch mother had with her baby. Only that time it was a large male baboon who kidnapped her child and went to the top of a sixty-foot tree. The baboon was coaxed down by a Bushman and the baby was not seriously hurt. Whereas Cheeta came to the Chimp Farm after her escapade, the poor baboon "paid with its life" for his escapade, in Africa.

Bob always tied Snookie out in the woods, across the road, where he could climb and play all day. I was across the road at the house when I heard one of the puppies yowling. I rushed over to see what was wrong with him and was horrified to see Snookie, sitting on the ground, with a completely placid-emotionless expression on his face, as he held the hind legs of one of the puppies, and was slamming him on the ground in a figure-eight pattern -- repeatedly. This was about 1946. It was not until I saw that marvelous painting by Jay Matternes in one of Goodall's books, depicting the killing of a young baboon by a big male chimp, that I realized that what I had stopped with a shout, was a purely instinctive food-gathering act. Whether Snookie would have attempted to eat the puppy will forever remain a mystery because of my instinctive rescue. From the Goodall account (**My Friends the Wild Chimpanzees**, by Jane Goodall), it is no mystery about that poor little baboon. The wild chimpanzees did, indeed, eat the little baboon.

Tobacco Road, Georgia is one of many areas so named in the South. This one was a small community in Eastern

Georgia where we put on our show in one of the early years with Snookie, our only "fighter" at the time. Bob was on the platform, talking over the microphone when a drunk forced his way past him and went into the arena cage. Bob continued talking as I ran around to the back and just got there in time to prevent the drunk from opening Snookie's cage and letting him out. He was shouting, "I can lick that G-D-S-B. Let me at him!" Bob got him ready to go into the cage above my protests. "The man's too drunk, Bob, he can't do that!" Bob said, "Let him go in. He's so sure he's so tough, we're going to let him try it." I had lunch bags in the truck and would say to each man, "Empty your pockets into this bag and give it to a friend. If you lose anything out of your pockets in there you'll never find it in the five or six inches of wood shavings on the floor." This got rid of any weapons they might have planned to use on Bob or Snookie, and saved us the trouble of hunting for rings, watches and small change after each show.

The drunk complied. He went in and Snookie "shellacked" him. His friends had to help him off the lot. The next day an old, old man with a cane came and shouted in his thin, quavering voice, "Ya'd ort to of had better sense than to 'of let a man in a cage with a varmint like that!" as he shook his cane at us. The drunk was not able to get out of bed.

One time, while we were working in the schools, Snookie tore his wooden cage apart. If he hadn't been chained inside, he would have been loose for hours during our absence. As it was, he was able to reach up in a storage compartment over his cage. This he did, and he took down a cartoon (500) of paper "V" cups (which we used for Snow Cones) and the two or three gallons of Snow-cone Syrup in glass jugs. This he drank until he was full. Then he poured a little bit into each cup, and laying them down on the floor when filled, he was soon in a sea of sticky, pink syrup. Not satisfied with that, he got down several gallons of paint. He probably tasted that and found it unpleasant, but he poured that in the cups, too, and had red, green and white paint all over himself and all

51

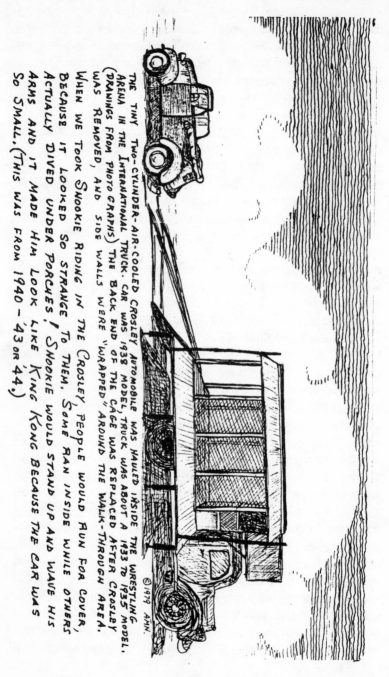

THE TINY TWO-CYLINDER-AIR-COOLED CROSLEY AUTOMOBILE WAS HAULED INSIDE THE WRESTLING
ARENA IN THE INTERNATIONAL TRUCK. CAR WAS 1938 MODEL, TRUCK WAS ABOUT A 1933 TO 1935 MODEL.
(DRAWINGS FROM PHOTOGRAPHS) THE BACK END OF THE CAGE WAS REPLACED AFTER CROSLEY
WAS REMOVED, AND SIDE WALLS WERE "WRAPPED" AROUND THE WALK-THROUGH AREA.
WHEN WE TOOK SNOOKIE RIDING IN THE CROSLEY, PEOPLE WOULD RUN FOR COVER,
BECAUSE IT LOOKED SO STRANGE TO THEM. SOME RAN INSIDE WHILE OTHERS
ACTUALLY DIVED UNDER PORCHES! SNOOKIE WOULD STAND UP AND WAVE HIS
ARMS AND IT MADE HIM LOOK LIKE KING KONG BECAUSE THE CAR WAS
SO SMALL. (THIS WAS FROM 1940 - '43 OR '44.)

©1979 A.H.

52

over the end of the truck when we got home. Fortunately, we had an oldtimer named Earl Woltz with us, and his quick-witted handling of the situation saved the day, but what a mess to clean up!

We decided that Snookie must be lonely not having his own kind with him. "Maybe," we agreed, "he needs a mate! Wouldn't it be wonderful to have a chimpanzee family on the show?" So we bought tiny twenty-one inch tall "Suzy Q" for Snookie's bride. We didn't know then what we learned later from Phil Carroll: it is always best to have a bigger female and smaller male to start with. The female will be gentle with the little male. A small female becomes a victim of a larger male, especially if he figures, as Snookie apparently did, that she was cutting in on our affections and attentions. Jealousy is the only motive I can conceive of for his show of brutality toward poor little Suzy. It took only a couple of tentative introductions to realize that this marriage was on the rocks before it started.

To make matters worse Suzy came down with the same kind of deep cold Snookie had when we got him. Again we had to run a "chimpanzee hospital." And -- fractious little Suzy had a nip at every one of us. She was a little vixen. It was hard to realize, years later, that sweet, lovable adult Suzy Q was the same one from infancy!

Bob's desire to own a Crosley automobile having been realized at last, we had to devise a way to transport it from town to town. Very early we had learned that it was safer for us to drive our own equipment and not to trust any of it to helpers. Because I was a "new" driver Bob drove the car and trailer and I drove the International truck. He was afraid I'd not be able to handle the longer rig. I designed the show equipment and came up with the idea to make the whole back end of Snookie's wrestling arena-cage removable. By dropping the tailgate-stage to the ground it was out of the way of the two ramps we used to load the Crosley into the truck. It was always an adventure when we pulled into a town to set the show up. People would laugh in amazement

53

when the truck would "give birth" to the funny little Crosley automobile. Then, moments later, I would open the trailer door and Bozo, our fawn Great Dane and Trouper, our Toy Fox Terrier would jump out. At one town a man's eyes bugged out when he saw Bozo tied to the truck.

"What kind of dog is **that**?" he asked in astonishment.

Bob was busy but he said, "A Great Dane."

A few minutes later a little boy came running up and the man grabbed him by the arm and said, "Look out, there boy! That man tells me that's a Great Dangerous Dog!"

After about a year we decided if Snookie would not marry Suzy we should get her a new husband. So when we saw an ad in the **Billboard**, (the world's foremost amusement weekly) saying that animal dealer Henry Trefflich in New York City had a trained chimp for sale, we bought him.

When the huge crate arrived from the Detroit Zoo, the man in the baggage car looked at the label before unloading and asked us if we knew the box was C.O.D. When we assured him we did, he then wanted to know if we knew the C.O.D. was four hundred dollars. We laughed and assured him that the four hundred was just the balance we owed, since we had sent a substantial deposit in advance. He shook his head and said, "No animal is worth that much money!" But we never regretted the purchase.

Chapter Two

When we got Joe home we thought, "Good Lord! He's so big!" He weighed almost a hundred pounds! But when he came out of the crate he was a perfect little gentleman. We were anxious to feed him but he refused all food. We tried everything we could think of with no luck. I was thinking, "Oh Boy! Here we go with another sick chimp!"

We had bought him from the Detroit Zoo, for $600, through the famous New York animal dealer, Henry Trefflich, but we didn't get any information about him. I wrote to the Zoo to find out what his name was, since we have always had too much respect for their feelings to change an ape's name. After we waited for several anxious days, his trainer wrote us a beautiful letter, outlining his whole routine, "And," he added, "His name is Joe." This may be hard to believe, but as soon as we started calling him Joe he started eating. He soon seemed like a family member to us, just as Snookie and Suzy seemed before him.

With Joe, a fully-trained chimp, we decided we had the perfect set-up for a school show. Here was a cute little chimpanzee who did a fabulous routine. He even called our attention to parts of his act which we had forgotten!

Joe was an enthusiastic performer who could ride a bicycle, tricycle, scooter, jump rope, walk a tight rope, walk on his hands, and wore overalls, striped T shirt, cap and tennis shoes. He ate with tableware and was very well behaved. Because of this, I went out and booked him in school assembly halls, where he became very popular. On the first performance, he perked up and "came alive." He was back in his realm. We had read and re-read his routine because, "after all, he was only a little animal who needed our guidance." But we left one trick out because we had overlooked it. It was a simple thing but it belonged in the act. The "trainer" was supposed to take Joe's hat off and toss it on the floor while Joe was circling the stage on his bicycle. On the next trip around Joe was to pick up the hat with his foot as he passed, and with his foot he put it back on his head without slowing down. It was a beautiful demonstration of the dexterity of his hand-like feet.

We couldn't figure out why Joe kept circling the stage and looking at Bob expectantly. Finally, in exasperation Joe threw his own hat on the floor and then retrieved it on the next trip around. It got a big laugh from the kids in the audience. Joe had simply refused to leave a good laugh out of his act. It was a simple case of the chimp teaching a human. Needless to say a single lesson was enough and it was kept in the act.

We had a lot of confidence in him, and trusted him enough to let him run free on the hillside at Bob's sister's farm. There was a very steep "gully" down the hillside, and we put Joe on his bicycle and headed him down the steep hillside for a fast ride. He revelled in it until it went too fast -- then he would jump off, and let the bike wreck itself at the foot of the hill. Then he would go to the bottom of the hill and bring the bike back up the hill for another "go." After about a half-dozen trips that little wise guy figured out how to steer the bike for a longer slower and safer ride by following the contour of the gully. It is my opinion that many a child would not have figured that trick out on his own, so quickly.

To make Joe feel welcome and to get better acquainted with him, Bob dressed him up one day and took him in the car to pick up a motorcycle that Bob had to leave beside the road a couple of miles from home, when it broke down. When we drove up, an old man was standing on the other side of the fence. Bob said, "Say! Look at this little fellow! Did you ever see anybody like him before?"

The old fellow peered at Joe in amazement.

Always the practical joker, Bob said, "He won't talk to us. He won't tell us his name. He is lost."

The animal was wearing tennis shoes, overalls, striped T shirt, and a little visored cap. The old man shook his head in disbelief and said, "No sir, Mr. Bob. I ain't got no idea who he is! You better take him to Lynchburg and turn him over to the police. They's something bad wrong wid dat boy! The police will know what to do with him! Don't you leave him here! They will find his pappy for him!"

When we presented Joe's act in the school auditoriums, we would finish the show with a "bicycle race" which Joe always won. The kids from the audience would get scared and jump off or run the bikes off stage -- anything to get away from that weird looking thing!

One small school in North Carolina had no auditorium -- as such. But the doors between rooms folded open and all the kindergarten and first grade tables were pushed together for a bumpy, uneven "stage." The bicycle race got too close to the edge of one of the tables. The animal, the tricycle, the table and Bob "went under." It was a mad scramble for a couple of minutes, but fortunately no one was hurt.

We booked another tiny school near Lynchburg, Virginia. There were only eighty children enrolled. We were told they were not allowed to have any shows in the daytime but could have "doings" at night. So, because the teacher was so anxious for her kids to see the show, we came back at night and put the show on. Because the school had no lights we had to buy a gasoline pressure lantern that cost us $8.00.

When we presented the show, all eighty kids came out and paid their dimes. We put the show on for them and earned a gasoline lantern for our efforts. No one ever enjoyed the show more than that little group.

While we were at Bob's sister's farm, Joe used to go back to the barn with Bob and carry back the bag of straw for his bedding, without a leash. Joe was an amazing animal. He was very smart. When he got older, however, he became quite "crotchety" and "cranky." He didn't enjoy the "foolishness" as of old, but this was to be expected since it is characteristic of the normal development of chimps (and when you think about it -- of some humans, too).

There were many young people who liked to travel with our show in the summertime and help us with our chores. Some would never get back in touch with us and others we would see – only briefly -- when we played their home-town again the following year. Of all of them, I think Leon Wood was probably the most appreciative. I asked him to write about his experiences on our show, and I received the following account of his experiences on our show from him in January of '79. It is a classic.

"One afternoon I stopped by Mrs. Harrison's country store on my way home from school. This was back in the late spring of 1943, and the memory is as fresh as yesterday's, because two strangers came into the store and both men insisted that everyone in the store should have a soft drink on them. I didn't have the 5¢ to buy one, so this was a pleasant surprise. This one man had a pleasant personality and won everyone over by showing us some magic tricks he could do with coins. He was very good. He introduced himself to us and said his name was Bob Noell and he asked Mrs. Harrison if he could use the vacant land she owned, across the road from her store, for a week to put up his show. He explained that he had a variety show, and had a wrestling ape. Then he showed us some pictures of the ape and looked at me and said, "You can be the first to wrestle the big one. His name is Snookie." I didn't tell him to his face, but I thought, "Not me! That thing would tear me up like newspaper." Instead, I said, "I don't think that brother Snookie and I have anything in common."

Well, he rented the lot from Mrs. Harrison and told us he would be coming in about two or three weeks. I never did know who the other man was because Captain Bob took over from the beginning. The other person didn't have no smarts and I found out later that I was dumb, too.

About two weeks later, here comes the show! Captain Bob -- wife Miss Mae -- and their two children Bobbie and Sister, and Snookie, Joe and Suzy the chimpanzees. Well, of course, no one knew the difference between gorillas and chimps.

Monday night was the first night of the show. There was a large group of people there and Capt. Bob knew just what to do. He said he would pay anyone $5.00 to put Snookie in the box. Everyone wanted to get the $5.00 but the gorilla meant a change of mind, so Capt. Bob got his five-year-old daughter to go in with that big ape and she played with him like he was a doll.

Me? Yes! I wanted the money because money was hard to get or earn, so I went in to try to put that chimp on his back. I found out very fast, that I couldn't do anything with Snookie, so Capt. Bob told me to play with him as I would play with a person. When I did as he told me Snookie rolled over on his back for me. Well, the people thought I had put that animal on his back. Capt. Bob gave me two or three dollars! Boy! Oh boy!

Then it was time for one more show. Well this person was a big man and he could not put Snookie on his back, but Capt. Bob gave him a couple of dollars, too.

The most important part of the show, to me, was that a lot of it was a free show. Capt. Bob and Miss Mae had the talent to perform acts for the people that had no money to see the animal act. They gave the people their money's worth and what I thought, at first, was a put-on was not.

They really did seem to enjoy the show as well as the audience. Yes, I thought that was an act, but they truly did enjoy putting on the shows. I found this out when I joined them later and stayed with them two different times. I learned quite a bit about the entire operation and learned to love them – even the animals. I was a young boy and could not make up my mind whether to stay with them or go back home. I didn't have much work to do while I was with Capt. Bob and Miss Mae. They were very good to me. Most anything I wanted they would give to me. They treated me as if I was their own.

I guess the best thing that happened while I was with them was that I began to learn something about the animals and their nature. Snookie was the best to play with."

(Leon confessed, in another letter, that he had opened Snookie's cage door to feed him unbeknown to us -- an extremely dangerous stunt.)

"Although Joe never hurt me, he would lose his temper sometimes. Now -- Suzy -- she was a female and so mean she would hurt any of us. I loved Snookie because he loved me, and he could have hurt me if he had wanted to. Joe could have hurt me too but he never did and he had plenty of chances. We took Joe to the schools to do lots of his acts. They were fun and you had to love him. I was not afraid of the animals – but I respected them.

Well, one day I got sort of homesick and left to return to school. Before long I had been drafted and was in San Diego for U.S. Navy Boot training. Got out of the Navy in '48.

About twenty years after I had left Captain Bob and Miss Mae, I happened to see them again in my wife's hometown. Then, the last time I saw them was about 1967, and hadn't heard of them for a long time after. So, about fall of 1978 I wrote to them at the old address in

Virginia and was sort of scared I might hear something not satisfying. The letter was forwarded to their Florida address and about a month went by – then my 'phone rang and it was "Miss Mae." I cannot explain how I felt. I knew that I loved them as a father and mother (my real parents are deceased). After all these thirty-six years, I'm still in contact with them.

I regret that I did not let them raise me up, and I am sure they would have made something good of me that I don't have now.

I hope to see them soon. They are getting up in years and I'd like to visit them at their Chimp Farm down in Tarpon Springs, Florida. I close saying may God bless them and keep them."

And he signed it, "Leon William Wood."

Joe was always an "escape artist" as a youngster. Once he escaped while Bob was gone and caused pandemonium at Annie's (Bob's sister's place). There were several strangers around and I was afraid someone might get into trouble with him. I had to work a trick on Joe to make him come to me; I gave George, Annie's helper, a blank gun and told him to fire it three times, at the animal, and to be ready to get in, in case the trick back-fired. George complied and Joe ran to me for protection and I rushed him "protectively" to his cage which he entered eagerly. During his freedom, this time, the group of strangers, who had just driven up in their car, complied with my request to remain in their car and run the windows up. Joe made straight for the car, jumped up on the running board and grabbed the door handle. They had locked it from the inside. Joe swung back and forth on the handle and shook the car threateningly. It was while this was going on that I got George to use the gun. The strangers piled out of the car when the coast was clear and asked, "Where is the rest room?"

Joe escaped another time, in a little town where we were showing. I threw a washpan of water out the front door of our trailer, and a few feet beyond where the water landed, there

WHEN WE STAYED IN NEW ORLEANS, WINTER OF 1945-46 WE SOLD THE INTERNATIONAL "ARK" AND GOT THE 1946 G.M.C. TRACTOR AND HAD THE 1937 FRUEHAUF REBUILT TO OUR SPECIFICATIONS. THE TAIL-GATE BECAME OUR "STAGE", THE TWO BACK DOORS BECAME THE BANNERS. BOTH SIDES HAD (HINGED-AT-THE-TOP) AWNINGS SO THE CROWDS COULD SEE INTO THE ARENA. THE FOUR NEST CAGES WERE BEHIND THE DOOR WITH THE WINDOWS. ENTRANCE OR EXIT WAS MADE VIA BACK DOORS OR THE TWO DOORS ON THE OTHER SIDE OF THE TRAILER. THIS UNIT WAS LATER "STRETCHED" TO ACCOMMODATE THE GORILLAS AND ORANGUTANS. WHEN WE HAD THE "CANDY SHOW", WE HAD TWO PLUSH-LINED FLASH CABINETS IN THE BACK END. THE CANDY PRIZES WERE KEPT IN THE CABINETS – ON DISPLAY – UNTIL SOME-ONE WAS LUCKY ENOUGH TO WIN THEM.

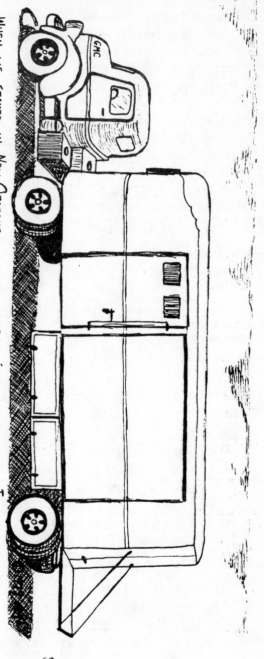

62

was Joe! I gasped, and when I did, he bristled up, then, catching myself, I opened the door wide and baby-talked him into the trailer. I have an old iron chair I've had for years. This was "his" chair when he came in the trailer. He climbed up on it as I closed the door. And all through my "animal business life" I have used a phrase that should become an international language to be used on animals; "I gonna git you some." Immediately the animal knows that food is coming, and he goes on his good behavior. I raided my ice box and cabinets (because, as always, the escape was performed in Bob's absence) to entertain him until Bob got back.

We have an agreement that the animal business is like mountain climbing and skin diving; it should be done on the buddy system. If the one who is handling the animal decides he needs something, he needs someone to run and get it for him (lead chain, a bit of food, etc.).

None of the escapes proved disastrous because we always made it a game until we could regain control, but we were beginning to get "fed up" with all the escapes and were wondering how long our luck would hold out. In 1946, we finally decided, "War shortages or no, we needed a new cage wagon if we were to keep the apes." In New Orleans we found just what we needed, a Freuhauf trailer, which could be rebuilt to our specifications. We went right to work on it. Because we had no other place to keep the animals, the man we traded with gave us permission to keep the old truck for three weeks while the new truck was being built. At the end of the third week the man came for his truck and our new one was not finished! We were parked right in front of a "metals dump" or junk yard, and that day they were loading a freight car with the stuff. I ran over and got permission from the boss of the crew to have his men set an old ship's hatch upright. This we could use for a cage for Snookie. Suzy and Joe could stay in the small wooden boxes until the new truck was ready. It was a lot more than three weeks before the truck was ready, and between times, we had two more escapes but this time in the heart of New Orleans.

First, Suzy decided to go for a walk. She went over back

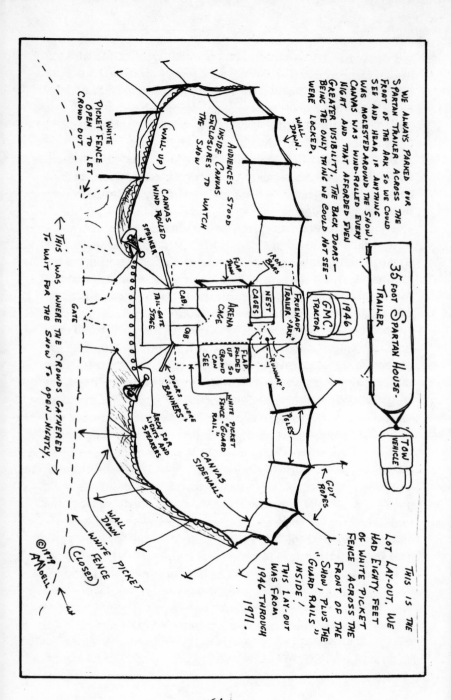

fences, under old frame houses, across streets, through back alleys, and stopped at a store with a big glass door. The people inside shut the door and held it shut in alarm. She grabbed the knob and shook the door fiercely.

A child came running, breathlessly shouting, "Hey, Mister! Your gorilla's a-loose!"

Bob ran back with the child. When Suzy saw him, she ran, screaming, back home, over the same route by which she had come. It was impossible to follow her and she got home before Bob arrived!

The second escape occurred one afternoon while Bob and I were at the shop looking at the new truck (which was still under construction). Bob had run over from the trailer park on his motorbike while I had stopped off after booking schools, in the car. I had been there only a few minutes when we got a phone call from the park that one of the chimps was loose. Bob jumped on the motorbike and ran over to the lot. When he got there, he found our twelve-year-old son, Bobby, holding the doorknob on the men's shower-room. The chimp was inside, turning the water on and off, kicking and stomping, and jerking on the doorknob and raising "General Cain." He had kicked the side out of his cage and then walked around the park a couple of times, passing within inches of several people, even letting a little three or four-year-old child pet him, before he went into the shower-room. Luckily, it was after school hours when it happened, or it might have been much worse, since no one but Bobby knew where we were, and no one else would have thought to have kept Joe shut up in the shower-room. One man even demanded that Bobby let him out because he might damage the fixtures.

Bobby said, "No! If he does any damage, my Daddy will pay for it! He's better inside. Just you call my Daddy. He's at the shop." He told them where the shop was.

After Bob put a lead on him, everyone relaxed and enjoyed the little fellow's antics. His cage was repaired and all was back to normal very shortly. This was a trailer park where nearly everybody who lived there was in show business, so everyone

Bob, and the crowd, waiting for the contestant. Sidewalls down - ready to open show

Show front in daytime - Canvas wind-rolled.

took this sort of thing in stride. If it had not been a Show-Biz Camp, we'd never have been permitted to stay there with the animals, in the first place.

That night, Bobby figured to have a little fun. He had a black leather glove on the end of a stick about three feet long. He had padded the stick, artfully, and wrapped it with an old piece of black fur. Whenever he wanted to scare someone, which was often, he would stick that "hairy arm" out in the direction of the "victim". The results were as varied as the individuals who were "victimized." After dark the night Joe got loose, Bobby, unbeknown to me, went around the park and scratched on the sides of trailers. He waved the arm over the window, when his victims looked out. Several people turned their lights out and shut all the windows. One man cured Bobby of any more nighttime shenanigans. (He was one of those who turned the lights out.) Later, Bobby followed up by knocking on the door. "Have you seen anything of one of the chimps?" he asked.

"I don't know what it was," the man said, "but next time it comes around, I am ready for it." He showed Bobby a pistol which he said was loaded. Bobby came home, and told us about it, soberly. This was the type person I was always afraid might shoot one of our escapees, and our son almost made a victim of himself!

While we were awaiting delivery on the truck, Snookie lived in the old ship's hatch. Bales of dry straw were used for a nice warm bed, and the porthole in center of the door top was exactly the right size for him to stick his head out after we removed all the broken glass from it. He was short, so he had to climb up to stick his head out. He would put one foot on each of the two hand rails and, looping his fingers over the window's rim, he would stick his head through and watch, for hours, the behavior of all the people he saw.

One man walked to within a few feet of the hatch, unaware that it was occupied. When he looked up and saw this sub-human face looking back at him, he almost had a heart attack. However, he got such a kick out of this experience that he victimized his own wife with it a few minutes later. Snookie took it all in as most amusing and entertaining.

Babies of practically all animals are, in their helplessness, quite lovable. But when a chimp becomes self-sufficient, he can (and usually does) become hard – if not impossible -- to handle. And when it is realized how big and how very strong they are when adult, it becomes very clear that a mere man is no match for an angry or determined ape.

There was a persistant "old wives' tale" (origin unknown) that we heard over and over again when we first got the chimp. The story went that "the reason a chimp becomes dangerous and subject to "fits of insanity" was because a chimp's brain developed faster than the skull and it drove him crazy." I always scoffed at this reasoning and now it is a known fact that chimps go through a lot of the same emotional changes during adolescence as humans do. The big difference is that inhibitions have played a big part in the development of the strength of the two species; no one has ever told a chimp, "Don't lift that, you might hurt yourself." So the chimp has all that primordial and primitive strength continuously at his disposal whereas man displays "superhuman strength" only on rare emergency or stressful occasions, and usually gets sick soon after such a display.

When Mickie Quinn was keeper of the Ape House in the Bronx Zoo in New York City, he showed us a male chimp (while we were **behind** the glass enclosure) who weighed 200 pounds!

The Guiness Book of World Records for the year 1977 tells of some tests that were said to have been made in 1924. A female chimp who weighed approximately 135 pounds was said to have registered a right hand pull of more than one thousand two hundred pounds during a fit of rage. And that a man weighing 165 pounds could pull only a little over 200 pounds, while a male chimp of the same weight, after bracing his feet and using only his right hand, pulled 847 pounds. Further information lists a "dead-lift" of 600 pounds with two hands by a 100 pound chimp!

Is it any wonder, then, that Kongo (85 pounds), Butch

(145 pounds), Joe (95 pounds), or Bamboo (100 pounds) found it easy to hang from the ceiling by one hand, and, hooking one finger in the back of a man's belt, sling him around the arena like a big rag doll?

The secret of training our fighting apes (if there was any secret) was in the fact that we started out with very young apes who were allowed to play with boys their own age. We knew that the chimp probably felt safer with little people when he was little himself. As he grew up the boys we let in the cage were progressively larger. Finally, men went in. I think the chimps actually thought all but the most obnoxious of men were playing with them. It took between eight and ten years to develop a really good animal for our show. This may be one reason why only three other people copied the show with varying degrees of success. Our show enjoyed one of the longest runs in show biz history -- thirty-one years! (1940-1971). It was successful because it featured audience participation and everyone wanted to get into the act.

"Joe the Boxer," as he came to be known, was very handy with his feet. He used his hand-like feet to pinch and bruise, so we had to outfit him with tennis shoes.

Most of the contestants thought that because we were show people we were lying to them, but it is true that everything we did was done to protect the man. We know now, and knew then, that no man -- even no four men -- can match the strength and cunning of an angry chimp.

Many times, early in the game, two men would go in to try to wrestle the chimp to the floor. It was too dangerous for the men and we stopped that. The chimp gave no quarter and, often as not would use the body of one man as a weapon upon the other. We have seen one of the chimps hang on the overhead bar with one hand, grasp the back of the leather belt of one man and swing him helplessly against the other man. Inevitably both men would be on the floor yelling, "Get him off!" as the chimp bounced gleefully up and down from one to the other. Weight lifters — Golden Glovers — black belts — professional wrestlers — town bullies —

— you name it — all have had a try at it at one time or another, and all have come away "believers."

There were times when I had to size people up and take precautions to prevent being hurt by some of them. Too many of our patrons and, often, our contestants were "loaded" and likely as not, stupefied with drink. When a man came out of the cage after a pretty rough go, if he was a bum sport, he might forget that I had tried to steer him right before he went in. In such an event, he might want to take his spite out on me. That was one of the reasons we hired policemen to stand by — to see that the show went smoothly. In one town in Virginia a muscular young man went in with Joe the Boxer and broke all the rules. The inevitable happened. He got the "be-jabers" beat out of him. I went in the cage and tried to stop the ape because Bob was having trouble controlling him after the guy had made him angry. At long last Bob got Joe into his cage and to my horror, the contestant remained, apparently unconscious, on the floor. I was afraid he was really hurt. Two of his friends ran into the cage and helped him to his feet. When they did he revived and saw me. It was fortunate that I was just out of reach when he swung a hay-maker at me. His friends grabbed him and said, "Don't hit a woman!" and he replied, "I just wanted to get even with her for what she did to me!" He apologized later when I reminded him that he didn't listen to my advice when I gave him the rules, and that I was not the one who beat him up. But that danger was always there. I've always said, though, "Thank God there are more good people on Earth than bad ones." Even so, we had to put up with our share of the "bad ones." It was just such an episode when I had to swear out a warrant in Virginia for the arrest of a man who harrassed us to such a degree that we could not allow it to pass.

We were showing in a mountain town at a country fair in Virginia and huge crowds were attending the show each night. It was not too far from Roanoke, and Bob's kinfolks were there that night. We had a contestant on stage and more

70

than half the crowd was already inside when two drunks came up and caused a commotion. One was a big guy who must have weighed 260 solid pounds. He was not fat but was big and muscular. His companion was a slightly smaller than average-sized man. The big guy blocked my gate – stopping traffic and holding up the show. He demanded that we let his man go in and fight the ape and that we take the rightful contestant off the stage. This could not be done without misrepresenting the show to the customers who had already gone in expecting to see the rightful contestant go in. After a few seconds he became abusive and Bob called over the microphone for a policeman. A gasoline powered carinval ride beside our show was running without a muffler and making so much noise that the two officers standing near it did not hear Bob's request for aid. Bob was not aware of the fact that they couldn't hear him and he said, "If you don't come and get this man out of the gate, I'm going to have to move him myself!" The policemen saw Bob pointing at the gate and thought he was telling them to come in to see the show so they nodded and waved at him. This infuriated Bob, who thought they were telling him "go ahead," and after the drunk made a couple of obscene remarks, Bob flew into him in a rage. The guy was a full head and shoulders taller than Bob and they tangled. Immediately the policemen took over, and because they had not heard any of the situation, they took both men downtown. Quickly as I could, I jumped into the cage and told the audience inside what had happened and explained that without Bob there could be no show. I asked them to please go out in single file and I would refund their money. As they were going out one of the men stopped behind me, as I refunded to the others, and said, "Mrs. Noell, that man is a trouble-maker everywhere he goes. He's been locked up in this town so many times you wouldn't believe it. You go to this lawyer and tell him what happened. They shouldn't have taken your husband in. It's too bad." He handed me a piece of paper that had the name of the culprit on it and the name of the lawyer. Underneath it he wrote,

71

"Bring charges against him, by all means." After the money was refunded I raced downtown and swore out a warrant for the drunk and brought Bob home. It was Friday night so they set the hearing for Monday. Under normal circumstances we should have moved to the new show lot on Sunday, in a new town, but we elected to stay over so we could appear against the drunk. We told the show owner to hold our space open and we would open Tuesday night. As fed up as we had become with the "drunk situation" we'd have stayed till doomsday to see the thing finished. I should have brought a lawsuit, but just wanted to see justice done. The lawyer turned out to be one who had defended the culprit in the past and who also was fed up with him. The Judge turned out to be a very old and wise man. I'll never forget him. "Mr. Noell," he said from his high bench, "You are dismissed." Then turning to the culprit he said, "Jones! (not his name) You have been more trouble to this court than any other man in this county! This is going to cost you a heap of money!"

Justice was done, as far as I was concerned, when Bob's name was cleared. When I first swore out the warrant he becane angry and said, "I'm not going to stay here for any trial!"

"O.K." I argued, "You go on to the next spot. Don't appear in court. You will have a jail record if you don't. Is that what you want? Right now, except for this thing, your slate is clean. Do you really want a blot on your name?"

That calmed him down and he decided to stay. We, as show people, had always had to take whatever was dished out to us by the local people and Bob was both elated and surprised when that fine old Judge did the right thing by him. The lawyer deserves a lot of credit, too.

Several local people appeared as character witnesses in our behalf because we had worked our little independent show in that town a couple of years before we joined the carnival. And Bob's kin came out from Roanoke and were "our" witnesses, too. The culprit had only his little drinking companion as a witness, who admitted that he had been too drunk to remember what did happen that night.

Drunks! The scourge of our lives.

In another place in Virginia we learned that we had to put a limit on how long a man should be allowed to remain in the cage. Until then, we had allowed them to stay as long as they wanted to because the chimp loved the exercise. At this place one man stayed for twenty-seven "rounds" with Joe the Boxer -- against our protests. We saw he was becoming tired but nothing would stop him. Finally, exhausted, he stopped, and we paid him and he went home. Later some of the spectators told us that he had a "fighting reputation" to uphold. They told us that he was once in a beer joint and started a fight and took on nine guys all at one time. Someone had to take a bar stool-top off its pedestal and beat him over the head before they were able to subdue him.

Later we were told that he had been unable to get out of bed for three or four days after fighting with Joe. But Joe was as eager to work the next night as he ever was. Because of this, we decided to limit the "fights" to five "rounds." A round was a start and stop whether it lasted ten seconds or the maximum of a full minute. But as time went on we discovered that even five rounds were too strenuous for the average man and we cut it down to three. And some of these bouts -- as short as they were -- were classics of contortionistic athletics, probably never seen before or since. And no two shows were ever alike -- no two men ever reacted in exactly the same way. Often as not a contestant would become frightened, and it would become a hilarious foot race around Bob. These the audiences loved. I've seen people fall flat on the ground and grovel with hysteria over a friend or acquaintance who lost his nerve and ran away from the chimp. But, chances are, the ones who laughed would not have had any more nerve, in the same situation, than the friend at whom they were laughing.

One time -- and one time only -- I saw Joe do something I would have thought impossible. A big guy went in to box

with Joe. The chimp sized the guy up, ran away from him --
ran three or four steps up the wall with flexed knees -- made
a catapult of himself and caught the guy in the pit of the
stomach with the top of his head -- and the fight was over.
Joe was none the worse for having butted the man with his
entire weight! All these tactics were the chimp's own natural
behavior. They were not "trained" except to wear the gear
and to stop when told to. The usual method the chimp used
for getting rid of a big bully was for the chimp to grab the
guy by his foot and flip him onto the floor, then to jump up
and down on him till he gave up. Sometimes, if the guy
caught the bars and didn't fall, (which happened quite a few
times) the chimp would disrobe the guy so fast that a couple
of them didn't realize they were in the nude until I turned
the lights out or until a part of their anatomy touched the
cold metal of the cage. Often as not when a chimp grabbed
the man's belt from behind, the belt would break and the
pants would be reduced to rags. And sometimes, when the
chimp put a finger under the pants cuff an inseam would
open up -- all the way around -- and make a "very revealing"
skirt.

One fellow was the town drunk. Everyone liked to make
fun of him and with him. He was well liked because he was
not a belligerant fellow. Someone dared him to go in, and he
took the dare. So in nervous anticipation he got drunk before
he went in. It was only a split second before he was in the
nude, because he had gone into the cage wearing nothing
more than a pair of old fashioned "strap and bib" overalls,
not even shoes. I always turned the lights out quickly if it
was a "nice guy" who got stripped. If he was a stinker I'd
wait about five or ten seconds before I flipped the switch.
This was a nice guy so I flipped the switch at once. But a long
unused spotlight was shining on him as if it had been
planned. As drunk as he was he was a decent man and had sat
down, knees up and head between knees, arms wrapped
around legs, modestly covering his nudity as best he could.
Since the light had been out of service for several years I had

a deuce of a time finding the switch. This was one of the episodes that I thought might have started the "streaking" fad, because the audience laughed unroariously and continued to laugh long minutes after the show was over. There's probably some kind of message for psychiatrists or psychologists in this, I think.

One policeman came to me and said as he laughed, "We ought to lock that ape up for putting on a lewd show, but you've already got him locked up."

Most of the contestants were people who had been dared to go in and fight. They could not back out, once committed to go in, for fear of the ridicule they might suffer for the rest of their lives at the hands of "friends." One man complained to me that he had smoked more than a pack of cigarettes in a couple of hours, before the show in nervous anticipation of going into the cage.

At a college town in New York State, college men fought, and it was a status symbol and a contest among themselves, all week, to see who'd have the most scratches or bruises acquired in the arena with one of our chimps. This caused an older man to gasp, "Shades of the Roman Arenas!" and I felt like saying "Amen" to that, because it went on for the whole week we were at that place.

There were many times that I tried to talk men out of going into the cage to box or wrestle because I feared they were too drunk and might get themselves hurt. But, for some reason, alcohol makes people feel they can lick an army and the more you say against something the more adamant they become. So, at last, in a lot of cases, I had to yield, against my better judgment.

There was just such an occasion in western North Carolina, in 1971, during our last year on the road. The man was determined to wrestle and equally determined to disobey the rules. As was usual in such cases, the "fight" was fast and furious with the man on the bottom yelling lustily for us to let him out of the cage. He was a bully and the police had been pleased to see him go in the cage. He came out in clothes that

75

(This is a sample of the release the contestants had to sign, before + after)

AFTER COMING OUT OF THE ARENA, THIS IS TO CERTIFY THAT, EXCEPT FOR A SCRATCH ON MY KNEE, I AM NOT HURT.

Johnathen D. Roe

5' 9½" – 146 – BLUE – BROWN – 1-16-1931
SCAR ON CHIN – TATOOED EAGLE RIGHT ARM; "L-O-V-E" FINGERS RIGHT HAND; "H-A-T-E" FINGERS LEFT HAND; "MOTHER" LEFT ARM.

I, __JONATHAN D. ROE__

in consideration of the sum of $1.00 to me in hand paid, hereby agree forever to release Noell's Ark Gorilla Show and/or any of its associates or affiliates or sponsors from liability and responsibility for any and all damages for injuries which I may receive as a result of entering into the arena with an ape and engaging in a boxing and/or wrestling match with said animal on its show grounds.

And I further agree that I have voluntarily entered into said match and that said sum has been paid and accepted by me as full payment and satisfaction for all such injuries as I may sustain in the arena while engaged in said boxing and/or wrestling match on the

__33__RD day of __OCTEMBER__ __1952__.

I intend to be legally bound by this agreement and have read same and know it is a release and not a receipt for money paid.

I hereby swear and affirm that I am over 21 years of age.

__Johnathen D. Roe__

__16   DOE STREET__

__JONESVILLE, IOWA,   12345__ $5⁰⁰

SHOWING AT WINSTON-SALEM N.C.

BUTCH

76

were pretty well messed up and with his hide pretty well bruised.

The next day a policeman came to tell us that the man had come to the police station to swear out a warrant for the arrest of the ape on charges of assault and battery. The policeman was laughing when he said, "We told him there's nothing on the books to cover that."

Some of the remarks the men made to the audience -- both before and after the "fights" -- were quite comical. Standing tall and arrogant one fellow pounded his fist on his chest and shouted, "I'm a veteran of **future** wars! And I'm gonna knock that ape's eyeballs loose!"

Another fellow whose nerve was probably failing him said plaintively, "Come up and see me at the hospital!"

And a fellow in the audience heckled another contestant until he said, "You're talkin' so big -- come on in with me!" Whereupon the voice in the audience replied "No thanks! I don't need no money **that** bad!"

When I had the men sign the release before they went into the cage to box or wrestle, I would take all the information about them that I could get off their driver's licenses and write it down. Whenever they did not have the license with them, I had to ask them a lot of questions. Here's a typical night's conversation. Please remember, the contestant usually had butterflies in his stomach and didn't always understand the question put to him.

Bob (over the loud speaker) -- "Is John Doe out there? He's the next fighter on the list. Is he here?"

Voice from audience, "If he is he'd better go home."

Mae -- "How tall are you?"

Contestant -- surprised -- "What's that for -- to measure me for my coffin?"

Mae -- "Of course not. I just need a full description of you."

Contestant -- "Five foot nine."

Mae -- "Any tattoos, moles or scars?"

Contestant -- "No, but I bet I **will** have."

Mae – "What nationality are you?"

Contestant -- by now thoroughly nervous – "Protestant! Protestant!"

Contestant turns to audience, laughing when he realizes he's made a comical reply and shouts, "It takes a good man to whip me – but it don't take him long!"

Voice from audience -- "Hey, John! I'll bet that's the last time you sign your name!"

Contestant – "Yeah! I ain't brave – just crazy!"

But the one I especially remembered was a young man who watched me write his name on the blackboard as a challenger for the following night. Standing on the platform beside me, he turned to the audience, pointed at the board and said, "See my name on the slate tonight, see my name on the tombstone tomorrow!"

I have always wondered why some people climb mountains, jump from airplanes, spelunk, or want to fight an ape. Is there a death wish there? That young man passed it off as a joke and got a big laugh from the crowd. But was that remark half in earnest? I wonder.

Kibitzers in the audiences sometimes came up with funny remarks too. One young fellow on stage and getting ready to go in was being teased by his peers. One of them said, "Hey! Can I have your watch?" Another said something about how the contestant should do it, whereupon he said, "If you think you can do it better than I can, you go in!"

The teaser said, "I ain't lost nothin' in there!"

Challenger said, "You've been talkin' awful big!" And the other fellow put his hand around his chin and said, "This is the only part of me that's athletic. All talk."

Still others, when dared by friends, to go in said, "How much will he pay me?" They said, "Five dollars just to try, man." – "Uh uh. No thanks. An office call is ten dollars. Uh uh."

At a little town in West Virginia, while we were with Hoxie Brothers' Circus, two drunks went into the cage and got roughed up. At that time we were giving everyone a dollar "to try" to put the ape's shoulders on the floor. After they came out, one of the drunks took the mike and said, "Ladies and gennelmuns, I went in that cage and I fought that ape. I got the hell beat out o' me, but I won a dollar!" Whereupon his buddy grabbed the mike and said, "Ladies and gennelmen, I **also** went in that cage, I **also** won a dollar and I **also** got the hell beat outa me, and I ain't too proud to permit it!"

Now that we are retired, people "discover" us and tell us about how much they enjoyed the show when it came to their town. One young fellow told me, "The first time I saw the show I was only sixteen years old. I wanted to wrestle the ape then, but I wasn't old enough. I waited five years until I was twenty-one and then you came back to my town. I came over to the show and you set the time at 8:30 the next night. I was real nervous before I went into the cage, but once I got inside and the ape hit me five or six times the nervousness went away. I wore three pair of pants, three shirts, a big heavy pair of shoes and a football helmet. The ape tore two of the shirts off with just one swipe of his hand. When I grabbed him by the shoulders I thought I had it made. He went right between my legs and jumped on my back and pounded me on the head. He jumped over and sat on the tire and I grabbed ahold of him again and he threw me on the floor. As I was leaving the cage he jumped on my head and knocked me down. I had a few bruises and a big red nose, but it was all worth it." **Holy Cow!** Worth it? Boys will be boys!

And an older man told me, "I was very excited and it was a thrill to get in a cage with an ape and box him as I did with Joe. One of the unforgettable highlights of my life."

A lady came to the zoo recently and told me that when their home burned down several years ago, her husband grieved more over his sportsmanship certificate than he did over any of his personal items, and would I PLEASE send him one to replace the original? The only way a sportsmanship certificate could be earned was by "emerging from the match without a scratch." If the man followed instructions they came away unscratched and the certificate was the only incentive I could think up to keep the men from being injured. When I stood at the door a lot of people thought I was hitting the door to make the ape rougher. But, actually, I did that to get Bob's attention and to stop the fights when they got too rough on the man. Most of the men **knew** I was working to keep **them** intact. I told them, "That little ape is strong and can take care of himself. Just don't antagonize him and you'll get the certificate AND the $5.00 and have fun doing it."

Another fellow who came to see us here at the zoo and told us he had gone in with the ape -- got the surprise of his life. He said he just got in the door good when Joe the boxer hit him. He said, "He hit me on top of my head so hard I thought my shoe soles were coming up around my neck! A friend of mine went in and got all his clothes tore off 'im. He stood there, just as naked as the day he was born. Man! I'll tell you! I never will forget how funny that was! That was a good show. Sure am sorry you folks have retired. I'd love to do it all again! It was the best fun we ever had."

A number of wrestlers have told me that because they believed all show people were liars, they thought they would find that the ape was a man in a monkey suit. One man told his friends he was "going in there and take that damned monkey suit off that guy and prove it was a fake." He told me later that when he got his hands on the ape and realized it was "for real" he nearly had a heart attack. We never knew about these things until long afterwards, sometimes not until the next year or even several years later.

Just recently a lady from Gainesville, Georgia, said to me, "Yes! I saw the show! I sure did! That monkey was knocking people east and west all week! There wasn't anybody could beat him!"

As an example of the power apes have in their hands, Dr. Temerlin (in his book **Lucy, Growing Up Human**), tells how frustrating he found it to be when Lucy would unscrew a nut with her fingers after he had tightened it with a wrench. Also he was surprised that when she put a nut on a bolt she could pull it down so tightly with a wrench that the bolt would break. Of course, these were almost certainly not the big oversized type bolts that we use on our cage doors.

My brother, J. W. Roach, and our son-in-law, Joe Deddo, have both commented on the awesome strength of chimpanzees. My brother had his own chimp show for about five years, and Joe went in the cage with Kongo one time just to see what it was like. He saw. His comment was, "I never dreamed that anything could be that strong!"

A hair-raising story that illustrates how very strong a chimp really is was told to me by a visitor to the Chimp Farm, named George Bruney, who lives in Orlando, Florida. He told me of a harrowing eight hours he and about forty other servicemen experienced in 1965. They were aboard a naval vessel, a "S.E.A.L. group."

Bruney gave me written permission to tell this story, so here goes:

Their C. O. went ashore on an African layover and while there, he bought a chimp in a bamboo cage from some natives. Once on board, the natives argued that the man had bought the chimp, but not the cage. As is so often the case, the servicemen thought they could handle the "cute monkey" (who turned out to be an adult male chimp with a full complement of formidable teeth) so someone opened the cage door. As anyone who knows the nature of chimps can tell you, an opened door is an invitation for a wild chimp to an explosion of fur and muscle and teeth. This one reacted according to the rules and several men were sent sprawling. One man was turned for a flip. And then the contest was on.

George informs me that the "S.E.A.L." group members are classed as "big brothers" to the green berets, and that they are well trained in combat. However, he admits that one "little" chimp kept forty men busy for upwards of eight exciting and exhausting hours. He says he doesn't know how many men got bruises and bumps and some even had broken bones. One man went aloft intending to bring the climbing

81

chimp down. Instead, the chimp threw him down a thirty-five foot drop onto a steel deck, and so seriously injured him that he was sent home.

George said that he and three other men had the chimp in their grasp for a few seconds, but that as well trained as they were, they were not able to hold him long, and when he got free of them he belted George and gave him a monstrous shiner. A black belt Karate man felt he could handle the situation and found he was every bit as helpless against this primitive fury as everyone else had been.

During his running, the poor chimp tried every way he could to get away from the men. Each time he started over the side, he realized he was above water and ran to another area. The ship was anchored out from the land and there was no way the poor guy could get away from the impossible situation in which he found himself. At last the C. O. regretfully ordered the men to shoot him. Too many of his men were being beaten. Also, there was no cage and no way to get him ashore, so there seemed little else that could be done. Poor chimp!

I'd like to know why this man wanted a chimp in the first place, and an adult at that! Sad to say, a lot of people who have owned chimps had no business having one. A couple of tragedies come to mind:

Some years ago a lady brought a nice young male chimp here to sell him. She left him with Cliff Faust and offered him a commission if he sold it. A sale materialized and a showman bought him. The chimp was a family member for a number of years, and was even used in the couples' act for a time. Then, one day, the chimp escaped and the man tried to put him back in his cage. In the ensuing scuffle the man was severely bitten and he had to shoot and kill the chimp.

Another bad episode concerned a performing chimp owned by a show biz couple. They wanted a big price for him and we couldn't afford it, so they left with the chimp, in a huff because we couldn't pay their price. A few weeks later, we read in the paper that they had **given** the chimp to some big horse farmer up north who shot the chimp after being attacked.

It is really too bad that people don't know that wild animals are not toys. Chimps are so cute and lovable as infants that it is hard to convince pet lovers that a chimp can grow to be as big as a man and five or six times as strong.

Chapter Three

I have always said that Snookie taught us most of what we know about chimps. (And we are still learning, after all these years!) But, to suppose that anyone knows all about great apes would be as fool-hardy as to say that you knew all about a certain group of people! Each animal -- believe it or not -- is an individual in his own right. Personality traits of one do not always match those of another, so that one must learn to "know" the individual animal, even as one learns to know an individual human! And, as with human friendships – one can not always come up with the right answers! Sometimes we guess wrong. And there is where civilization comes in! Animals have no inhibitions about flying into a rage or a tantrum, as most people do. Therefore, you might make an old friend quite angry (intentionally or otherwise) and you would not, necessarily, have to suffer physical harm. On the other hand, if you anger a chimp enough, you are almost certain to be bitten and maimed! It's true, he may suffer true remorse when he sees he has really seriously hurt you -- but then, of course, it's too late!

It was a dreary Sunday afternoon in March, 1953. We were

with a small carnival. The weather had been very bad. When we pulled into Heidleburg, Mississippi, we were confronted with a huge sea of red mud on the lot. The entire show was having an awful time in mud up to their knees and the axles of the equipment. Our big red cage truck weighed more than fifteen tons and as soon as it got on the lot it sank axle-deep. All the men on the show came and were struggling to get the thing to the back of the lot -- an almost hopeless project.

For some reason, I had a premonition that we should not put the show up there. Bob came to me and said, "We won't be able to put the trailer on the lot this week," and went back to the job of trying to budge the truck onto the lot.

We had made an agreement, years before, that we would never park our animals separate from our trailer, because we feared vandalism in our absence. Caged animals are defenseless and, I felt, needed our protection. I had this strange, ominous feeling and decided to try to convince Bob he should not work that week if we could not park our trailer near the "Ark."

I went over to where the men were digging in the sloppy red mud, and said, "Bob, I want to say something important. Listen me out, then whatever you say will be law. I don't want any argument. If you say, "Yes," I'll be happy, if you say, "No," I'll be distressed. But whatever you say -- we will do; you are the boss."

"I have a bad feeling about this place. Please, if we can't get the trailer on the lot with the Ark, let's not work this week. I'm afraid something horrible is going to happen here. Let's take the stuff off the lot and lay off."

His reaction was one of impatience and I stopped him before he could get started. "Remember -- no argument. You have said **no,** so no it is. But I have to say one more thing then I'll go: whatever it is that is going to happen is going to be very bad. In fact too bad to say, 'I told you so.' So--when it happens, I won't have the heart to say it -- remember that I'm saying it now; **I told you so!**"

All the men had stopped working to listen in on what we

85

were saying, and when I walked away they went back to their digging.

I walked away feeling very strangely upset, because we had to park the trailer nearly a quarter of a mile away. The only thing that kept me from putting up more serious resistance was the fact that at least part of the family had already been parked on the lot -- our son Bobby and Jean, his wife.

It was Friday morning. I had planned, all week, to go to Laurel, from Heidelburg, a distance of eighteen miles, to pick up my mail and express, because I figured I could not go Saturday since we often have to work Saturday afternoons. Also, I wanted to pick up a beautiful ring I had bought for my husband (I'd made a down paymment on it and wanted to close the deal).

Leaving the lot with a list of duties to perform that was "as long as my arm," I had no feeling of impending doom.

When we awoke that morning, Bob had been in one of his rare good moods, and we had a wrestling match, which comprised of my trying to get away from him because he was bent on tickling me "mercilessly." I was limp with laughter when I jokingly said, "You're in too good a mood this morning; you'll be foul before night!" Then I kissed him and got dressed.

Little did I realize what an evil day this was to become for both of us. I drove down to the lot and called to Bobby, "Do you want to go with me to get your birthday present today?" He declined, and I went on without him. His birthday was the day before -- March 19 -- the day the swallows come back to Capistrano!

On this Friday, March 20, 1953, I bought the tiny shoes for Dorothy's little boy, bought the animal food, got a much-needed pair of shoes for myself, sent Sister and her friend to the movie, while I got the express package, the mail, polly feed and several other things on my list. As I walked past the jewelry store, I noticed that they had not put another ring box back into the window; there was an odd little space where Bob's ring had been removed, only a few hours before.

I thought of him fondly, and how it was going to be an awful job to keep that beautiful ring hidden until -- what was Father's Day – June 15? Anyway, it was the ring I had been waiting for and now it was bought -- paid for, and would soon be tucked safely away in my desk at home. When the time came for its presentation, I knew I was going to feel all fluttery inside, because – if he didn't like it – or if he felt I was too extravagant -- I would be crushed. But no -- he had to like it! As a means of self-assurance, I had shown it to several businessmen who were Masons and asked, "Would this ring be proper for a Blue Lodge Mason?" And each time the answer had been the same: "Madam, your husband will enjoy that ring" – or, "It's perfect – wish I had one like it." I was happy.

I picked up the two kids, and we had lunch at a large table in a little restaurant I had eaten at once before. As we drove out of town, Sister asked, "Are we forgetting anything?"

I said, "I sure hope not. This is a nice little city but I'm seeing it now for the last time in a long time, I hope. I just wish I knew for sure where we are going next week so I could have left a forewarding address for my mail."

We rode along, laughing and talking -- playing games about the clouds in the sky – seeing all kinds of cottony forms. I was pleased with myself; I hadn't missed a single thing on the list and to make things even better, I was getting home much earlier than I had dared hope I would. I drove up to the trailer camp where Sister's girlfriend was staying and as we drove into sight of the place the kid sang, "Home Sweet Home." I caught her in the middle of the first line -- "Don't you know that song is taboo on a show?" I asked.

"Why?" she wanted to know.

"Because it's strictly bad luck. That's one thing I am superstitious about -- and strongly so. It sends cold chills over me everytime I hear it. "I know," I added, "it seems silly, doesn't it? But everytime that darned thing is sung where I can hear it, it brings a fearful feeling to me because something nearly always happens!"

"Scuse me", the kid said sheepishly, but we all laughed it off and I said, "It's alright. I think I caught you in time."

She waved at us as we drove off. When we got over the first hill I said, "Wouldn't it be funny if Doc Etling pulled in while we were gone?" (He was Bob's foster-father.)

Sister's reaction was one of disbelief. "Aw!" she said, "Do you really think he's on his way?"

"Why, of course," I answered, "Why did you think I had the telephone service assistant take the filling station's number down? That was so if Doc called up he wouldn't have any trouble locating us. He should be in today or tomorrow."

"Oh, Boy!" she exclaimed.

We both cackled with delight as we pulled onto the lot and saw Doc's trailer parked, near our own. He was at the back end feeding and watering his performing birds.

After a joyful greeting I asked him, "How long have you been here and have you seen Bob yet?" He answered, "I've been here three or four hours and saw Bob as soon as I landed. I've been asleep until a few minutes ago. It was a long drive and I was tired out."

Greetings over, I went to Dorothy Mackey's trailer to deliver the shoes I had brought back for her baby. But try as we might, we couldn't get his chubby feet into them. It was then decided that my grandson could wear them since he was younger and not nearly so chubby.

Then Bob came up in the green panel truck. He was delighted with the shipment of huge enlargements of the gorilla, and was eager to take them to the lot to show to Bobby. He drove off with the pictures in the truck and called to me as he left, "Mae, try to get down early so we can have an early show." It was only about 5:30 p.m. but I was tired and maybe a little cross, and called, "O.K." as he rolled away.

Dorothy called me and said, "Mae, would you like a cup of coffee?"

I sighed, "You bet! And have you got a bite to eat for a poor old tramp?"

She uncovered a huge bowl of potato salad and said, "Derned if that ain't all I've got, Mae, unless you want some peanut butter."

So I reached for the salad, a slice of bread and with a knife I spread some of the potato salad on the bread and poured myself some coffee. I had just swallowed a big swig of coffee and still had half the potato salad sandwich to go when Jean drove up in the green panel, and Dorothy said, "Oh, oh, Mae, here comes Jean. Guess your old man is in a hurry to open the show."

Jean stepped into the trailer and Dorothy said, "No! I know what she wants! She came after her potato salad."

"No," Jean warned, "I got bad news!" I looked at her, started and noticed that her face wore a strange expression, and had turned a peculiar color.

"My God! Jean! What is it?" I gasped.

"Joe got him," she said simply.

"Got who! Good Lord, Jean! Who did he get?"

"Your old man."

"How bad? Where is he bitten? Where did they take him?" I wanted to know. She came to life and said, "Glen took him to the doctor -- I don't know how bad he's hurt, but I do know two fingers are off because Joe handed them out of the cage to Bobby."

I jumped into the car frantically and started to the lot -- then backed up and called, "Which way did they go?"

By that time Doc realizing something was wrong came out of his trailer. I called, "Doc, get in the car, quick! Bob's been hurt and I'm going to him. Go with me!"

Almost before I had finished he was in the car.

I turned it around and sped up to the little town of Heidleberg. There I asked a filling station attendant where the nearest doctor could be found. He pointed back the way I had come to a white two-story structure. When I got there I could see there was no one around. I called across the road to some men who were fixing a flat tire on a truck and they said that Bob and Glen were only a few minutes ahead of me on the road to the nearest hospital, which was at Laurel!

I turned around once more and sped to Laurel. At the outskirts of town I went into a filling station and called up to find out which hospital had admitted him. When I arrived at the hospital I met Mike Mackey, Dorothy's husband, and Glen. They said that the doctor was preparing to operate, and I couldn't go up.

But Doc was allowed to go up and Bob told Glen to give Doc his diamond ring and his billfold. Then Doc came out into the hall and offered them to me. I told Doc to take my keys and put the stuff in my desk and lock it up.

Suddenly I remembered the ring I had bought for him! I told Doc, "I've always admired Bob's hands! Today I bought him a beautiful Masonic ring, and now he has no fingers to wear it on!"

I told Doc to go ahead and ride back with Mike and Glen, that I would come home after Bob's operation was over.

I waited nervously in the waiting room for what seemed like years. There were several other people waiting. They were waiting for an old, old man to regain consciousness after a dangerous operation. They were friendly and we chatted about our troubles. The receptionist signalled to me and I went into the office to take a phone call. Bobby wanted to know if it would do any good to bring the fingers. The receptionist called the operating room and relayed the message. "No." I told Bobby I would come back with news about Bob as soon as he got out of the operating room.

As I hung up, I heard the operator say, "Dr. will you please hurry up here? Dr. has a very bad emergency case and needs you right away! Can you come quickly?" "Yes." "Thank you!" Then she called another room and said, "He is on his way."

I then went back to the waiting room and wrung my hands worriedly. "A very bad emergency case." That was Bob!

After what seemed an eternity, but was actually five hours,

a startlingly loud bell rang near the elevator and nurses appeared from nowhere. I jumped up and went into the hall just in time to see Bob wheeled out of the elevator and down the hall. I stood transfixed with horror – he looked so pale, and had a big black rubber tube stuck down his throat. The doctor walked up to me and said, "Are you Mrs. Noell?" I nodded dumbly -- almost ready to cry. Then I asked, "What is the picture now, Doc?"

"Well," he sighed, "I may have done the wrong thing. He has two fingers entirely off the right hand. And I left the two damaged fingers on the left hand and am going to try to save them. If infection sets in and gets too bad, we may still have to take those two fingers off. But until we have to, I'd rather try to save them."

"No, Doctor," I said. "You didn't do the wrong thing! If I could have seen you before you operated that is what I'd have asked you to have done. Was he bitten anywhere other than his hands?"

"No," he replied, "There were a few minor scratches, but none had broken the skin, on his abdomen. One or two scratches elsewhere, but nothing serious. Only his hands, but let me warn you, it is bad. All the nerves, leaders and ligaments are torn loose from all eight fingers. I had a deuce of a time getting them all sewed back together. I just hope we don't get a lot of infection and have it all to do over again!"

"When will he wake up? And when can I see him?" I wanted to know, "And how long will he be confined?"

"Madam, in this hospital, we don't put up with visiting hour foolishness. Whenever you get ready -- day or night -- you can see the patient. But after you look in on him tonight, you had just as well go home and get a good night's sleep because we had to give him a long sleep since working on fingers and toes is tedious and very painful to the patient. So he won't wake up till around eight in the morning. He will be here at least two weeks."

"Thank you Doctor," I called back softly as I ran on tiptoes down the hall to the room into which I had seen Bob wheeled. A nurse came in and asked me, "the "Doctor has ordered that someone stay with your husband every minute all night long. We advise a special nurse. Do I have your permission to get him one?"

"Why, of course," I exclaimed. "Whatever he needs, be sure he gets it!"

"Thank you," she said, and was gone.

I looked at Bob -- he still had the tube in his mouth. I looked at the nurse who was there and whispered, "How long do you think it will be before he wakes up?" She whispered back, "Several hours." I then told her that I would leave since there was nothing I could do but would be back very soon. She nodded and I left.

I hurried back to the lot, the lights were still on and the crowd was almost all gone. As soon as I got out of the car, a goodly number of the showfolks ganged around me.

One of the working men said to me, "Boy! I want you to tell my fortune!"

I was surprised and said so. Then I asked him what had ever given him the idea I could tell fortunes?

He said, "Well, you told Bob something bad was gonna happen and four days later it happened. You even said it would be so bad you wouldn't want to say 'I told you so' – and now you're tryin' to tell me you can't tell fortunes?"

I felt the blood drain out of my face. I had completely forgotten the episode, but what the boy said was true. I had expressed fear over a premonition!

I went to the back of the lot to report to the family and to friends. The whole show was concerned over Bob's welfare. I made my report and then told them that I would probably not see any of them again for some time since the Doctor said he would be confined at least two weeks, and I might not get back the next day. I told them all so long.

I then hastened back to the hospital. The doctor had told me I could come in anytime, and though it was now around midnight, I tiptoed into his room – a four-bed ward. He had been awake, and when I came in he looked at me feebly and said in a tiny wan voice, "Boy, Mae, it's tough ain't it?" I wept.

I stayed by him and the special nurse told me to curl up on the other bed and I got a few minutes sleep but he suffered nearly all night.

When morning came he couldn't eat. I left long enough to eat and call up his brother-in-law, who didn't seem too surprised at the news, and then I ran back to Bob. Bob kept worrying that they might not make the most of their opportunity that night by showing the animals, and kept insisting that I go back to the lot and see that his orders were carried out. As the shadows of night fell, I reluctantly left him.

I hastened to the lot to tell Bobby that his father wanted him to show the crowd his torn and bloody clothes, and to explain that they are trained wild animals and to let the people walk past Joe's cage and look at him. Bobby already had the gates open and a few people had already filed through during the day. I knew Bobby would have everything under control so started back. But everyone on the show gathered around me in small clusters, group by group until I got off the lot. I said my farewells to all of them and told them sincerely that I regretted having to part company with so congenial a group.

As I walked past the elderly gypsy's stand he called me over and tried to slip something to me he had concealed in the palm of his hand. I backed away and said, "No, thanks a million! You're really swell to offer to help, but we are lucky – I have a hospital policy that will take care of this. Please don't worry about us. And thanks again!"

Tears filled the old man's eyes and he said, "You're wonderful people, bot' off you – I loff dat husban' off yourrs – it mak's my heart hurrt to know he iss soffering. Please! Take dis and git him a box off ceegarrs!"

I smiled and said, "I'll tell Bob you offered -- he will

93

appreciate it just the same as if I took it. More in fact. And thanks again. You're pretty swell yourself."

And I walked away and waved at him as I left. Up on the road, when no one else was near, his son-in-law tried to make me take some money for Bob. I refused and thanked him too. Then I found Glen and told him, "Bob has been moaning and groaning, 'Mae, pay Glen for the way I bloodied up his car. Pay him for the sheet, too.' So how much will it cost to fix up your car, Glen?"

"Mae, that car has plastic seat covers and we wiped it all off with a damp cloth. It didn't hurt a thing," he answered me.

"Well, then, here's the money for the sheet." I paid him. He took it reluctantly.

Then I said all the rest of my farewells and went to the Boss' trailer. He very kindly assured me that our equipment was going to be off that lot before the show left town. I was deeply grateful and relieved since it had been a tremendous ordeal getting the trucks on and I was afraid it might take us days to get them off.

I rushed back the nineteen miles to the hospital, eager to be with Bob every spare moment. And he needed me. He had a lot of fever and when they gave him a sedative he would perspire until he was miserable. I wiped his face dry every few minutes, gave him the ice water he craved so lustily and helped him with other things since he was unable to get out of bed.

At the time I was unaware of it, but he was practically in a stupor. He kept telling me things over and over that I should do; and I kept assuring him that all was well -- those things that were yet undone I would see to and those that were done I told him about. He repeated himself over and over as he tossed feverishly. Too many times to recollect he asked for something to put him to sleep because his hands were hurting so badly. I feared he couldn't stand the pain and worried the nurses to death. Once a nurse had to come in and assure him that it was too early -- by some twenty-five or thirty minutes — for him to have another needle. He begged her and she refused; then he threatened, "If you don't give me something to ease this pain I will jump out of the window — then you'll be sorry!"

"Oh, no I won't" she replied, "You're the one who will be sorry!"

And with this she walked out on us.

Another time when I went "up front" one of the nurses assured me that it would be better for the patient if I stayed away from him for awhile because "husband's expect their wives to baby them," she explained. So I innocently decided maybe she was right and sat in the reception room and wrung my hands, when Lo! here came Bob parading up the hall in that short "see-more" bed jacket affair that is considered proper hospital attire! The nurses rushed around and decided maybe I'd better stay with him after all, and gave him the sedative he had requested.

It was several days before the dope was taken away from him without ill effect.

On Sunday afternoon Bob's brother, Lawrence, came to see him — all the way from Virginia — some seven hundred odd miles away! Bob was delighted; it was the moral support he needed. Saturday I went to the dime store near the post office and quickly bought a beautiful bouquet of artificial flowers. They were so cleverly made that people actually thought they were real!

Sunday a huge beautiful bouquet of real flowers came. I read the card attached and found that some of the show folks had made up a collection and bought Bob flowers. They were exquisite. Then Mike and Dorothy came and told us there were two bouquets — the second would be delivered later, and there were also three boxes of cigars! When they mentioned the cigars I knew who thought of that — the elderly gypsy! He had wanted me to get Bob some cigars!

After about six or seven weeks, Bob took Joe out of the cage, with hands still bandaged, and played with him on the show lot, when we rejoined the troupe. Joe showed regrets, but, of course, it's too late to say, "I'm sorry," to an amputee.

The "accident" to Bob's hands happened in 1953. Our show was then "thirteen years young." I became worried about the future. Bob's fingers -- bitten off by a chimp! Hands that had once done magic, juggling and balancing acts -- mangled, yes, ruined. Harrowing, despair-filled days and nights at the hospital, watching him suffer, trying to help him. He couldn't scratch his eyebrow, wash his face, comb his hair, feed himself -- I did it all for him. Because the hospital at Laurel, Mississippi, allowed me to stay with him night and day, I was with him every possible minute.

During those sad, uncertain days, I did a lot of thinking. We were nomads. No real roots anywhere, except to visit our relatives and friends in North and South Carolina and Virginia, and to camp on their places with our animals. I feared we might never settle down and have a home. Oh, we owned property, alright, but it was rental property, not a real home.

I made up my mind, "We're not getting any younger, and we need to have our own winterquarters somewhere far enough South for the 'weather to suit out clothes.' "

That winter I told Bob, "You've had five trips with Doc this winter while I stayed here and took care of the animals. I'm taking the next trip -- with you or alone -- and I'm going to buy a place where we can winter without freezing." He was agreeable and we came to Florida to do just that.

After searching all over Pinellas and Hillsborough Counties we bought three acres (which we enlarged years later to about six acres) that was already a "Mom and Pop" zoo. Bessie and Jimmy McVay had some monkeys, peafowls, alligators and chickens and were charging nine cents admission to avoid having to pay the state 4% tax.

We bought the place in February of 1954, almost a year after Bob got hurt. We liked the location because it was not too far from a big city where produce for the animals could be bought at reasonable prices, and at that time, it was still

96

'way out in the country. We felt it was important to buy a place as remote from neighbors as possible because the apes often make a lot of noise. Many times their noise made it difficult to find a place to park.

For instance, we could never have hoped to put our equipment in a trailer park. We would be asked to leave the first time one of the animals "kicked up." This is why we selected the site we did for our little sanctuary. With a busy highway in front of us and a railroad in back, the local people did not find it hard to become accustomed to one more occasional noise.

Some of the stories about the noises they make are quite amusing.

I remember one Spring when we were on our way North with our show and had reached Live Oak, a little town in North Florida. I always drove the house trailer unit and took the lead. As he rode along behind me, Bob noticed something wrong with the axle of my trailer. He turned his headlights on (in a pre-arranged signal to stop) so I stopped. He looked the situation over and decided to go back to a city we had just passed through to get a part. He pulled up to a wide place in the road and made a "U" turn. Sensing this was an unusual manuever, the animals started banging on the truck and screaming. If you never heard it before, you'd be certain you had just heard a horrible wreck.

When he did this, a woman came screaming hysterically out of one of the houses. Almost instantly she had a crowd around her. She was raving: "Someone screamed! I'm sure that child across the road was just hit by that big truck, and they've turned around to take him to the hospital! I've told her to keep that child in the yard! Now it has happened just like I said!" About that time, another woman came out of the other house and called, "What's all the excitement?" Whereupon, the first woman screamed at her, "Your baby! Your baby is on his way to the hospital! He just got hit by a truck!"

The second woman looked amazed. "That's not so; I'm

looking at him! He's sitting in the house, here!"

The first woman then became furious and asked, loudly, "Well then, why did you scream?"

"I didn't scream!"

"Well, then who did?"

I saw it was about to get out of hand so I called over, "If you'll wait a minute, I can explain."

With this the first woman pointed an accursing finger at me and shouted, "**You** screamed!"

I replied, "No, nobody screamed. That was a truck load of trained chimpanzees."

After the first surprised moment, everyone, including the hysterical woman, laughed heartily and extracted a promise that I would show them the animals when they got back. Of course I did, when Bob returned.

Another example of how these outbursts can be hair-raising I remember, happened with a frightened policeman. Bob was going along in the big, red truck, and a patrolman signalled for him to stop. Obeying the officer meant pulling off onto a very narrow shoulder with part of the truck still on the pavement, but Bob complied anyway. Both men got out of their vehicles and started walking toward each other, when all at once the chimps started screaming and banging on the metal. The poor officer was right beside the door when the noise started. Jumping, and grabbing his gun reflexively, he ran to the car and had his microphone in one hand, gun in the other, when he saw Bob laughing. He put the gun back in the holster, looked all around, put the mike back on its hook, and returned to Bob, who then explained to a very embarrassed officer what it was he had just heard. The policeman told Bob he thought they had caused a wreck. With all that metal banging and all the screaming, it does sound as if something catastrophic is taking place. The policeman then wanted to see the animals and said he forgot why he stopped the truck in the first place.

Still another time, we were camping on a friend's property at Clearwater, Florida. Because Mr. & Mrs. "Dutch" Duefrene had insisted we spend Christmas with them, we camped on their acre tract for several Christmases. It was through them that we "found" Pinellas County, and learned to like it so well.

Their place was about the distance of two or three city blocks from the Gulf-to-Bay Highway. Not far from where their lane intersected the Gulf-to-Bay Highway, there was a small cafe. One of our acquaintances was sitting at the counter when the chimps let loose with one of their "serenades." All conversation in the place stopped as everyone looked at each other in open-mouthed amazement. One of the waitresses said, "That does it! This is the third night in a row that I've heard that man beating his wife! I'm going to call the cops! If someone doesn't put a stop to this, he will kill her. Why there can't be a stick of furniture left in the place the way they bang around back there!" As she spoke, she headed resolutely for the pay phone fishing in her apron pocket for a dime.

Our acquaintance laughed and said, "Wait a minute! Don't call the cops. You'll have a red face if you do! That's not what you think it is. It's a bunch of animals."

"You bet it is," she said. "Anyone who could carry on like that for three nights in a row must be an animal!"

"No - No! You don't understand -- that is a bunch of trained, wild animals! That is not a fight! Those animals are 'singing!' "

The waitress looked at him as if he must be insane. She held the dime poised over the slot with the receiver in her other hand. But by now the noise had stopped and she wasn't sure if she were being kidded -- or what. So the acquaintance said, "Tell you what. When you come to work tomorrow, come a little early and I'll get the Noells to show them to you."

This did the trick. She did come to see them. After that, when they "kicked up" the people at the cafe would laugh. They soon became as accustomed to it as we were. And our neighbors at the sanctuary don't even hear them anymore. The highway and trains outdo them.

When a chimp is angry or excited his screams are piercing and painful to the human ear. When wrestlers or boxers were in the cage and the animals screamed, the fear that struck the man usually caused him to want to leave, poste haste.

Southern soldiers were taught to scream the "rebel yell" in Civil War days, to intimidate and frighten the enemy when they were charging. I can readily see how this would be a successful maneuver after watching the chimps demoralize "big brave bullies" with their screams on our show. When they scream and at the same time bang on metal, it sounds horrendous.

Soon after we got the Chimp Farm, a couple rented a room in the tiny motel next door to us (now gone). During the night the chimps kicked up with their metal-banging and screaming. Both the man and his wife leaped out of bed and ran to the window to see the horrible automobile wreck on the highway. Not wanting to get involved, but curious, nonetheless, they sat for more than an hour, watching out the window for police cars and ambulance that never came.

Next morning they asked the motel manager about "the wreck" they heard last night. The manager laughed when he told them it was the animals next door at the Chimp Farm who had made all the noise. Within the year, that couple bought the motel!

Very recently, I was innocently sitting on one of the benches at my front gate, reading, when the chimps let fly with one of their screaming fits. A little girl, who was coming out of the zoo, became frightened and climbed all over me, bruising me in several places. She was so frightened by the noise she went momentarily berserk. Poor kid. Poor me!

In his book **Almost Human** Dr. Robert M. Yerkes mentions this noisy trait. He says an adult chimp at Madam Abreau's compound in Havana, Cuba, "was subject to periodical outbursts", and that his owner claimed that the adult male chimps could not be trusted because they have "crazy spells" during which they become dangerously rough

100

and extremely noisy. (And I might add, unpredictable.) We see this behavior daily in our big males and it is almost certainly comparable to the frenzied behavior described by Goodall as "the rain dance." Many times the noise is made to attract attention to himself, but I think it is done most often to "let off steam."

Some chimps use hand-clapping and a variety of noises to attract attention. And my young adult male twin performs for tourists with his hand clapping. It is a noisy "show-off" stunt done only for spectators. With a style all his own, he claps his hands as he bobs his head up and down in rhythm with the claps -- slowly at first, then faster and faster until his head is a blur and the claps are so fast that they almost blur into a hum. After one of these displays the little fellow sits down, exhausted.

Most chimps start their "rain dances" by singing, "Wooo, Wooo, Wooo," faster and faster as they sway their bodies to and fro in rhythm to the "song," climaxing the song with "Wha! Wha! Wha!" in a higher pitch and slamming hands and feet against the nearest object -- (animate or inanimate) -- that will make the most noise.

One day Bob read in the paper that some friends were appearing at Ocala, Florida, about a hundred miles North. Bob went to visit the show, and I knew he could not get home before two or three A.M. I told him to drive carefully as he left. At about nine or ten P.M. all the chimps started "war whooping" and I knew something was amiss out there, so I went outside with the hair on the back of my neck a-tingle.

There are any number of reasons for this sort of pandemonium, the most dreaded being that of an escaped chimp on the rampage. The moon was bright, and I walked -- cautiously -- toward the zoo area. I peered down the path toward the zoo, and at the other end I saw a big chimp -- all bristled up to nearly twice normal size -- heading, threateningly, in my direction. I had always been "playmate" to the apes, and Bob was "boss." I was "low man on the totem pole." I never attempted to force issues with them. In short, I feared the outcome if I failed to show them the proper respect. Knowing that any chimp could run me down, effortlessly, I did the only thing I could do. I pretended I hadn't seen him and went, slowly, back to my trailer, with a "creepy feeling" on my back. Once safely inside the trailer, I nearly collapsed. (I didn't know it then, but turning my back on him was an "act of submission" and the very best thing I could have done.)

There were three big males out there, any one of whom could literally dismember me with his strong hands and fierce-looking canine teeth. I didn't know who was out there: One; if it was Joe, he had bitten Bob's fingers off the year before, but had always been a nice playmate to the whole family before. I could figure a way to work things out safely if it was 95 pound Joe. Two: there was Butch, a 150 pound mass of brawn, made timid by a past history of medical experimentation. If it was Butch I could fire a gun and he would run back into the cage. Three; then there was 85 pound Bamboo! "Dear God," I thought, "If it's Bamboo -- he's "gunning" for me! What can I do?"

I thought hard. "Ah!" I surmised, "It has to be Butchie! That was a big big chimp! Yes!" So, I scrambled around and found the guns Bob keeps on hand. I opened my trailer door, aimed at the ground, closed my eyes and gritted my teeth, then using both hands, I pulled the trigger, "Blam!"

If the noise was deafening before, this time the chimps nearly raised the roof!

Not sure if my plan was working, I tried to fire it again but the gun wouldn't go off.

I frantically picked up the shot gun. For some reason, a gun should be fired three times in rapid succession to affect a chimp, and I had failed on my first try. The shot gun went off, alright, but in so doing I accidentally blew my light line, which was temporarily lying on the ground, in two. Now I was in the trailer, in the dark, panicked. No flashlight! I was in fear for my life but felt duty-bound to do something effective about the escapee. But what? Then, a knock at the door! Chimps don'g have that much manners, so I opened the door and saw Mr. McVay (former owner of the place who was staying on, with his wife, as caretaker) standing there.

He was about six feet, two inches, and no lightweight – I grabbed him by the collar in my panic and said "Good Lord, Man! Don't you know there's a chimp loose out there?" as I 'lifted' him inside. "Yeah, that's what I came to tell you. Joe's loose," he said calmly. "How do you know it's Joe?" I asked.

"Because his cage is empty."

"You mean you went down Chimp Alley?"

"Sure," he said casually, "he wouldn't hurt me."

I was so sure he could have been hurt I felt weak.

"Do you know how to use a gun?" I asked.

"Yep."

"O.K. Take this one. It's loaded. Get Bessie, and both of you get in your car. Sit out there with doors locked and windows closed. Don't let Bob walk in here without knowing what's going on. I've got a chance to keep Joe entertained if I work it right. Don't come in here, no matter what happens, until Bob says to," I ordered.

He shrugged and said, "O.K." and left.

Now -- I had definitely taken the wrong tack with the guns. They had only served to rile Joe up. I had to figure out a way I could "backtrack" with him. To walk out there, now, would be stupid to say the least. So I decided to go to the transport truck (The Ark) and get in one of the empty cages, then talk baby talk to Joe to calm him. These cages were in a position to give me an excellent view of what was going on in Chimp Alley.

Once inside the cage I could see impish Joe, running up and down in front of the cages--and I could imagine his taunting remarks to the other chimps, "Ha! Ha! Ha! I'm out and you're in Ha! Ha! Ha!" By the response he was getting he

103

was successful with the barbs. Then I spoke to him, "Hi, Josephus! Hi there!" Absolute silence settled on the place, and -- I knew then, as I know now -- that it was fortunate for me that I was behind bars! Joe charged, angrily, in my direction. When he saw I was in the cage he went past, with hair all on end, making his dark image in the moonlight appear more like a 400-pound gorilla than that of a ninety-five-pound chimp.

It was "now or never," so I went to the opened door of the truck and stood in it, some four to four-and-a-half feet off the ground, near where he was strutting impudently. I kept up the baby talk patter as he walked past the door. There was a bushel basket of tangerines in the truck, so I picked some of them up and tossed them so they rolled on the ground in front of him, repeating, as I did so, the familiar, "See? I got you some!" Each tangerine made his hair go a little flatter until I felt it might be safe to go out and take a chance on entertaining him. He had pretended he didn't see the tangerines before, but I knew they had "turned the trick" along with the baby talk. I stepped out of the truck onto the ground, and when I did, Joe spun around and charged for me. I stood frozen and continued the baby talk. Joe stopped at my feet and sat beside me! I patted his shoulder and told him what a good boy he was. He then decided to put on a "silly chimp" show for me. He charged toward the puppy that was tied out. My heart did flip flops again -- "Don't hurt the doggie, Joe," I wheedled. As I spoke, Joe cackled his chimpanzee laugh and jumped over the cowering pup. Then he ran to me for approval. I patted him again and this silly business went on for some twenty minutes or so, until Joe tired of the "sport."

I sat on the step for quite some time and peeled tangerines for him "till he was full," then cautiously followed him, in the eerie moonlight, determined to stay with him until Bob got home. Toward the front of the place we had a spigot sticking up out of the ground. A tub of water was under the spigot, and an enameled cup hung nearby. One small light bulb dangled overhead, competing feebly with the bright moonlight.

Chimps are fascinated with a pan of water, a rag, a cup, and soap. Joe took the cup and scooped a cupful of water out of the tub, then, holding the cup aloft, he slowly poured it back into the tub, watching the sparkling cascade with total concentration. This took up another twenty to thirty minutes and this is where we were when Bob got home. I had my arm across Joe's shoulder, baby talking and saying, "Wheeeee!" every time he poured the water.

Bob came in, gun in mangled hand, and whispered hoarsely, "Mae! Mae! Where are you?"

I "wheedled" – "we're right over here by the spigot and he's been a real good boy!"

Joe jumped up and rushed over to Bob with a happy "Hello" bark, and the ordeal was over.

Joe was tired of his freedom. Bob pocketed the gun, and after we muzzled him, we played with Joe another ten or fifteen minutes and then he was happy to go back to his cage and to bed.

I had been out there with him at least two hours. My main job was to keep him entertained on the premises. If I had tried to get him to "go home" this story would have had a tragic ending. As it was, it taught us a valuable lesson: that padlocks, alone, are worse than useless on a chimp's cage. They have all day and all night in which to experiment, and Joe is not the first one of our chimps who has picked his lock open. And it makes no difference what kind of a "key" they use, wood, straw, or whatever, pure chance will finally trip it when so very many hours are put into the effort. Cages are now padlocked to make other **people** feel secure, but the real "locks" on the cages are huge bolts that are double "nutted" and tightened with wrenches. The locks and bolts are also out of the animals' reach where possible.

For all his young life, Kongo, Joe's son had seen us lock his cage with a padlock. Then when we came to take him out, we poked something inside the padlock and "Presto!" It was opened. One day Kongo came strolling out of his cage and we were "flipped out," as the young folks say, because we knew he had been padlocked in. On examination we found that he had used the wood shavings on the floor of his cage and had worked at it until he sprung the lock! A professional locksmith could not have "picked" it open any better, but the lock was ruined because we could not get the shavings out of it. After that we put a shield behind the locks to make them inaccessable -- but better yet -- we have since used the lock to keep humans out and huge bolts to keep the chimps in!

Chapter Four

Fortunately for us it was "Love at First Sight" with Suzy and Joe. Bob reported a lot of love-making but it never seemed to come to fruition. We had carried Suzy Q. around as what we felt was a "free-loader" for eight years. It didn't look as if she were ever going to have a baby. Bob wanted to get another young male to train up to be a wrestler. We needed a young one to do the foot races with the kids that the audiences enjoyed so much, because we were afraid Snookie and Joe were getting too big for the kids. Then, on February 25, 1948, we both agreed, regretfully, that Suzy was probably never going to be a mother, therefore since we used only males in our boxing and wrestling matches we decided to trade her for a male. We drove down to Dania, Florida, to the Denis-Roosevelt Chimp Farm and looked at several males. The owners agreed to the trade and Bob selected his male, a little fellow who had, they told us, been used for medical research. At the last moment I broke down and started crying. "We just can't let her go after all this time!" I begged. Bob pretended exasperation but I think he was dreading the parting, too. "Alright!" he said impatiently.

"Get me the money and I'll buy the male!" I got it quickly and in a couple of hours we were in Miami setting up camp at the Tropical Bird and Monkey Farm on 79th Street, and shaking hands with our old friends, Mr. and Mrs. Addison, and showing them our newly purchased male: "Butchie." We had camped on their place, each winter, for several years. On February 28, 1948, at Addison's place, (three days after we nearly traded her off) Bob reached in the cage and said "Give me that cat!" He thought she had kidnapped a kitten the way she had so often done before when we were at Bob's brother's place at Lone Pine, Virginia. But instead of a cat Suzy handed him a beautiful little male baby chimp! We had almost traded two chimps for one!

* * * * *

As I write this, there are more than twenty chimps on our place, and forty-five babies have been born in our colony. We believe we may own a world record for ape births in a "Mom and Pop" (privately owned) public Zoo. Probably the most famous of all the babies that were born here would be Lucy Temerlin, the Oklahoma chimp that has been taught sign language under Roger Fouts.

It didn't take little Butchie long to learn what was expected of him because we made peep-holes from all the cages into the arena so all the animals could watch the "fights." ("Monkey see, Monkey do.") It's amazing that so very many people wanted to have a try at wrestling or boxing with the animals, even women!

Snookie and Butch were the two animals we used when we put ladies in to wrestle. It never became anything like a wrestling match with a really effeminate lady. We even supplied a chair for ladies to sit on because Snookie used to love to remove bobby pins from their hair. Then he'd untie or otherwise "open"their shoes to remove them. Several times he tried them on and tried to walk in them. Instead of wrestling, he liked to "smooch" them.

Some of the women saw the beautiful certificate we gave to the men who were good sports and decided they could not let their husbands outdo them. So we would give them careful and explicit instructions and it was always a funny but safe show. Some women got scared and would run away from the ape – running around Bob, who stood in the center of the cage virtually helpless with laughter. Even if the ape caught the squealing victim, the worst he would do would be to try to remove shoes, earrings, beads, bobby pins or whatever caught his eye. When the contestant was not aggressive the ape made a game of tag of it. Only **the ape** was always "IT." Several years ago a man came and was supposed to see our show so he could write about it in his forthcoming book, which shall remain nameless for the obvious reason that I am **not** promoting it. He admitted to me that he could not read his own notes when I was "interviewed." He spent his time watching the carnival girl-show girls strip and did not see our show that night. Then, because he pleaded for us to put on a "command performance" for him, we called one of the girls out of the concessions who was our stand-by and put on a token show for him. This was a mistake. We should have chased him away. He wrote about the show, alright, but it was the sort of tripe you'd expect someone to write who was under the influence of an hallucinogen of some sort. He was probably remembering the nakedness of the girl-show women because "our" contestant wore dungarees! And the chimp has **never** acted the way he said it did. The law now protects people who lie this way in the name of "freedom of speech." All I can say about imaginative muck-rakers such as he -- I hope he gets exactly what he deserves in the here-after for telling such whoppers.

Butch and Snookie were two chimps who looked a lot alike in body structure and had about the same disposition. When children went in the cage with either of these two big fellows, they played gently with them. They showed the same kindness to women, always. Butch was not quite as gentle as Snookie was, but he certainly was more gentle with

MONTEZUMA 22"x28"

FRI. APR. 23

—ROXIE TUCKER PRESENTS—

UNDER THE BIG TENT!
—ROBERT NOELL'S—

GORILLA SHOW

—Featuring the—

WORLD'S ONLY
ATHLETIC APES!

See Your Friends Box and Wrestle
With These Big Animals!

One Night Only

—ALSO—

MUSTARD AND GRAVY
PERSON! —In Their Big— STAGE REVUE!

14"x28"

8:30 P.M. **WED. JAN.**

OLD JUNIOR HIGH SCHOOL AUDITORIUM
FT. MYERS

10 Round Boxing Bout With Gloves

Wright to receive $100.00 if he can answer the bell for the 10th Round
$1000.00 if he can knockout Joe.

Also 'SNOOKIE' the WRESTLING APE
IN A WRESTLE ROYAL WITH 7 BOYS

After his bout with Wright, Joe will meet any volunteers from the audience
(Nobody in the world barred). $2.00 for each minute in the ring with Joe
will be paid the man for either fighting or running.

Prince OMAR vs. Walter KAMEROFF

GENERAL ADMISSION $1.00   RINGSIDE $1.50   CHILDREN 75c   INCLUDING TAXES a woman than with a man, and never did anything to a woman that could embarrass or offend. Figuring to play on his tendencies towards gentleness to ladies, a young fellow in New York State went to elaborate ends to dress like a girl. He got a nice wig, tied a ribbon in it, wore a pair of Bobbie sox and ladies shoes. A proper length dress and tasteful makeup completed the illusion. He came up to the show front ahead of time and I told him we would start in thirty minutes. He didn't speak but merely nodded, for fear his heavy voice would expose the ruse to the by-standers who always waited at the front of our show. He turned and walked up the midway with his friends.

A man in the audience said, "She's gonna wrestle the ape! Boy! Look at the legs on that girl. I gotta see that fight!"

When the boy came back and went in, Butch was gentle with him. (He had even put on some perfume!) Butch wanted to see what was under the dress and managed to raise it a couple of times, but the boy had on long bloomers which hid his turned up trousers. Butch must have suspected something was "not quite right" about this "girl" from the start, because he had never tried to peek before. But the boy was "modest" and held the skirt down. However, it became a foot race around Bob and the boy didn't squeal. This just was **not natural**, so the race got a little faster. Finally Butch managed to catch him and was smelling his "hair" when the wig slid off. The crowd roared because until that instant, they had really thought it was a girl. As soon as Butch saw he had been "taken" -- the fight was "on." And it was one of the funniest shows we ever put on, with the boy trying desperately to remain on his feet and Butch determined to knock him down. It was as if Butch were saying, "You no good rascal! All the time I thought you were a nice lady!" No one was upset over the ruse--they all loved it instead!

At Cayce, S.C., across the river from Columbia, we were on a small lot--showing independently. Most of our contestants were usually people from the working classes -- nearly all "blue collar" types. So we were quite surprised at Cayce

111

WRESTLING
8:15 P.M. **MON. 9**
MUNICIPAL AUDITORIUM · TAMPA APRIL

BROUGHT BACK BY POPULAR DEMAND

BOXING GORILLA

TO BOX A COLORED FIGHTER AND OTHERS

$1000 REWARD IF YOU CAN KNOCK OUT JOE, THE BOXER

OFFER OPEN TO ANYONE, EITHER PRO OR AMATEUR

SMALL GORILLA & 7 COLORED BOYS

IN A WRESTLING BATTLE ROYAL

DOUBLE MAIN EVENT

GOLDEN TERROR vs. PAT O'HARA | ANGELO MARTENILLI vs. JOHNNY DEMCHUK RETURN MATCH TO A FINISH

PLUS ONE OTHER GOOD MATCH

RINGSIDE 1.50   GEN. ADM. Any Seat In The House Except Ringside 1.00   CHILDREN .25 TAX INCL.   WRESTLING OFFICE—THOMAS JEFFERSON HOTEL Or Call 2-2132 For Reservations

THIS CARD SHOULD HAVE READ "--7 LITTLE BOYS."

THIS CARTOON WAS MADE FOR NEWSPAPER ADS.

112

when a "professional man" insisted on going into the cage to wrestle.

We carried extra clothing to put over top of the men's clothing. We could buy shirts by the hundred from Goodwill, Salvation Army or Saint Vincent de Paul Stores for only a dime each. And pants were seldom more than a quarter a pair. So when a man went in the cage he was usually covered with our cheaper garments which could be soiled or torn and not be something to grieve over.

The professional man was an attorney, and he had been drinking. We tried to talk him out of going in the cage but to no avail. He raised a fist in the air and shouted to the audience, "I'm going in there to teach that ape the law of the land!" I went ahead and helped him cover his nice business suit with our second-hand clothing, and we let him go in.

As usual, the 'fight', didn't last long and our second-hand clothes were torn to shreds. Leaping high in front of the man, the ape dared him to strike the first blow. This the ape always did to let the man "set the pace," and the lawyer was no different from any other man who had imbibed a little too freely. He "swung a haymaker" that didn't connect. That's all the ape wanted to know. The intent was there, so the little ape just went to work on butting, kicking and pummelling the disoriented and confused contestant until he yelled for mercy. Every time the man would swing the ape would be somewhere else -- usually in back of the man – ripping his clothing, gleefully. When it became obvious the man was whipped, Bob stopped the ape and I opened the door to let him out. The lawyer had quite a few minor bruises for his pains. However, he went away a good sport -- just like the greater majority of our fighters did. When he came out, he took the microphone and said, rather humbly I thought, "I went in to teach that ape the law of the land, but he taught me the law of the Jungle!"

The next morning we were awakened by the lawyer and his wife.

"Hey!" he called, "I need you to come out here and talk

113

to my wife."

We went out and he told Bob, "My wife doesn't believe me; she said she was going to leave me if I couldn't prove to her that I got my pants torn by an ape. She thinks I got in a bar room fight."

She spoke up and said, "I've heard so many of these stories he'd better be telling the truth this time."

Bob said he felt sorry for the guy, so instead of showing them Butch, the chimp he had wrestled, who who weighted 135 pounds, he showed them Tommy, the gorilla, who weighed about 500 pounds.

His wife gasped and said, "You mean you went in the cage and fought with that big thing?"

Because he had been drunk the night before, he was confused and said, "Yeah and he almost killed me."

She said, "It's a wonder you **weren't** killed!"

That made a hero of him and they went home happy.

Kid Gavelin, the boxer, caught the show at one of the towns when we were showing in Cuba. When he was asked if he would challenge the chimp, he laughed and said, "there wasn't enough money in Cuba to get him in that cage."

Probably most of my readers will not be familiar with the format of our "Gorilla Show", so I will describe it as briefly as possible;

When we were appearing as an independent unit, at small towns and cross-roads locations, we had a platform, or stage, which was actually a large tailgate on the back of our truck, on which we presented our free shows. We did a lot of the oldtime medicine show acts in those days, but instead of selling medicine between acts as we had previously done, we sold tickets and put on a boxing or wrestling match between one of our chimps and someone out of the audience. Later, we got lazy and used a 16mm movie sound projector and showed "shorts" (that ran from twelve to fifteen minutes each) as our "free show" between bouts. When we went on Carnival lots, in later years, we did not have to give the free show. We found it very hard to get the people to leave and

114

walk around the grounds between bouts. Some (but not all) of the carnival people thought we were trying to hog all the business because the people were afraid they might miss one of the shows if they walked away, and there was always a crowd waiting in front of our show until "lights out."

Carnies said, "Your show is too strong. It kills everything else on the midway!" But the people knew what they wanted to see, and these complainers didn't realize that most of these were people who would not have come to the midway if we had not been there. It was something over which we had no control, try as we might. But most knowledgeable show-owners were happy to have us with them as a "drawing card," and some even paid us to be on their midways!

Probably the most widely read spectator's account of the show would be the one in **Newsweek** back in July of 1970, the next to the last year we were on the road, written by Malcolm MacPherson:

AMERICANA:
Son of King Kong

For quite some time -- particularly in the century since Charles Darwin spied the monkey in the human family tree -- man has had it in for apes. **Homo sapiens** will go to almost any length it seems, to establish his primacy among primates. Consider the circus chimpanzee, stripped of all human dignity by being decked out in a satin jacket and plopped on the seat of a bicycle. Consider King Kong, invented by man only so that he could be sacrificed to biplanes upon the alter of the Empire State Building. And consider the nightly goings-on at Noell's Ark Ape Show, now touring the tidewater country of North Carolina.

"Everybody come on up to this end of the midway," boomed Bob Noell one recent evening when the Royal Blue Carnival, with which his Ape Show travels, was playing in a field outside Beaulaville, N.C. "The fight's about to start. Tonight we got a marine who says he's

115

116

going to whip the ape." Noell was standing at the end of a trailer truck that doubles as transport and fighting arena. Under a large sign announcing "Gorilla Show," there was a smaller notice: "Wanted -- Athletic men to earn $5 per second ($20 limit) by holding ape's shoulders on the floor. If you **don't** throw him, you get $5 to try."

Punch: The crowd gathered excitedly around the truck -- the Gorilla Show is the top attraction on Royal Blue's scrawny midway -- and Noell began to outfit the marine, a 21-year-old named John Hebert from nearby Camp Lejeune, for his bout. He made him don an old-style leather football helmet, change into a tattered shirt and choose whether he would box or wrestle. "You're going to punch the ape, aren't you?" Noell suggested. Hebert nodded. "Well, when you draw back, that ape's got you. He'll put a sucker punch right on you." Hebert did not seem intimidated. "I'm going to fake him good," he announced, "and make him believe I'm a gorilla." He had watched a previous contest. We came up here to see the broads," he reported, meaning the Royal Blue's two mini-skirted go-go dancers. "Then we saw the gorilla. Some dude got his lip busted, and I knew I had to come back. You just got to do it once you've seen it."

This instinct seems widespread enough among human-kind to supply a full card of challengers for Noell's apes. No one, according to Bob Noell and his wife Mae, has ever been badly hurt in a bout -- the worst injuries have been scratches, bruises, and a few cuts here and there. But neither, in what they estimate to be 22,000 matches since 1952, has man ever bested ape; they have never paid off more than the $5 they offer anyone simply for stepping into the ring. The Noell's ever-victorious apes include two gorillas – one of them an impressive 600-pound male named Tommy -- three orangutans and five chimpanzees. Upon this brood, Mae

117

and Bob Noell lavish heaps of food – Purina Monkey Chow, plus such treats as green peppers, cantaloupe, bananas, Coca-Cola and pound cake – and considerable affection. A few years ago, two of the animals fell ill and died. "We thought so much of them," says Mae, "that we didn't want to bury them somewhere that they'd be plowed up by a farmer." So she had them pickled in formaldehyde and temporarily stored in a shed near New Bern, North Carolina.

Chimp; But once the carny crowd has assembled and the ape fight is ready, the Noells are all business. Mae collects $2. a head to admit spectators to a fenced-off area around the truck. Bob picks up a muzzle and a pair of light boxing gloves and goes off to collect the monkey. He returns not with a gorilla or an orangutan – either one of which could doubtless wreak terminal damage upon the strongest marine -- but with one of the chimpanzees. The distinction, however, is often lost upon the spectators.

To face John Hebert, he selected Butch, a rangy, four-foot tall, 135 pounder. Hebert advanced cautiously into the cage, his impersonation of a gorilla none too convincing. Butch pawed the sawdust and screamed, causing Hebert to stop, momentarily off balance. Suddenly the ape hurled forward, knocking the marine to the floor, grabbing the leather helmet off his head, and beating him with it while keeping him pinned with a sneakered foot planted on his face. It was all over in fifteen seconds. Bob Noell led Hebert out to a lawn chair he had charitably designated the "winner's seat" and held up the young man's arm. "Here's a guy who's going to Vietnam," he told the crowd, "and he's already had practice with gorillas." Hebert assessed the scratches on his face and arms. "I'm going to get some tennis shoes and come back tomorrow," he said. "Pops, that's all I need to whip that bastard."

118

Hebert wore our pants over his own, and before the "fight" was over, the top pants were torn to shreds.

Bob's bally was always "loud and clear." We had one of the most powerful amplifier systems that money could buy. Many times people would come to the show from several miles away because they could hear the audience laughing at the show and could hear Bob announcing the names of the contenders.

One of the things that Bob used to say during his announcement was, "When the show starts, don't turn your head. Keep your eye on that ape, because no show is guaranteed to last more than five seconds, and the maximum time is five minutes." We even had that on a sign out front. A classic example of why one should not turn his head was when our friend, Emily Hahn, the author who has written fifty books in fifty years, came to visit the show while we were in North Carolina. I asked her to write an account of what she remembered of the show for inclusion in this book. She very graciously mailed me the following vivid account for my readers:

"WANTED," said the sign outside the sidewalled trailer. "Athletic men to earn $5.00 per second by holding 85 pound ape's shoulders on floor. ($20.00 limit).

It sounded easy, but as I have never thought of myself as athletic and I'm not a man anyway, that was not the reason for my interest. This was in 1970, and I was there as a friend of the Noells, whose show it was. I stood in the middle of the carnival ground at Beaulaville, North Carolina. It was early evening. All around me in the dusk the carny people were setting up shop on their allocated sites, and the sound of speeding up electric motors, hurdy-gurdy music and a few experimental bellows from barkers was exciting, at least to a greenhorn like myself. Here and there lights were tried out, flashed a little, then settled to a steady glow.

Down the main pathway I could see a sort of shadow play in which scantily dressed girls kicked the air, then disappeared as the lights behind them went off. I turned back to the sign about athletic men and apes, and studied the lay-out. Bob and Mae Noell own a chimpanzee breeding establishment at Tarpon Springs, Florida but they used to vary the year's routine by going the carnival route at the appropriate season, and here I was, watching to see how they did it.

I knew something about their outfit. Beyond the portable white picket fence was an enormous Fruehauf trailer in which lived some of the Chimp Farm's most prized animals -- three gorillas, an orangutan family, and the most important performers in the show, the battling chimpanzees. Built into the big trailer was a 7' x 11' cage-arena which would be open to that portion of the public that paid their way in when the time came. The viewing area was surrounded by a ten-foot high canvas wall, and there was a pleasant smell of grassy meadow. At the back end of the arena-cage was a door that led into a private area, a dressing-room, as it were, for the chimps. Opposite, or up front, the view from the midway was obscured by the canvas sidewall and by the picket fence. Mae stood at the front door of the arena and was able to watch proceedings through a spy-hole. The entrance gate was surrounded by posters and pictures of the chimps.

Early as it was, I was not the only person whose attention was attracted to the WANTED sign. A few Marines from nearby Camp Lejeune, exploring the grounds, paused to read the poster and discuss it, laughing and daring each other to have a try at wrestling an ape.

"Twenty dollars just for that?" I heard one of them say: "Gee, that ought to be easy. Jim, you go along and collect the money."

"Why don't you?" retorted Jim.

120

"Well, gee..."

A friend of theirs, I gathered, was obviously the first one who ought to try it. His name was Hebert (pronounced Ay-Bair) and he was evidently a favored athlete in any game at all. After a minute or so he came on the scene. The others told him about the proposition, showed him the sign, and egged him on. Hebert looked thoughtful.

Up at the entrance, I saw Mae open the gate, and the Marines went over to ask her questions.

"You sign up and get your chance in the order you apply," she told them. "We don't have time in one evening to put on more than three or four fights, so better make up your minds now, before some of the others get in ahead of you."

Still thoughtful, Hebert proved himself a canny customer. Mae handed him a release which, she said, must be signed by applicants before they could go into the cage with a chimp; it absolved the Noells of any responsibility for injury which might result. He took a long time reading it and he argued over various clauses until Mae said, "Well, make up your mind. Nobody says you've got to go wrestle a chimp, you know."

"Sure, but don't I get a contract, too?" asked Hebert. "How do I know you'll pay me what you owe me when I've got the animal pinned down?"

"That's fair enough," admitted Mae, and another paper was signed.

"Let's have some action," said one of the Marines at last, "Come on Hebert, let's get going. Or are you afraid of a little monkey?"

Hebert was ushered up onto the platform to get ready, and the rest of us – the public – stood in line for our tickets, then filed into the enclosed meadow. It was quite dark now, and the lights around the arena shone brightly as I jostled my way to the front row. There, jammed against the picket guard rails and surrounded by grinning farmers and yet more Marines, I had a good view.

First, Bob Noell came into the middle of the cage and gave a short talk about chimpanzees and their fighting abilities. He explained that they often didn't realize their own strength, but on the whole, he said, they were nice enough animals. One chimp, named Joe, had been on the circuit for years; a real trouper, said Bob.

"He did forget himself once, and bit off my fingers," he added casually. "See?" He held up his mutilated hand, and the crowd murmered respectfully. "But Joe didn't really mean any harm," said Bob, "it was just that chimps are quick-tempered."

"Just remember that, Hebert," called a voice in the crowd. Somebody else yelled, "Is Hebert going to fight Joe?"

"No," said Bob, Joe wasn't on first. Hebert's opponent was to be a chimp named Kongo.

"Where is he? we heard Hebert call. "Where's that monkey? Let me at him!"

The Marine entered the front door of the arena, as Bob went into the back. There was an expectant silence and then the door swung open and Kongo came in. He leaped rather than walked; three leaps took him to the center of the cage. I was awed. Every one of his black hairs stood on end, which gave him the look of a huge, fierce, black flea — a flea with boxing gloves on his hands and a pair of shorts around his hairy waist. Kongo stood there in fighting stance, glowering at Hebert.

"Attaboy, Hebert," yelled my right-hand neighbor. I must say that Hebert was game, at least at first. He moved slowly toward the chimp and took a swing at him.

Kongo reacted swiftly. It is hard to say just what he was doing — boxing or wrestling.

Perhaps snatching would be a better description. He grabbed at Hebert's leg and tugged. Every time they got

122

close to one another the chimp pulled the man's pants, and it seemed as if each time more of the pants disappeared. First the left leg was ripped up, then the right came to grief. Hebert's singlet hardly lasted at all.

"Cream that ape!" screamed the Marine on my right. I gave him a withering glance, thereby missing the dramatic moment when Kongo removed the last bit of Hebert's pants. Now the Marine was in full flight, running round and round the arena with Kongo at his heels. The audience was in an uproar. At last Hebert collapsed against the steel wall of the arena, and Kongo closed in. I held my breath. Was it to be sudden death, or a slow mangling?

In fact it was neither. Kongo, amazingly, put his arm around Hebert's shoulder and nuzzled his face, as Bob, in proper referee style, lifted the chimp's other hand and held it in the air as a signal of victory. The fighters then shook hands and the bout was over.

Later, Joe the boxer, appeared. He wore tennis shoes as well as boxing gloves because, as Mae explained to me, it wouldn't be fair otherwise. Joe was as good with his feet as most animals are with their hands.

The Noells didn't have to pay out any money that night, except the guaranteed five dollars each. "Sometimes we pay an extra five if there's the slightest question as to whether the shoulders touched the floor," said Mae, "just to put heart into the boys, but nobody has ever gone away with the full twenty dollars."

Of all the people who boxed or wrestled with our animals, I think Bob Talbert related his experience the most humorously. He went in with Butch while he was a columnist for **The State and The Columbia Record** newspaper in Columbia, South Carolina. I mailed a copy of his very funny column "An Ape Made a Monkey Out of Me," (11-3-63) to **Argosy Magazine** and he did another version of the story for

123

Top photo shows front as painted by author. Bob prepares P.A. set for committee-man's bicycle give-away.

Lower photo shows front as painted by O.D. Abston. Bob standing on tail-gate stage.

them "Monkey Get Off My Back" in the April 1964 issue. I have been given generous permission, by both publications, and that of Bob himself, to include this material in my book.

The newspaper article is pretty self-explanatory so I'll just let Bob tell what happened to him that night:

"An Ape Made A Monkey Out of Me"
(Bob Talbert At Large)

Rule Number One in ape fighting:
Don't.
Butch the Ape made a monkey out of me. That arrogant anthropoid made me feel like a chumpanzee. My head is still ringing and if you think I walk bent over like this all the time you are crazy.

At the Colored State Fair which ended Saturday there was a sideshow called Noell's Ark Gorilla Show. The show owners, Mae and Bob Noell, offer prize money for anyone who will stay in the cage with one of their playful primates.

One brave...[fellow]...offered his services last Monday. He stuck his head in the cage door, took one look at that hairy rascal Butch and set a record for the shortest match on record — three-fifths of a second. The last seen of him was his heels as he rounded the corner at the Ferris wheel. He may still be running.

The Noells and their athletic apes winter in Tarpon Springs, Fla. They have been playing fairs and carnivals all over the country for 23 years. When I heard that they were getting no takers, my community spirit rose. After all, you can't have them traipsing around the country telling one and all that there's not a single ape fighter in South Carolina.

Playing and Praying

I picked Halloween to grapple the gorilla. If you've got to fight one, I figure that's about as good a time as

125

any. If you get mangled you can always go trick or treating as Frankenstein or something.

Things went pretty good at the start. Noell put me up on the stage in front of the cage and started his bally to build a crowd. "In 23 years," he told me, "no one has ever been hurt by one of our apes." He forgot to add that no one has ever beaten one either.

About this time Butch, a 165-pound black ape, started rattling the door of his pen. "Remember this," Noell said, "they are only playing." Yeah? They may be playing but I was praying. It is too late to back out.

Noell has two other monkeys that can wrestle -- Thomas, a 300-pound gorilla, and Kongo, an 85 pound ape. I took one look at the big fellow and got a pretty good idea why they can't keep one fellow playing Tarzan for long in the movies. And the little ape, Noell said, was just too mean for anyone to fight.

Didn't Come To Debate

"Butch is real gentle," Noell said. Yeah, and a black widow spider looks harmless, I thought. Noell promised Butch would be muzzled and would wear gloves over his hands. I was to wear a football helmet.

Mrs. Noell said, "You'd better read these rules and learn a little about apes."

I told her, "I'm not going to debate him, I'm going to wrestle him."

"I'm glad you have a sense of humor," she said and sighed.

Noell climbed in the cage and got Butch ready. Just before I climbed in Mrs. Noell confided, "Look, whatever you do, don't grab the ape with both hands and squeeze. He'll panic. He'll try to trip you and pull your pants off." She didn't say anything about if I panic.

When I got into the cage it looked like an overmatch.

126

I'm 250 and 6 feet. The ape is 165 and 4 feet – each arm is four feet long. But the crowd was with me. "You can take him," they yelled. To the hospital maybe I can take him. He'll be visiting me.

Came Out Frightened

Butch and I shook hands and I came out frightened. Noell stood between us so Butch would get used to me. "Chase him around," Noell advised. We went round and round Noell for a few moments and then Butch ran over to the corner of the 8-by-16 foot cage and hung from some bars on the ceiling.

"Go pull him down," Noell said. I know how the first soldier off at Anzio Beach felt. I felt like saying, "Pull him down yourself."

I grabbed hold of Butch's arm and it was like holding onto a hairy slab of concrete. I guess if you swung by your arms since you were three weeks old you'd have muscles, too. Trying to budge Butch was like trying to make the faces on Mt. Rushmore smile.

The next thing I know I was spun around and Butch's feet were banging me in the belly. He kept spinning me around with his feet as if I were some sort of top. Then came a left cross that sent my helmet flying and a right foot to the chest that sent me flying across the cage.

Now I can usually handle the old one-two combination. But Butch had a one-two-three-four combo with a Congo kick. "Yes, sir, he's playing all right," I thought while I tried to find my helmet.

Make a Buzzard Cry

Butch came over and sat down beside me. "He wants to make friends," Noell said.

"I sure don't want to make enemies," I assured Noell and Butch who was listening I hoped.

I sort of started to put my arm around Butch and he was all over me again. And some of Butch's best friends ought to tell him about that breath. It would make a buzzard cry.

Noell pulled him off of me and by this time I was beginning to wonder which of us had the most sense — Butch or I? His playful little taps were like being nudged by a locomotive.

Butch squatted and I stood. He started hopping up and down and making a "whu-u-h...whu-u-h" noise. In ape circles this means somebody is going to really catch it in a moment. Butch dove for the peephole where our photographer, Dave Underwood, was snapping away. Butch bounced off the door and into me.

He grabbed at my legs and fired a shot that hit me in the lower breadbasket. For a moment the cage turned into a planetarium. If the astronauts thought they saw funny-looking lights, they don't know the half of it.

All I Needed

"Butch is right frisky tonight," Noell said. "The flash bulbs are getting him excited."

If there's one thing I do know, when an ape gets excited it is no place for me to be. I told Noell I had all the first-hand knowledge I needed and I wanted to get out while I still had my hands and limbs intact.

Outside the cage, the Noells told me that no man, no matter how big or strong, can whip an ape, even a little 85-pounder. I noticed Noell was missing the middle fingers on his right hand. "How did that happen?" I asked.

"One of my chimps bit 'em right off. Clean as a whistle," he said, proudly looking at the stubs. I checked my hands.

I can tell you one thing. The next time you see Tarzan or The Phantom or one of those jungle fellows

128

whip an ape in the movies, you can take it from me --
they do it with mirrors or something. I even whispered
the magic jungle words -- "Um-gah-wah" -- in Butch's
ear and all it got me was a one-two-three-four to the
chest and stomach.

The Noells did say this. I stayed in the cage with the
ape for ten minutes, which is about five minutes longer
than ayone ever had before. Which is also ten minutes
longer than I ever will again.

When the **Argosy** editor saw this writeup he got Bob to try
one more time, only this time Bob was to box with Joe the
Boxer. But I'll let **him** tell it the way he did in his story:

"MONKEY GET OFF MY BACK!"

"In this corner the champ -- ninety-five pounds of
hairy muscle. And in this corner, the challenger -- 250
pounds of fearless reporter who'll do anything for a
story. There's the bell, fight fans. Get set for the fight of
the century!"

I've got news for Sonny Liston. He may think he's
the world's heavyweight champion. But I know a
ninety-five-pound little five-year-old (sic) that could
make Sonny get blue real quick.

His name is Joe. He's the ape that made a monkey
out of me. This arrogant anthropoid made me feel like a
chump-panzee. I spent a day with a monkey on my
back, on my stomach, on my head, on my legs, on my
arms, all over me. It might not sound probable, but take
it from me, you can be completely surrounded by one
ninety-five-pound chimpanzee.

I write a first-person human interest column for **The
State** newspaper in Columbia, South Carolina. One day I
let this statement slip: "I will do anything within reason
at least once."

When you write a newspaper column six days a week,

you keep looking for the offbeat things to do and write. People send in their suppressed desires and you arrange to perform them.

You know these little go-karts? Yeah, those tiny machines that look like a power lawnmower gone wrong. Well, a fellow in Columbia has one that will go 100 miles an hour. It's powered by eight engines. I rode it, or rather bounced a quarter of a mile in it, trying to keep it from flying. That's an example.

I've ridden rapids in a rubber life raft. I once sat down and ate seventy-eight fried catfish which I claim as the world's indigestion record. I've lived with contestants in beauty contests (chaperoned, of course). I played Santa Claus for a day and got kicked in the shins by some little girls whose names obviously weren't Virginia. To help promote a "Stop Polio" oral-vaccine campaign, I lived in an iron lung for a day to see how it felt. I rode a 427-horsepower dragboat eighty miles an hour over water. I've spelunked in caves, scrimmaged with football teams, spent a day blindfolded to find out how the blind feel. Things like that. That's what my column, "Bob Talbert at Large," is made up of day by day.

And when you do this sort of thing every day to get a column, you become trapped. How do you top what you did the day before?

So this telephone call came from **Argosy** Magazine. "How," they asked, "would you like to box a ninety-five-pound chimpanzee?"

If you ever get a call like that, either hang up immediately or pretend it's a bad connection and you can't hear so well.

But not me. Bob the Boob answered, "A chimp! Sure, I'll box him. Ninety-five pounds, eh? I think I can take him."

After all, I weigh about 250 and am six feet tall, twenty-seven years old and in pretty good shape except for my catfish-eating days. There's a little suet, to be sure, but it makes for good padding. I figure I can spot any monkey 155 pounds in a fair fight.

Argosy explained that Bob and Mae Noell own a gorilla show -- a troupe of fighting apes -- they take around the southeastern fair circuit, offering prize money for anyone who can stay in the cage with one of their athletic apes. The Noells' playful primates winter at Tarpon Springs, Florida.

The Noell's Ark Gorilla Show has been playing fairs and carnivals for twenty-three years. During that time, some 20,000 frisky humans have ventured into the ring with the Noells' muscular monkeys. Approximately 18,211 have been carried out. No one has ever beaten one of the apes. There's a sign on the front of their truck that says: No Show Guaranteed to Last Over Five Seconds. Maximum Five Minutes.

This appealed to me. I can stay in the ring with any monkey for five minutes," I figured. "Let's face it, what does an ape know about fighting."

I was to find out.

I didn't quite know how to go into training for ape fighting. What do you do? Eat a lot of bananas? Swing from tree limbs? See a whole bunch of old Tarzan movies?

I went to a sporting-goods store in Columbia to get some equipment. I asked one of the owners, Charlie Todd, if he had any kind of ape-fighting equipment.

"Fresh out," he told me.

He's a funny fellow. Everyone is a comedian when you say you are going to box a chimp. Todd fixed me up with a pair of personalized trunks and someone suggested they write the name of the store across the seat. George Moore, the other owner, held them up.

"From the size of these," he said, "we could get 'Todd and Moore, Sporting Goods' on one side and 'Columbia, South Carolina' on the other." See what I mean about comedians?

Anyway, with equipment in hand, I arrived at Tarpon Springs. This is a pretty unusual town -- one big Greek salad on top of a lot of sponges. If you don't have an "x" or a "z" or a "k" in your name, turn around and go home. I finally found someone that talked English and asked him where the monkey farm was. He grinned.

"You gonna fight the chimp?" he said.

I told him I was and asked him why he was grinning.

"I'm the undertaker," he said.

This monkey farm is a sight to behold. It looks like the back lot for the Tarzan movies, coupled with a carnival either putting up or taking down. There are animals all over the place – dogs, chickens, five species of monkeys, mandrills, baboons, orangutans, chimpanzees, a 300-pound gorilla named Tommy, and about the meanest goose you'll ever see.

Bob Noell warned me: "The most vicious thing on the place is the goose. Watch him. He'll sneak up on you from behind." Now I know where the phrase came from.

Carnival props, many-colored wagons and trailers, cages and an assortment of in-repair machinery covered the place. Noell and photograhper George X. Sand had set up a ring off to one side.

Have you ever heard a chimpanzee scream?

Well, let me tell you, it's enough to turn you stone deaf. Not only did my blood curdle when Joe let out a holler; it turned to milk.

"Joe is using psychological warfare on you," Noell said. "He screams like that to scare you." Joe had won round one and we hadn't exchanged a lick.

They insisted Joe and I do some road work, and I got my first look at the chimp. He may weigh ninety-five pounds, but he looks heavier. He stands about four feet and each arm drags the ground.

Some human beings, to demonstrate their strength,

132

tear up telephone books. Others pull freight cars with their teeth. Some bend crowbars. Chimps, I found out, tear people. I've seen telephone poles with more fat on them than Joe had. But I guess if you had swung by your arms since you were two years old, you'd be muscular, too.

After we got the road work out of the way, signed the contracts (the part about losing my limbs didn't set too well) and weighed in, we got ready for the bout.

My second, I must admit, was a refreshing and beautiful young lady named Velda Deddo, the Noells' daughter. She could stay in my corner any time. Joe's second was owner-trainer Bob Noell, who also served as the referee.

Mae Noell said, "Bob's got to be right there at all times or Joe may panic and get a little rough."

Joe may panic? How about me?

Joe wore a leash and a muzzle, which is just as well. Some of his best friends ought to tell him about that breath. It would make a buzzard cry. Not only that, chimps are afraid of water. They won't go near it. And you can imagine what you'd smell like if you hadn't had a bath in five years!

"When he pounds his chest, he's happy," Noell told me.

Later, I found out when he pounded my chest he was happy, too.

Joe and I touched gloves and I came out frightened. We sort of shuffled around, and Noell said, "Take a swing at him."

I felt like telling Noell to "swing at him yourself." I put out a little straight jab and Joe dodged it easily. The next thing I know I'm sitting on the canvas.

That hairy little devil jumped straight up six feet in the air and caught me in the mouth with a right foot. Now I figured I could handle any one-two punch Joe had. But I forgot he'd have a one-two-three-four combo

133

with a Congo kick.

And once ol' Joe got me on the ground, he began to roll me around like I was a log or something. Noell pulled him off and Velda rushed out to comfort me. This I like, and would have liked even more but my lip began to grow.

I got back up and Joe and I squared off again. This time Joe sort of squatted and dropped his hands and began to hop up and down and say, "Whu-u-h...whu-u-h!" And when an ape begins to make "whuh-whuh" noises he means somebody is going to catch hell in a second.

Did you ever run into a tree in the dark? Well, that's what it felt like when Joe crawled me again. That's when I felt surrounded by chimpanzee.

Noell smiled. "Joe's just playing."

"Yes, sir, he's playing, all right," I thought as my lip continued to swell and my left eye began to close. "Boy, is he ever playing! For God's sake, don't tell him to go for real!"

Once again, we squared off and this time Joe decided that boxing was no fun and went for my leg. He grabbed hold of it and flipped me on my back.

Now, Joe figured it was time to get a little cheesecake in the game. He started pulling off my trunks. I don't know if you've ever been in this situation or not. There I am with boxing gloves on, and a chimp is pulling my trunks off with two hands and slapping me in the sides with his two feet. I was torn between decency and death.

Well, he got my trunks off before Noell could pull him away. I got the feeling all match long that Noell was a little slow with that leash.

Velda retrieved the trunks and I got ready again. This time, Joe trotted across the ring and put his arm around my waist.

"He wants to make friends," said Bob.

"Tell him for me that I certainly don't want to make enemies," I assured Noell and all the folks standing around.

Joe began making with the **"whuh-whuh"** noises again, and I began looking for the quickest way out of the ring. Too late. Everything I did seemed too late. Joe had me on my stomach this time and was jumping up and down on my back. And if you think you've got a monkey on your back, you don't know the half of it.

I was getting pretty sunburned and all I could think of was something the Noells had said earlier. The only meat apes will eat is meat that's been cooked. By this time, I resembled a well-turned leg of lamb. Muzzle or not, I knew it was way past Joe's regular feeding time.

Noell got Joe off my back and I staggered back to my corner and Bob Noell, Jr. took one look at me and threw in the towel. He'd have had to throw me in to get me back in there with that ape.

It was ruled a TKO at the end of the first round. They could have ruled it anything they liked. I just wanted to get the hell out of there.

Outside the ring, the Noells told me that no man, no matter how strong or big, can whip one of the chimps. "Chimps don't know just how strong they are."

"I can assure you I do," I told Noell and noticed that the middle fingers on his right hand were missing. "How'd that happen?" I asked.

"One of my chimps bit 'em off," Noell said, "Clean as a whistle."

I checked my hands. All fingers accounted for. I had an extra three pounds of lower lip, but nothing missing.

I can tell you one thing. The next time you see one of those Tarzan fellows of the jungle whip an ape in the movies or on TV, you can take it from me – they do it with mirrors or something.

As I was leaving the monkey farm, I noticed a

taxidermist's shop across the street. I wondered what he gets for stuffing a people. One more round with Joe, and the taxidermist could have done business with me.

And if **Argosy** gets any more bright ideas, give me a day or two to sleep on it. They sure have a lot of nerve asking a fellow to do these crazy things."

Chapter Five

Baby chimps are born with their hair already parted, and I've been accused of fibbing when people asked me why I parted Kongo's hair that way when he was a baby. Chimps are also endowed, the instant they are born, with a tremendously powerful grip in hands and feet. This is necessary for the survival of the animal; the moment one is born, it attaches itself like glue to its mother's fur and starts nursing soon after birth (if it is normal). This leaves the mother's hands and feet free so she can go on living as she did before, but now and then, she may wrap one arm protectively around the baby as she moves along the ground or in tree tops. Babies never seem to tire of holding on. These powerful little hands can give a nasty pinch if they grasp a handful of "meat" instead of hair. Although we have had forty-five chimps born in the collection as of this writing and **all** were kept in the trailer for awhile, only a few were **raised** in the trailer.

Kongo was our first one. He was born February 28, 1948, at Miami, Florida, in our truck. His mother was Suzy Q. Noell, and his father was Joe Noell. So, we named him Kongo

ALL LINE DRAWINGS (EXCEPT CARTOON) BY
AUTHOR. ↓ THIS IS A HANDBILL ON COLORED PAPER.

Joe Noell the First. Suzy had six live births. Only one of these (Kongo) was a boy. When Suzy died, she was "expecting" number seven. When Kongo was only ten days old, we "chimp-napped" him because when we went up into Georgia where it turned cold, Suzy had laid him aside on the straw. Because she had tired of holding him we were afraid he might get chilled, even though we had heat in the truck.

When my children were growing up, money was not too plentiful, so we did not go in for anything really expensive or fancy in the way of clothing. There were baby clothes for which I wished, but I had to forego the frivolous in favor of real necessities. I had to carry buckets of water and wash the babies' clothes with a scrub board. It was the only way we knew then. Often my knuckles would be rubbed raw from washing baby clothes.

Naturally, when Kongo came along and money was a little bit freer, I bought several really nice outfits for him. Because I always took my children with me everywhere I went -- never trusting them to "baby sitters" -- it was only natural that I did the same with an infant chimp. Because Kongo went everywhere I went, I had quite a lot of fun with him.

His birth was such a happy surprise that even our friends enjoyed buying things for Kongo. We were with a big tent show which featured a famous and popular comedy team known as "Mustard and Gravy." Both the men and their families were thrilled with "the baby." When he was one year old, we had a birthday party for him with one candle on the cake. The team got him a doll highchair, which "just fit."

All the "babies" I raised in the trailer were always fed with fresh, homogenized, Vitamin D milk mixed with strained baby foods in a nursing bottle. Recently science has discovered (after much research) that animals that are with their babies constantly after birth have a weak milk and those that have to leave the babies for hours at a time have a more potent, concentrated milk. Perhaps the milk I fed was a bit strong, but my chimp babies really thrived on it! It matters not which type of animal is being fed, but what governs the

139

strength of the milk is the length of time the mother and baby are separated daily. This is a good thing to remember, because if one knows what an animal's normal habits are in searching for food, one would then know how strong or weak the formula should be to raise the infant successfully.

It would be impossible to over-emphasize how important it is to love the great apes when they are tiny. They feel this as keenly as does a human child. I am afraid, though, that I over-loved Kongo! He was most precious and not mean or spoiled. However, just like a little sleepy-headed kid, he would refuse to lie down, no matter how sleepy he got. Often as not he would be found sitting, nodding, in a most uncomfortable position. I'd place him comfortably when I found him thus, and, like a human baby, he'd sigh contentedly and sleep on.

He weighed less than five pounds when he was born and was wrinkled and almost completely hairless. In a few weeks, though, he was covered with long, black "baby hair", and it was about this time that I started taking him everywhere I went.

We thought we might travel with the Hunt Brothers' Circus, which was playing in the New York-New Jersey area in the late 40's and early fifties. We were with them less than a week, because in New Jersey we found it almost impossible to work because of the way the kids came under the walls, opening the way for adults. While in that state, we were close enough to the Bronx that I decided to go by bus and visit some of my kin. Kongo was just a few months old and still in diapers. We took him along because I never left him behind when I went anywhere. He needed food and attention at short intervals.

On the way home we got hungry and stopped at a Horne and Hardart Automatic Restaurant. We had selected three nice meals for my son, daughter and myself. I thought I had the baby securely covered, but, as usual, the little stinker got an arm out of his blanket, at my back.

An attendant came by and nearly went into shock.

"Lady!" he gasped, "You can't stay in here with an animal! It's against the law!"

Not wanting to cause a disturbance I told the kids to go ahead and eat their meal and I would wait outside, I had to do without my supper.

But later, when it came time to get on the bus, it was different.

We had missed the bus I had intended to catch and it was getting cold. We were waiting in line in the bus depot when the driver came down the line to tell us the bus would be a half hour late. I was exhausted and scared to death that I'd not be allowed to get on the bus with a baby chimp so – again – I thought he was well concealed, and again that little black hairy arm had snaked its way out of the covers. The driver came straight to me and said, "Where did you get the little baby chimp!?"

I told him, and told him too, how tired we were.

He said, "Come with me." We followed him and he said, "Get on the bus. It won't be loading for another half hour, but you can get on with your kids, now."

We got on the bus and rode around in it while it was serviced and gassed up.

Because of my baby chimp I had lost the right to eat my supper at the Automat, but he got us a seat on the bus that was crowded with standees when it left the bus depot.

We travelled, also, sometime later, on the Hoxie Brothers Circus, and since a Circus usually stays only one day in each town, it was a short season for us. We were not equipped to put up and tear down every twenty-four hours as they are, and we were soon exhausted.

Some of the places I took the baby while we were with Hoxie were "episodes to be remembered." Like the day in Franklinton, N.C., when I was uptown doing my grocery shopping. I always made it a point to keep the baby covered so people would not breathe on him. I was aware of the chimps' weakness where respiratory diseases were concerned, so did not "show him off."

My children were born before World War II in a farm-house, more than twenty miles from the nearest hospital. The doctor charged $15.00 to come some eight or ten miles to deliver a child and to make two "follow-up" visits. We owed the doctor for several months before we could pay him. My babies wore cotton flannel garments I had sewn by hand. Store bought baby dresses cost 50¢ to a dollar and we could not afford such expensive frills. So, when Kongo came along after the war I was able to buy pretty baby clothes for him. I satisfied my maternal instincts for beautiful baby clothes by decking him out in finery. Also, this kept nosey people back because everybody has seen a human baby and wouldn't usually be pushy to look at one.

However, in Franklinton, it was different. While walking along the sidewalk window-shopping – with the "baby" carefully wrapped in a lovely white, loosely woven woolen blanket, a tall skinny woman came running across the street. She ran right up, startling me. A young girl was behind her. The older woman very rudely grabbed the edge of the blanket as she said, "Oh, I've just got to see that baby! I know it's the tiniest thing!" (Kongo was about four or five pounds and only a couple of months old at the time.) She flipped the blanket back before I could stop her, almost knocking the little guy out of my arms. When she saw the little, wrinkled, brown face she fainted dead away as the young girl caught her on the way down. The girl looked at the baby, horrified. I've since been criticized for what I did, but I would do it again under the same circumstances. I covered the baby back and told the girl, "Now! Because she was so rude as to snatch the cover off my baby without first asking -- you can both wonder, for the rest of your lives, what is wrong with my baby!" And I walked away with the girl still standing, mouth agape as she held the older woman under the arms, half suspended off the sidewalk.

I've often wondered since, "what they did think was wrong with 'my baby'?"

When anyone asked, politely, to see the baby, I would

142

always say, "Wait a minute, now, this is not a human baby. It's a pet and I'm very proud of him. I don't want you to think you're going to see a baby, then get a shock!" And then I would uncover him amid "Ohs" and "Ahs", because once warned, people realized what a cute and precious thing he was. So I always felt (and still do) that that woman got what she deserved.

At a drugstore, one day, I was looking at post cards on a card rack. That hairy little arm was hanging behind me again. I "felt" eyes staring at me from behind. I turned quickly and saw two young women staring wide-eyed at the arm. One had a hand over her mouth as she was whispering something in the other one's ear. Both were "electrified." I "discovered" the arm, flipped the blanket over it and stomped out of the store in pretended indignation. Again, I wonder what they thought was wrong with "my baby."

Anytime anyone acted rude they got no satisfaction from me. On the other hand, decent people always got to see the baby and they loved him. Once, when Kongo was a pretty big baby, a store man came to the lot to ask me if I would take Kongo over to see his wife at the store. Because I had dealt there and they were nice people, I decided to take him over. Standing and talking to the store people, I hardly noticed when a middle-aged woman walked in and stood staring at him. Kongo must have sensed something was wrong with her because he returned the gaze. When I turned to go back to the lot, the woman said, "I'm gonna knock his head off." Then she swung her handbag. I just barely jerked him back in time to miss being hit by it. Then I proceeded to tell her just what kind of an idiot I took her to be, and that I thought somebody somewhere was at fault for letting such a person run loose on the streets. After this experience, I decided Kongo was more intelligent than some people, and I'd not bother to accommodate anyone that way again. Had Kongo been a vicious animal, he could have jumped on her (justifiably) and could have done a lot of damage. As it was, he seemed to be silently agreeing with me.

When Kongo was about three or four years old, I decided to take him to the beach with us for an outing. I got the scare of my life that day. Thinking he might enjoy a dip in the salt water, I took him on my back and waded out into the small breakers about waist deep. Kongo warned me several times by barking the danger signal not to go out in the water. I ignored his plea. I had him on my back and also held the end of the lead chain. Kongo panicked and tried to jump back to shore. I watched in horrified amazement as he seemed to freeze into an immobile statue, as he sank to the bottom! Never a single effort did he make to swim! I jerked the chain and got him back on my shoulders and headed straight back for shore. He was a relieved little chimp when I put him back in his cage. I was surprised because all my life I had thought all wild animals could swim. Not the great apes!

I have seen a Baboon swim, but never an anthropoid ape. The Baboon, named Charlie, was one we owned. Our Great Dane jumped in a moat around a small island and left the Baboon on the island. Charlie didn't want his playmate to leave him and followed without the least hesitation, swimming better than the dog.

As this is being written, in 1979, Kongo is thirty-one years old and still "Mama's baby" even though I can't carry him around anymore.

When Kongo was a couple of years old, we had our show in Valdosta, Georgia. We were not far from Orange Park, Florida, where the Yerkes Laboratory of Primate Biology was located. Because I had heard they had quite a huge collection of chimpanzees there, I was anxious to visit them. I got the opportunity when we went to Jacksonville to get some new truck tires and had to wait several hours for them to be mounted on the wheels. I called the Lab and asked if we could visit them. Dr. Nissen told me to "come on."

I had no idea we were getting into such an interesting adventure. When we drove up, we noticed a tall (six or eight feet), chain link fence encircled the premises. We parked in the parking lot and walked over to the gate. We used the push

144

button bell rather with misgivings. The buzzing sound at the gate startled us. Then, when we made no move to respond, we heard a lady's voice at the building at the end of the walk, "When the buzzer sounds, open the gate. It is an electric lock."

We were delighted! We thanked her and went in. She led us down the hall and out to the back where we were introduced to Dr. Keith Hayes who very kindly "guided" us around the entire chimpanzee area. He cautioned us about letting our ten-year-old daughter near the cages. I assured him that she would not get close because she knew the danger. As he showed us around, he watched her with growing approval. Finally, as we got ready to leave, Dr. Hayes said, "Would you like to meet a young chimpanzee who is being raised like a human child as an experiment?" Of course, we were delighted. He added, "I've watched the little girl and am anxious to see what kind of a reception the little chimp will give her."

We got in our car and followed him a short distance away to his home. As we rode, we talked excitedly about the many chimps that were at the Lab and how well fed and contented the animals seemed. Most thrilling to me were the many babies that were being bred and raised there.

We drove down a long lane to a cozy little house and found Mrs. "Cathy" Hayes in the yard, reading a book by Belle Benchley (**My Friends the Apes**). Mrs. Benchley was due to visit the Lab in a few days and Mrs. Hayes wanted to read the book before her arrival. The chimp was on a child's swing, contentedly swinging back and forth. When she saw the cars come into the driveway she "hooted" her happy greeting to her "Daddy." Mrs. Hayes shook a restraining finger at her and said, "Now, Viki, behave! You have company, so behave yourself!"

I said, "You are a gal after my own heart! My family laughs at me for talking to my 'babies' so much. But Vicki's restraint and good behavior show she does understand you!"

"Oh, yes! Didn't Keith tell you that is part of the

145

experiment with this animal. She says three words!"

I was surprised. Only a few days before I had seen a newspaper story concerning a chimp that was "speaking" — (and I did not find it hard to believe because I knew that an experiment had been conducted some forty or fifty years earlier, in which an Orangutan had been taught to say "Mama," "Papa" and "Cup.").

I said, "Oh! Are you the young couple whose chimp says "Mama," "Papa" and "Cup?"

"Ah, you saw that newspaper article," she said.

"Yes, but it wasn't as friendly an article as it should have been for this sort of an experiment."

Someone had said that the animal was not really "speaking," and the Hayeses had felt offended (justifiably so) by the remark.

Mrs. Hayes went on to explain, "When she wants food, she says 'Papa' to Keith or 'Mama' to me. When she asks for a drink, she says 'cup' to whichever one of us is near. She definitely associates these words with the proper people and objects."

"How long did it take you to teach each word?" I asked, remembering how tedious the book had said it had been to teach the Orangutan, so many years before.

"A safe estimate is something like six months per word. But, we hope that once she gets the idea, subsequent words will come easier and more fluently."

While we were talking, "our daughters" were hitting it off together very nicely. Velda Mae was making chimpanzee sounds to the ape, who found this little human playmate something of a surprise. She was corrected, from time to time, by a very watchful Mrs. Hayes when she got over-enthusiastic or too rough.

Finally, after extracting a promise before we left the area that they would come up to see our show at Valdosta, we said reluctant good-byes. On the way home, we agreed that this had been one of the most rewarding days we had experienced since we had had great apes! And, in retrospect,

146

I feel that Viki and her "parents" opened the door (figuratively speaking) for all the sign-language experiments with great apes that have since proved so successful and revealing.

A couple of nights after our visit to Orange Park, the Hayeses came up to see the show and to "introduce" Viki to Kongo. However, both the "mothers" (Mrs. Hayes and myself) were a little bit afraid to let them actually get hold of each other. We were not sure whether they might hold to each other or fight. Deciding it was not worth the risk, we put Kongo back in his cage and enjoyed Viki.

I served a "midnight snack," as was our custom after the show, and Viki sat at the table with us. When Velda Mae reached for something, Viki bit her suddenly on the chest. For this she was spanked over everyone's (including Velda Mae's) protests. She was put on her best behavior and made to say, "Papa," "Mama," or "Cup'. for each thing she got at the table. Mrs. Hayes had complete control, for which I still admire her, because that size chimp could as easily have been her boss! Viki did not use her vocal cords to "speak" but used a hoarse stage whisper. Anyone who heard these words, however, would have to admit that they were perfectly spoken.

I never felt the constant effort needed to train one this way would ever be repaid in "showmanship" value. As a scientific experiment, this was a tremendously valuable piece of business. It "clinches" what I had been advocating ever since I'd had Great Apes; learn to speak their "language" – it is much easier for us to step down ten or fifteen steps than it is for them to step up one step. It took six months to teach a bright little chimpanzee one word. A reasonably intelligent human being can "master" the whole "chimpanzee vocabulary" in a matter of minutes or hours!

As they prepared to leave that night, Mrs. Hayes was so impressed with our daughter (aged ten) playing with (adult chimpanzee) "Snookie" that she said, "I simply must mention this in my book! This is fabulous!"

147

WANTED!

**Athletic Men To Earn $5.00 Per Second By Holding
85 Lb. Ape's Shoulders on the Floor (up to 4 seconds)
Also Wanted: Boxers To Earn $1.00 Per Minute**

AT THE GORILLA SHOW

WRESTLING 8:15 P.M. MON. JAN. 29

FORT HOMER HESTERLY TAMPA

10 ROUND BOXING BOUT WITH GLOVES

JOE GORILLA
WORLD'S ONLY BOXING

VERSUS

RUBE WRIGHT
"KILLER"

Wright to receive $500.00 if he can remain the bell for the 10th Round, $1000.00 if he can knockout Joe.

Also "SNOOKIE" the Wrestling Ape, in A WRESTLE ROYAL

RETURN GRUDGE MATCH—WINNER TAKE ALL
FREDERICK VON SCHACHT vs. DANNY "HOT SHOT" DUSEK

DAN O'CONNOR vs. JACK BERNARD
JIMMY RAY vs. PAT O'HARA

Ringside - - $1.25 | WRESTLING OFFICE—THOMAS JEFFERSON HOTEL Or Call 2-2132 For Reservations | Gen. Admission - 80¢

"You're writing a book?" I asked, excitedly.

"No, it's already written, and is already being set up. But maybe I'm not too late! Maybe I can slip a few words or a paragraph in. I simply **must!**"

The book **The Ape in our House** (1951) by Cathy Hayes contains the following paragraph on page 240.

> The question often arises in the village drugstore as to whether Viki will "turn on" us as she grows older. Among our acquaintances are the Noells, who operate the traveling Gorilla Show. We have seen their ten-year-old daughter playing with an unmuzzled, unchained adult chimpanzee. When she tickled it, the ape rolled on the floor and chuckled like an overgrown Viki. I would also like to point out that both the late Gargantua and his "mate" Toto were raised by human foster parents without assault. On the other hand, the newspapers carry many an account of a berserk human who has murdered his gray-haired mother or father or both. It's a chance parents have to take.

For many years our chimps proved themselves unbeatable in unorthodox boxing and wrestling matches. How could we explain the Marquis of Queensbury rules to a chimp? They used their own tactics and the only training we gave them was to stop when told to. But if the man had riled the animal enough it was often hard to get the animal to obey as quickly as we wanted.

Most of the "fights" lasted considerably less than five minutes. Some lasted only ten seconds! We were visited by S.P.C.A. people on several occasions and they always went away shaking their heads and saying, "There ought to be a Society for Prevention of Cruely to **PEOPLE!**"

Kongo and Joe were **leapers**. They could jump up, kick a man's shoulders with such force that the man would find himself sitting on the floor and wondering how he got there. Then the second leap would land the chimp on the man's midriff – flattening him in a twinkling and the fight was over. Or – if it was a big man who wouldn't go down so easy, the ape would get a grip on the back of the man's belt and swing on it. A good strong belt was good for a dizzying swing of at least eight or ten revolutions, round and round the cage as the man helplessly flailed arms and legs in a vain attempt to remain on his feet. If the belt broke, the man would be standing in his birthday suit -- or, if he was lucky -- in his shorts. The ape would then take the rags and use them as a whip, often leaving the print of the buttons or belt buckles on the hide of the contestant and/or Bob, or both of them.

One big man was toppled so fast, years ago, that as he fell backward, the back of his open hand accidentally caught Bob across the mouth and knocked his two front teeth out.

Another time, when we had the old original wooden cage on the International truck, Snookie kicked one man against the door so hard that the door to the cage was "turned inside out" and we had to use wrecking bars to get it open!

I have seen men (who intended to use their helmeted head as a weapon) charge at the ape, head down, only to hit the steel wall when the ape swung aside, and almost knock themselves out. When this happened the ape usually closed in on him quickly and the fight was over suddenly.

It had nearly always been a source of annoyance and sometimes of amusement to hear the stories that started after we left a town where men went in to "really cream the ape." As I have said before, at no time in our entire career have we ever seen one of the apes "bested." But you can bet that as soon as the gorilla show left a lot of towns, there were any number of people who were anxious to back "their man" up and to argue that, "old John Doe sure whipped that ape!" Then when someone who had **seen** the show would be **truthful** about it the storyteller would always "back water," and – to save face – would say, "Well, maybe he just stayed in the cage with the ape longer than anyone else in town!" I always agreed that this could be true so that they **could** "save face."

We even hear some of these fantasties to this day, when people "find" us at the Chimp Farm!

At Matewan, West Virginia a goodly number of people saw the show in which one of the Hatfield boys wrestled with Kongo. It went fast and furious as usual when a strong man went in. When he came out, the contestant was asked how it went. He answered his friend by saying, "That's the first time I ever got punched in the nose and kicked in the butt at the same time!"

It was always my job to do the publicity work on the show, whether we were working on a carnival or independently. I was always on the alert to see the many different ways I could make the public aware of the fact that the gorilla show was in town. Knowing this, I think it will be easy to understand why I "flipped my lid" at Bob over the following incident.

It was also my job to stand at the gate to take the money as the people came in to see the show. On the night of this incident the volunteer was out on the bally platform talking to Bob. I was not in on the conversation because I was busy with a big crowd who had come to see this fight between their black-belted Karate hero and Kongo. The man told Bob that he would give the belt to the ape if he earned it. If I had known about this in time, it could have been a priceless piece of publicity. Naturally, the poor guy got "shellacked," as usual, and when he came out he was true to his word; he offered Bob the belt, "to give to the ape. He earned it." Bob refused it, of course, but I would certainly have had a cute newspaper story out of it if I had known about it in time.

In one of the towns we came back to a year later, a man told Bob he had wrestled with Butch when we were there the year before. If Butch didn't like a contestant he often pulled a dirty trick on them. This man was one Butch didn't like and the missile he tossed was especially smelly. The poor guy was laughing – almost hysterically at the memory when he told Bob about it.

"I didn't mind smelling like an out-house," he said, "half as much as I did having to circle the house twice before I got in

151

safely and then being **treed** in **my own house** by **my own dogs!**"

We had a local hermit on stage, waiting to go into the cage with Butch in one small town in Pennsylvania. He lived somewhere out in the woods and it was said that his only companion was a mongrel dog, and when the police took him to jail for being drunk he would not go unless they locked the dog in the cell with him. He was the pathetic target of brainless people who teased and tormented him, even though the poor man was on one hundred percent disability for service-connected injuries received during war times. As he sat on the platform, waiting to go in, Bob suddenly said – angrily, "Close the gate! I'm not going to try to work when people are throwing rocks!" The crowd outside was so congested that we could not discover where the rocks were coming from, so I refunded to the few who had gone inside and closed the gate. The show's manager, Mr. Eddie Dietz was our "protector" and friend. He got the police to stand guard and we were then able to let the man go in the cage with Butch, who played gently with him and they put on a funny show.

There were many times when radio stations would send someone to the show lot to do interviews, or when I would go uptown to the stations to be interviewed. Most of the time the interviews were done live on the spot, and were, therefore, never recorded. But back in 1968 we were at the Jefferson Town and Country Fair in Sykesville, Pennsylvania where a radio-man came out to the lot to tape Bob's interview. I have the permission of the interviewer, Charles Moore, to include it in this history:

INTERVIEW – WCED

"This is Ben Finger and Charlie Moore –

"Here in Sykesville, if you can wrestle a full-size chimpanzee, a monkey that big, we think you're a pretty good man. We have a gentleman who has for many years been a veteran on the road with road shows and his name is?"

"Robert Noell."

"Robert Noell. And what is the show called in Sykesville?"

"Noell's Ark."

"Noell's Ark. Robert, where are you from?"

"I was born and raised in Bedford, Virginia."

"Bedford? You have that old Southern accent so I know y'all are Royalty. I was gonna say "is it Virginia, North Carolina, South Carolina, hog jaw and black-eyed peas and squirrels head? You call me 'Hey, Charles' and I'll call you 'Hey, Robert.' Tell us just a bit about where our program is emanating from today in Sykesville."

"This is in the cage where we have the wrestling and boxing matches. We've got eleven apes with us; we've got two gorillas, three orangutans and five chimpanzees that take part in the program."

"You now have thirteen. This is Mr. Finger – Charles Moore -- we're gonna join the act and we're leaving town with you come Friday night! Tell me about yourself, Bob. You have a rich heritage; they say there is no written manuscript as far as show business is concerned. It is only the living people, such as yourself who have done a tremendous job down through the years. How many years, Bob, have you been in show business?"

"I'm fifty-seven years old and I started on the road when I was eleven. I've been with animals – with apes for thirty-eight years."

"You're looking at me like I'm one of the crowd so you're making me feel right at home, Bob. Where did you start out – and traditionally did you as a boy of eleven run away from home?"

"I ran away from home to join a medicine show in Bedford, Virginia, near my hometown and I've been going ever since."

"Can you tell us now, when you left Bedford, Virginia, how far did you travel in those days with the medicine show?"

153

"Ohio and Kansas and Missouri and back to Ohio."

"Then would you come home in the Winter, or would you stay continuously on the road?"

"I was on the road four years; when I came back I had my own show."

"Tell us how you got in this particular section of show business."

"I bought a chimpanzee that weighed fifty-five pounds and he got to where I couldn't put him in the cage and people laughed at me and I had to give two men ten dollars to try to put him in the cage, and the first show he ran the two men in the cage and upset the cage and it was the funniest of all the shows -- the first show. And then we got another one and he liked to hit so we made a boxer out of him and started out that way. Now we have eleven with us and nine more in Florida."

"Where at in Florida?"

"Tarpon Springs."

"The sponges. I used to be in Tampa at Phillips Field, when the Phillips shows were there. I worked with two stations in Tampa. Did you winter in Tampa many years?"

"We bought a little place there fifteen years ago and we've got a little zoo there now -- at Tarpon Springs."

"Tarpon Springs. I used to -- in the old days -- in 1950 -- I used to deliver Holsum Bread to Tarpon Springs at three o'clock in the morning. That was quite a time -- before I got my radio station. But I want to talk about you. Am I right -- I have heard -- that chimpanzees are pretty easy to control until they get to the age of six or seven and then the trouble starts. How old are your chimpanzees?"

"I'm working one that's thirty-eight years old, one that's twenty-eight years old and one that's twenty years old. And the big gorilla I'm working is eleven years old, and the little gorilla is three years old."

"We have a gorilla at our station -- his name is Ed Ball. I think he's about forty-three. I wish we'd have brought him with us tonight. Bob, tell me, seriously, I have seen

154

different acts -- as far as animal shows are concerned -- do you compare this to be much -- er -- are they much more temperamental to work with chimpanzees, gorillas and apes, than the big cats?"

"You couldn't pay a "cat man" enough money to walk in the cage with a big chimpanzee. You couldn't get one – nowhere for no price. You can take a stick and a chair and bluff a cat, but you take a stick or a chair to a chimpanzee and he'd take it away and beat you to death with it. It's altogether different. You can bluff a bunch of cats with a chair but you can't bluff a chimpanzee."

"What are some of the shows you've been with, Robert?"

"We worked mostly by ourselves – 'in the sticks' in the little towns up until the last twelve or fifteen years. Then we've been with just -- pratically the same carnivals all the time; Page -- five years, then with Frankie's for two years. We don't jump around from one show to another."

(We were also with Esther Speroni, "Beam's Attractions", "Deggellers", Eddie Boone's "Royal Blue", "Penn Premier" – among others -- Author.)

"Strictly carnie? Or did you do any circus?"

"Circus, too. Hoxie Tucker out of Miami, Florida and Hunt Brothers, but we always did better by ourselves – even better than the fairs but it's a lot more work."

(Plus Sam Dock's "Silver Brothers" Jimmie Heron's "Famous Robbins" – and Rogers Brothers – Author)

"They tell me it is a vital thing to have someone around a chimpanzee who is in complete control to reassure the chimpanzee. I've heard tales told by people who run zoos and the like -- things can be going real well -- the owner can leave and the animal senses they leave. In fact, I knew a man one time that said he lost his index finger. A chimp bit his finger right off. Did you ever have that happen? I see you're missing some."

"The one that's going to fight tonight bit two fingers off and threw them at me, and bit this hand off --"

"How many times -- down through the years -- have you been scratched, nipped, bitten -- I'm not going to say kicked --"

"...I've got scars all over me. I've got both eyelids torn off -- teeth knocked out -- fifteen stitches in one leg -- it's a little bit rough."

"I noticed you have powerful arms and powerful shoulders and chest, you're about my size -- about 5'11" -- what would you weigh, sir?"

"A hundred ninety-eight pounds."

"What did you weigh -- thirty-eight years ago when you started with the monkey --."

"I would say a hundred forty pounds."

"Do you find that the contributing factor toward getting people to come in -- do they always go in thinking someone is going to beat the animal?"

"Oh yeah! On account of their size. You see, most of them (the apes) that fight weigh about ninety pounds a lot of times. We have some three hundred pound men go in. In fact, tonight, we've got a 270 pound man and the ape will handle him like a rag doll."

"I think I'd rather wrestle one of the chimpanzees than to take you on -- you look in pretty good shape tonight. Have you always lived in the Eastern part of the United States?"

"Florida to New York and back. Some towns sometimes for fifteen years. Each year the same people come out to see it, only we have different fighters."

"Then there's always the same interest even when they know you're coming back."

"That's right."

"How about the Southlands up through the Okefanokee Swamps -- Douglas, Georgia, Waycross,

156

Baxley, Lyons, Jessup, Vidalia, Valdosta, Georgia? I'll bet that's home territory to you?"

"Every one of those places we have showed in them over and over again. And we'll hit them again this fall."

"Hey Robert, when you hit those small towns such as Alma, Baxley and Jessup do the crowds always come back the same year?"

"Every year and every night too. They follow us from one town to the other. Right here we had people come one hundred twenty-five miles night before last to see our show. "

"You are a living testimony, Bob, that you don't have to have seventy-five rides, forty or fifty other tents -- in other words you can go in and do a single in one town and still have a crowd! Right?"

"I've had people say it would stop the Ringling Show; if we'd get in front of it they would stop to see it before they would go to the Ringling Show. That's the truth!"

"Have you ever done any television work?"

"No sir, we've never tried. We've had a lot of offers -- we don't like to work that hard. We don't want to be on the big fairs where we've got to work hour after hour."

"I understand you've almost got to be a veterinarian as far as the care of the animals is concerned -- in other words -- when the animals get sick what is your percentage -- ratio-wise -- of losing animals? Do you lose one animal a year -- one in five years? You mentioned some that have been with you over nearly a thirty-year period. Is the respiratory system similar to a human being's? Do they get heavy colds?"

"No sir, we never lost one with pneumonia or anything like that."

"Bob, you have travelled, virtually, a lifetime with tent shows, doing a single. You've been up and down the country, there isn't a small town you haven't been in. What do you think of the young people of today as opposed to the forties? Do they have just as much guts to get in and wrestle or box?"

"Yeah, they've got the guts, but they're all mostly teen-agers. They want to go in but we can't put them in unless they're twenty-one because they're not old enough and they have to sign a release in case they get bruised up – which they do – and its not legal to put them in unless they're twenty-one and sign that release. We had four ladies week before last at Rocky Grove, we had two ladies last week at Rimersburg, and I think we'll have one here tomorrow night – I'm not sure."

"I could name a couple of ladies in DuBoise don't weigh more than a hundred and five pounds, could really tear up melons as we used to say."

"Bob has it been worth it all? You've been in a rough end of show business – I mean it's been strictly legitimate – you've never used the shell game, as far as the marks are concerned you give a dollars worth of value for the money invested. But tell me – has it been worth it all, down through the years? Would you have done anything else with your life?"

"I've enjoyed every minute of it. Every minute. And I'm just figuring now how I can change things so when I get older I can keep on going."

"Oh, man! That's not gonna be for another forty years! Oh, no! Now listen, when you had both the fingers nipped off your hand -- and I don't mean the end of the fingers, I mean clear back to the hand – how long was it before you were back in action?"

"I wanted to get out of the hospital the next day but they kept me in. I was all doped up. I was in the hospital a couple of weeks, but as soon as I got out I went to work with him again."

"Did you keep the animal? You didn't destroy him?"

"He's working! He's here now!"

"Still working! Right!"

"He's thirty-eight years old, now."

"Many of our listeners will be wondering about the

158

element of feed. How do you feed the animals? And in the off-season do they require as much feed – I know they would require care Christmas Day – Easter – New Year's Day – the Fourth of July – it would be the same amount of care – what is your story as far as feed and care is concerned?"

"They eat a lot of fruits and vegetables, bananas, oranges, apples, grapes – now the big gorilla will eat a bushel basketful at one feeding – it will take him two hours -- he eats slow, but that's celery, lettuce, apples and things like that."

"Bob, we're going to have to end this program right now, and I want to thank you for being with us. I want the folks to come in and see you – and the name of that act once again -- it's the best thing in Sykesville -- is the Gorilla Show. I'm turning back to you, Ben Finger."

Very soon after Mr. Moore completed this interview on tape, we put on a couple of shows and Mr. Moore's blow-by-blow description of the "fights" are classics that I firmly believe are necessary to show how fast the show was. We put on two shows that night and were "out and over" with both performances inside of one hours' time.

(Ben Finger:) "Back again at the Jefferson County Town and Country Fair and our pre-recorded broadcast. We are continuing here on the grounds at the Gorilla Show, and Charlie Moore, in just a few seconds will be telling you just what's going on here at the Gorilla Show -- and I think that Neal Secula is going to wrestle next. Ready?"

(Moore:) "We'd like to give you a word description here this evening. We are beside a big semi-trailer truck, the truck is parked onto the fairgrounds at Sykesville, the entire back half of the trailer is enclosed in heavy mesh wire so you can see through it. A very good crowd

159

is here and they have just let the chimpanzee out, and this chimpanzee is now throwing sawdust on the crowd, and I mean he's really throwing it through the cage and the people are really getting a big kick out of this -- and he's as full of spitzerinctum as a seven day Christmas turkey! He's twenty years old – he goes from one side of the cage to the other and I don't know too much about Geritol but if I could feel that good after coming out of a cage, I'll tell you its a wonderful thing! He's coming now from the left side of the cage to the right side of the cage! The cage where the chimpanzee is, I would say, about fourteen feet long [actually eleven – not a bad guess] and the width of the cage is the width of the tractor trailer, and the chimpanzee, of course, has a...[muzzle] on that they use for this particular type of animal..."

"Alright! We have a boy in the cage now. As we continue this broadcast from Sykesville, Robert Noell has just turned the chimpanzee loose, he weighs ninety some pounds, and he's going after -- he took the boy down that weighed about – roughly -- two hundred and thirty pounds. He has a football headgear on and this lad is tatooed on both arms and has on a big shirt that says "Ex-lax" on the front of it. I don't know if that shirt's going to help him, but I do know that chimpanzee is after him for wild. The chimpanzee jumps clear up to the top – at least the height of six or seven feet, touches the roof and comes down and makes a bound for this boy. The boy – just been in the cage a couple of minutes -- is breathing very hard. He has a short white shirt with "Ex-lax" written on the front – and the chimpanzee stays in the far corner, he minds his own business -- I think -- until he is given the signal. When he's given the signal he just comes out like a bolt of lightning.. Alright, the boy now -- 230 pounds -- young boy -- appears to be in his early twenties, powerful chest, great big arms. He's been knocked down once by the chimp. He was taken to the floor, he's taking his time now and he's coming at him -- uh -- cautiously. The chimp is sitting on the floor now -- and he's doing -- uh -- push-ups. Now he's stalking his prey -- coming over close and the boy is visibly moved -- uh -- the chimp goes back and forth across from one side of the net to the other side of the cage -- one! Two -- three -- he's ready to make his play -- he's swinging back and forth now and with a move faster than the eye can take he starts after his opponent. The boy -- now -- is backing water, he's coming in now in the wrestler's stance -- down to the wrestler's position. The chimpanzee is down, now, on all fours, he's moving to the left, moving to the right -- very evasive! This is something I have never seen before! Never seen anyone move as fast as this animal is moving! And the boy -- now -- is shaken! The chimp reached for his leg and would have taken him down with a leg dive, but he let him go and the expression on the boy's face is much more of concern. He tried to jump for a leg takedown and he barely got away. And now -- coming and picking him up -- picking him up in the fireman's, a fireman's ladder -- getting behind him he tried to back heel him -- pandemonium has broken out! The crowd is screaming -- he's up on his shoulders, now, and he can't get him off his shoulders! All I can see is the football helmet -- the boy -- he's pulling his pants off now! Not the chimp! The young man who I'd say weighs about two hundred and thirty pounds! His shirt is now ripped -- and he is in complete retreat over in the corner and he is smiling only because the crowd is smiling and I've never seen an animal move as fast as this chimp has done! It's **true**! I mean in thirty seconds he took him off his feet! They only keep them in there so many seconds and they're taking him out of the cage, now and as far as the performance goes from its start to its finish was only twelve minutes, but this was one of the most thrilling things I've ever seen at any

161

show regardless of its size. The animal is very well trained – you can tell. As far as Noell is concerned this animal has done this over and over and over. It's back to the old fashioned gladiator "will the man take the beast?" And invariably, of course, in this act the beast is the winner. Uh -- the reason we are interrupting our broadcast – he cannot get the chimpanzee back in the cage unless we leave; in other words he's a real ham and he will stay just as long as anyone's out here so we're going to pick up our microphone so they can get this animal back in the cage and leave at this point."

"As far as wrestling is concerned, and boxing -- this is faster than any wrestling match you've ever seen and far more exciting. Some one hundred sixty-five people have come through the gates in the last forty minutes for this second one; this gentleman's name is -- he's from Sebula and the chimpanzee now is swinging from a bar, he approaches his man very slowly. This fellow wouldn't weigh any more than one hundred seventy pounds. He's trying to protect his face; the chimpanzee works counter clockwise back and forth, he bounces up, he bounces down and continuously bounces up and down. He took the boy down with one sweep – and now the boy has just escaped -- he just escaped -- his shirt is ripped – he's backed – uh – and his face is white -- he's afraid, this boy! He wishes he was back in Sebula. Oh, if anything -- he does! He wishes he was way back in Sebula! The chimpanzee is looking at him now -- up on his perch – a rubber tire and he's putting his finger up -- the boy said – from Sebula – "One more time and I'm gonna leave!" This boy -- in the yellow shirt is as far back to the wall as he can get. If he goes any farther back he's going to be outside the arena. Alright – they have stopped the action here – but this is one of the fastest things we've ever seen! The chimpanzee is sitting up now -- on the tire -- resting. He swings back and forth, he has a large bar welded to the ceiling that he

162

can swing back and forth on. Of course he is mobile as a goose when he moves it's just like lightning. Alright, the lad with the yellow shirt and a football helmet, about six feet tall, one hundred seventy, comes closely in, he isn't moving from his corner. And back and forth the chimp goes from side to side and he just made one spang up and pulled his shirt completely off his back! He's rolled him over, now he has him completely on his back. He's ripped his shirt completely off of him and the boy got up. He didn't even know what hit him. He said, "That's enough!" He put his hands up. He didn't have time to put his hands up until the chimpanzee was on his back. They opened the door and the boy from Sebula escaped! He put his hand up and he said, "That's it!" and he said, "One more time!" And still the world champion...[Kongo]. He's twenty years old, weighs eighty-five pounds and we've seen him take on a man weighing two hundred thirty pounds here tonight, and of course, after every performance is the reward. He brings an assorted bag of fruits—bananas, oranges, apples, anything like this, but the deal is the chimpanzee will **not** go back in his cage, he's been trained, as long as there's one person -- the show is over but the chimpanzee waits for his reward."

"Ben, how many times have you see this?"

"Just twice, Charlie, I'm with you!"

"What would you say to our WCED listeners? That it's well worth the money to see it, anything you've ever seen and you've been covering fairs over twenty years."

"Charlie, it's a dollar and they tell you out there it's a dollar for adults and fifty cents for children ten and under and they say "it's one show, short or long." Two of them have been short but they've been worth it -- I'll tell ya!"

"Bob Ray of Brockway Glass, and a big sports enthusiast -- Bob, have you ever seen anything like this?"

"No, I haven't, I'll tell ya – I wouldn't get in with that thing! And fact is I'm trying to get him for my football team this fall."

"To play the Charlie Moore Chickens?"

"To play the Charlie Moore Chickens!"

"We've got a couple that look like him but they couldn't move that fast. Bob – did you bring your wife and children in to see this?"

"Yes, I did – yes I did! And Mary got a couple lessons from this and I'm afraid to go home tonight with her."

"I imagine you'll be sitting in a chair when I go past up and down Olive Avenue to the "Spit and Whittle Club.""

"If I see you're eatin bananas I'm gonna get out of there – I'll tell you now!"

"Thank you very much Robert. This program has emanated from Sykesville. And this is one of the most thrilling things that we've seen and I assure you it's well worth your time when you're in Sykesville to see the Gorilla Show here at the County Fair. Ben Finger, I'm turning it back to you."

Probably the most unorthodox "fight" that ever took place in our "Ark" was one not seen by the public, when Kongo victimized a very nice newspaper reporter from the Newberry (S.C.) Observer Oct. 5, 1970. Four days later he wrote about the experience in his column and has given me permission to share the column with my readers;

IT'S ALL NEWS TO ME
by Bayne Freeland

WHAT TO DO WHEN GRASPED BY A HOSTILE CHIMPANZEE

"Well, I went out to the Fair and wrestled the ape.
I didn't go out there with that in mind. It was the

164

The remarkable action pictures of Kongo on the following pages were made by Floyd Jillson for the magazine section of the Sunday edition of the Atlanta (Ga.) Constitution & Journal.

The first thing you know I jump up at him...

ape's idea. It would take more than $5 a second to get me in the ring with an 85-pound chimpanzee. The chimp, however, was willing to take me on for nothing.

It was a private performance, late Monday evening. I had stopped by the gorilla show to say hello to Bob and Mae Noell, whose Noell's Ark was the subject of an "All News" column the other day. The show was closed for the night but Bob Noell asked me to step inside and say howdy to Tommy, the larger of two gorillas who inhabit the Ark along with three orangutans and five chimpanzees.

I thought it was too late to disturb Tommy, not knowing how a gorilla feels about being waked up just after he's gone to bed. But Bob said Tommy would feel terrible if I left without saying good night so I said okay, but just for a minute. (Why needlessly offend a 600-pound gorilla?)

The gorilla's room is at the rear of the trailer and you get there by traversing a narrow corridor lined with steel plate. Bob Noell led the way and I had taken perhaps two steps when my progress was arrested by an ape. He had, I realized instantly but not soon enough, snaked his tricky fingers out through the bars which covered a small opening in the wall and had seized me by the coattails.

There ensued a brief but lively wrestling match with me on one side of the wall and the ape on the other, intent on drawing me into his cage through a two-inch gap in the bars. Frankly, this was a new situation to me and I was unprepared, never having given much thought to what I might do in the circumstances. With surprise in his favor, the ape got the upper hand in the first few seconds. He also got about 40 per cent of my suit jacket by ripping it up the back seam from hem to collar.

This gave the ape a further advantage, since I was still sort of wearing the coat. He twisted the material into a rope, braced his feet and leaned back, hauling me up

166

and work him over before he has time to think.

against the bars with considerable emphasis. It became clear to me that what this simian assassin wanted was not my coat, but me. He was in there just holding on while he tried to figure a way to slide me through the bars.

Possibly the same thing has happened to you. It's an experience, hey?

I'm told there was quite a lot of hollering going on, whether by me or Bob or by the ape I do not know. Probably by all three of us, but I assure you that if I shouted, it was in rage and not in fear. I am a man who smiles at adversity, chuckles at catastrophe and sneers in the face of doom. What's more, I didn't think the ape could really pull me through that little hole.

But being clutched by a stir-crazy ape might make anybody edgy, and I was naturally concerned about my suit jacket which contained two ballpoint pens, a package of pipe tobacco, a parking ticket and my notes from a meeting earlier in the evening.

Those Primitive Instincts...

I don't know what Bob did to make Kongo (that was the ape's name) let go. Bit his knuckles, maybe. Anyway, the chimp screamed and let loose of me and I just laughed the whole thing off, as though being assaulted by carnival chimpanzees was old stuff with me.

Coattails flying more than ordinarily, I went on down the corridor with Bob and said hello to Tommy, the gorilla. He greeted me pleasantly enough, considering that it isn't easy for a gorilla to look cordial. I also exchanged pleasantries with a silky, sad-eyed female orangutan while, down the hall, Kongo was trying to kick his way out of his bedroom so he could get a square crack at me.

The ape clutched at me when we went back down the coorditor to the exit. I snarled back at him from the far side of the passageway -- primitive man, with

and then about the time he thinks he has me...

civilization's thin veneer stripped away and his suit jacket in tatters.

The coat looks terrible from the back, but it never did lie quite right across the shoulders, anyway. And I think it fits a little better around the collar than it did before."

A young man was laughing recently, about one of hi friends who went in to wrestle Kongo.

"Two buddies of mine had been drinking and bragging what they could do with that little ninety-five pound ape. The more they drank, the smaller the monkey got. They decided the bigger one of the two would go to fight the ape. When he got ready to go in he told his buddy, "I'm gonna give him a haymaker and soften him up. I'll bet I get his shoulders on the floor."

"He went in with 'the little one', (Kongo), and that little rascal wasn't there when my buddy swung, and before he knew what happened the ape was hanging off the roof and had lifted the man off the floor with one foot, holding him by the shoulder! While the man struggled to free himself from a most painful grip, the ape was hitting him on the side of his head with the other foot. He said he's never have thought anything could be that strong! And he was a big guy, too!"

We were showing at a place in North Carolina near an army base. On opening night it had rained and the crowd was too small to justify putting on a show. A big man (a civilian) came on the lot with seven or eight other men following him. He came to our gate and demanded that we let him fight the ape. I explained that we were taking names for the next night because we would have no show, due to the weather, until then. He gave me his name and I wrote it on the blackboard for all to see. He and his group then stood in front of the show talking and clowning. A few minutes went by and two

I let him have it with both hands and feet...

green berets walked up to our show front and read the signs. We had thought we were going to have trouble with him and his gang, but the green berets appealed to him more so he started taunting them. One of them walked away, and the gang leader then knocked the other one to the ground. His Army training stood him in good stead, because he turned as he fell, landed on hands and feet -- running! He ran away from the mob with the bully close on his heels, slashing at the boy's back with a switchblade knife and missing him by inches. The soldier ran around a tent and into the arms of the law. The policeman made the bully and his gang leave the grounds for the night.

Before "lights out" two policemen came to us and one of them said, "Did that bully sign up to fight the ape tomorrow night?" When we told them he had, they were happy. Then one of them said, "That guy is the bully of the county. We have trouble with him all the time! Do us a favor and give him the meanest ape you've got! He needs a whipping!"

The next night, I gave the man his instructions. We had a definite set of rules for each of the three chimps. When a man was cooperative he could get a big kick out of the experience, and there were many men who went in to "fight" as many as ten or fifteen times, night after night and year after year. But this big bully as good as told me to "go to Hell." When this happened I got tough with the men, too. My usual talk went something like this:

"Look, Mister, I don't give a damn if you **don't** follow the rules! The rules are for your safety! That little ape can take care of four of the likes of you at one time! **Don't** follow the rules if you don't want to -- it's **your** funeral -- not mine! But, you are going to listen to the rules or you don't go in that cage. That way, when you get the hell beat out of you there's no one else to blame but yourself. Furthermore, I will have done my duty and even if you're carried out on a stretcher, I will be able to sleep tonight. My conscience will be clear. So, Buster, you just listen and then do as you damned well please!" I was serious about it because I really did not want

172

and, well, I guess you just ought to see him...

to ever see anyone or anything get hurt.

As a rule, this little speech got electric results, no one got hurt, and the audience loved the show. But this night the speech didn't faze Mr. Bully. He didn't even want to wear the helmet we provided for his protection. He listened to the rules with a sneer and when he went in I knew what he intended to do. He was the type who thought he was going to make a hero of himself before his sheep-like gang by killing that little ape. I also knew that he had no chance of success. I took my position at the small round window in the iron door. I had to be available to open the door in any emergency, since it could be opened only from the outside where I stood. As soon as the bully got in the cage, he rushed his 260 pounds of muscle and brawn at little 95 pound Kongo. When he arrived, Kongo was gone and before the bully could recover his balance Kongo, who was hanging over the man's head with one hand, had caught his belt at the back and was swinging him roughly around the floor. Wood shavings were on the floor as a "cushion" to keep the men from hitting the diamond plate iron floor, and shavings were flying in all directions. The crowd (except for his seven or eight buddies) were screaming with laughter. In the background I could see wide smiles on two men in uniform. Clearly the crowd loathed this man and were all rooting for the ape.

The stress on the belt became too great and it broke, taking the shirt, overalls, and underpants, leaving nothing on the man except his socks. The crowd roared. Some of the people fell to the ground -- literally in hysterics. I yelled to Bob to stop the fight, but there was no way he could hear me in the uproar. Kongo must have realized the crowd wanted more because next thing we knew the man was swinging around again -- arms, legs and head flying wildly. At last I grabbed the light switch and put out the lights, and the fight was stopped. The man crawled out of the cage in the nude and I threw some clothes over him. His friends carried him away amid the screaming laughter and derision of the crowd.

when he realizes what's happening to him.

As angry as I had been at him earlier, I felt sorry for the humiliation he must have suffered. And, too, I knew he simply **had** to be hurt to some degree because Kongo had grabbed a delicate part of his anatomy with which to swing him around. We stayed in that location about two weeks. Many other people boxed or wrestled the apes during our stay, with no further mishaps.

About two days before the fair closed, Mr. Bully came back to the show, on crutches, followed by his several buddies. He came to our fence and said to me, "Lady, I want to shake your hand." I thought, "Oh, boy! Here's where I get jerked over the fence." But I shook hands with him anyway and asked, "Why?" He replied, "Because you told me the truth and you're OK. I want to shake your hand, too, Mister," as he reached over to Bob, who shook his hand too.

Then the bully turned around and said, "You guys can all keep on doing mean things if you want too, but as for me, I've learned a lesson here. And I dare anyone to bother these nice people. If you do, you'll have me to answer to." And he waved at us and went back off the lot with his little gang trailing behind.

We came back to that place the following year. The first people we saw were the two policemen. They were delighted to see us and when we asked about Mr. Bully they corrected us and said, "He's not Mr. Bully anymore! He's Mr. Nice! Do you know, he stood up in church and said that while he was in that cage he thought he was being killed. And all he could think of afterwards was, "What if I had died that night? Just think of all the mean things I had done all my life!" And the policeman added, "You know something? He hasn't missed church a single Sunday since you were here? And if he sees one of us policemen in trouble he comes right to our assistance! And most of his gang have stuck with him, too! That little ape did what no cop or preacher could ever have done with that man! He's a good citizen now."

176

Chapter Six

One of the greatest things about trouping was the way we got to see so many different places and things. Before we had our animal show and while we were expecting one of our babies, we went to the Cincinnati Zoo in Ohio, in 1932, or maybe it was 1933. When we came to the ape house Bob admired Suzy, the female gorilla who had been flown into the U.S. on the Graf Zeppelin. I had read a lot of the terrible stories that had been written about the ferocity of the gorilla, so I was petrified with fright at the sight of her. She had a cannon ball for a toy. When she threw it against the bars of her cage I could think of nothing except, "That horrible thing is going to get out and kill all of us!" I wanted to leave. Bob laughed at me and when we went inside we saw her sit at the table where she used a fork to pick up the slices of cantaloupe. She poured some milk from a pitcher into a glass. After the glass was emptied, she drank from the pitcher, to the vast amusement of the audience. The trainer then stood behind her to tickle her and she laughed. He had to sneak out hastily or she'd have held on to him. I was relieved when we left the ape house. If anyone had told me, then, that the day would come when I could actually feel love for one of these creatures I'd have had to laugh in his face. But that is what did happen with all my "gorilla children": I fell hopelessly in love with all the critters.

We started off naming our animals after Biblical characters. After a time we decided it must be sacreligious to do so -- even though that was the farthest thing from our minds. Two baboons we named Sampson died, David and Delilah -- two (infant) chimps died, and Goliath, a gorilla, died -- all within about three years. The last animal I gave a Bible name to was a gorilla we were to get in 1951, from Henry Trefflich in New York. Phil Carroll came into the City from Africa, by plane. When he took the animals to Henry's place at 228 Fulton Street I was there, waiting for him. Phil handed me a beautiful infant boy-gorilla and said, "This is the gorilla I have hand-picked for my friend Bob Noell. I want him to have this animal because he's a fine speciman." I took the little tyke and cuddled him. He was gorgeous. I said, "This is Sampson. That's the name we have decided on. He's going to grow up to be as strong as Sampson."

Henry interrupted and said, "Mae, I'm sorry. You can't take him home now. He has to be in quarantine for ten days before he can leave here." Phil argued with him a moment but gave up. I had to be back in North Carolina for the show within a few hours. Henry said I should call him in ten days. It took seventeen hours on the passenger train to get back to Goldsboro, empty-handed. I was met at the station by a disappointed husband. We were both somewhat peeved over the fruitless trip, but we trusted Phil and Henry so were not worried. Just annoyed. When the ten days had passed, I called Henry. He said, "Mae, I have bad news about the little gorilla!" I said, "Henry! That was a beautiful, healthy baby! If you tell me that baby died I'm coming to New York to punch you a good one!"

"Well," he said hesitantly, "I was going to say he died, but I guess I'd better tell you the truth. I had a zoo director in here after you left and he fell in love with the baby. He bought an awful lot of animals from me so I had to let him have your baby. But I'll make it good. You can have your pick of any of the other ones you want."

Naturally, we were frustrated and disappointed about this, plus a bit peeved at having to go all the way back to New York City -- this time in our panel truck -- to pick up the substitute animal.

When we got to New York, Henry handed me a very sick little gorilla. He must have weighed all of ten pounds and had as severe a cold as anything or anyone I've ever seen. We took him because we felt so sorry for him. Bob and I tucked him in bed between us to keep him warm, at the hotel that night. Then, the next day Henry sent a veterinarian to the hotel to look him over and the doctor ordered us to bring him to his hospital downtown. We did. The baby died that night of pneumonia. Henry then gave us M'Bam (pronounced Ombahm) a little forty-pound fellow who was also sick, although he didn't show it at the time. They were afraid of him because he was so big. But he was a sweet gentle "child" from the very beginning. They put him in a bag when they wanted him to go into his cage, then put bag and all in the cage. Within about a half minute he got out of the bag -- crying -- wanting to come out and play some more. We never had any trouble with M'Bam -- he lived only to please his human pets -- Bob and me.

The baby that I named Sampson is still named Sampson without the "P" and is a magnificent fellow at the Milwaukee Zoo -- as I write this. We decided Bible names should not be used for our pets, ever again; after all, every one we had named after Bibilical characters was soon lost or died.

We were wintering at Clearwater, Florida, on the Duefrene property, and our precious little gorilla, M'Bam, was dying. The veterinarian was making a heroic effort to save the little fellow. We were staying up nights to attend to his needs. At about two in the morning, Phil Carroll came in with a young fellow named Bill Said. We were glad to see Phil and hoped he could help us -- some way -- with our sick little boy. Bill

179

Said had just been featured in a big story in Life Magazine, with a shipment of animals he had brought in from Africa. Phil told us he brought Bill Said because he had a female gorilla, named M'Jingo (pronounched "Mah-Jingo"), for sale. Phil said we should buy the female because M'Bam would need her companionship when he got well. We were in no mood to buy another gorilla because of the bad luck we were having with them. But, between the two of them, they convinced us M'Bam needed a mate – and we bought her for $2500, a ridiculously low price for a gorilla. A few days after we bought M'Jingo, our precious little M'Bam died in spite of all we tried to do for him. We buried him in a Pet Cemetery in St. Petersburg, Florida. We were told there would be "perpetual care" – just like in regular cemeteries. But it was razed and a housing development now covers the spot.

Back in the fifties, when we had so much bad luck with the gorillas, they were coming into the U.S. with advanced cases of a lethal type of microscopic intestinal parasite called strongyloides stercoralis. It seems there was not too much known about the treatment of this problem at that time because every doctor we consulted gave us a prescription for "enteric-coated gentian violet." Those pills were actually worse than nothing, because when M'Bam was autopsied by Ringling Brothers' "Circus Doctor," J. Y. Henderson, whole, undisolved pills were found all the way through his digestive system, along with the live worms, and we had even seen him pass whole pills! Today, a liquid containing thiabendazole keeps this serious problem under control when used about twice each year. Furthermore, the liquid is mint-flavored and goes down easily whereas the pills were a traumatic experience for the poor things.

M'Jingo had not been with us long when one day I was standing on the ground, looking up into the cage. M'Jingo turned her back and walked away from me. I gasped and cried, "Bob! Oh, Bob!" He came running and I said, "Our little girl is a little boy!" Bob couldn't believe it, not until she turned and walked away from him the same way she had done me. "Yep," Bob admitted, "I'll be derned!" It's a boy, alright."

It is a well-known fact that for many years people had found it notoriously hard to tell the difference between the sexes of gorillas. M'Jingo was just old enough when we got him that we could actually see, from our low vantage point on the ground, that he was actually a boy. He was a happy chest-beater.

When M'Bam died, I was glad Bob had another gorilla to console him. Bob used to ride M'Bam in the cab of the truck over the runs from town to town. No gorilla ever loved to ride in a car or a truck more than M'Jingo. When we drove through smaller towns, it was a sight to see the crowds standing by the roadside, waiting to see the truck go by, after their friends had phoned ahead to tell them it was coming. Bob drove a tractor with a long-low semi-trailer that housed four of our apes in what is called a "walk-through exhibit." When he had to make a right turn around a corner, M'Jingo would run the window down and lean out to watch the back wheels. They seemed to fascinate him for some reason. The effect this had on the spectators was amusing. They'd shout, "Look! He's telling the driver it's O.K.!" And, indeed, it did look as if that was what he was doing.

Bob said M'Jingo must have been from the same clean tribe of gorillas as Tommy came from because he never -- ever – "dirtied" the truck. He always rolled the window down, and putting his feet on the windowsill, he backed part way out of the moving vehicle, and got rid of his "dirty" that way.

Because the animal was in the cab and Bob might have needed my help if he had to stop, I brought up the rear with my Chevrolet panel truck and Spartan trailer. I could see a lot of what was happening up front, and it was usually very funny. M'Jingo, like all gorillas I have known, was a born practical joker with a vast sense of humor, only he was a little more of a show-off about it than others. He enjoyed scaring people, and the way he did it was very effective and never

181

failed to get the desired results. Bob had filled me in on what was going on in the cab. He said M'Jingo had a wrench that he hammered on the dash with when he was bored as they were going down the road. Bob said it was rythmic and was "M'Jingo's music." However, when a likely victim came into sight, M'Jingo would toss the wrench aside and run his window down if it was up, then just as they drew alongside the pedestrian, 'Jingles would crawl half-way out of the window, slap the roof noisily to get their attention, and reach for them to scare them. If he could have touched them, he would not have hurt them. He just loved to see them run because his sense of the ridiculous was delightful. It was a hilarious tableau every time we moved. The effect I got riding behind them was never-to-be-forgotten. First I would see a person – or people – walking toward us on the right side of the road. Then the truck would hide them from my view for a brief few seconds. But when I arrived to where they had been, I would see them running across the fields, kicking mud up on their backs as they beat a rapid retreat in search of safety. It was always the same whether it was one or a dozen persons. He had the top of that old jalopy truck caved in from beating on it with his ham-sized hand. The dent that he made held between three and four gallons of water every time it rained. He got as big a kick out of this mean little trick as any ten or twelve-year-old prankish kid would have, and it was all done in fun. Someone said, "That sounds dangerous to me!" But if that person could have known M'Jingo he'd never have doubted his harmless intent for a moment.

As we were leaving Roanoke, Virginia, one summer, a newspaper reporter took a picture of Bob and M'Jingo in the truck. That was one of the first two Associated Press wire photos ever sent out over the new wirephoto apparatus there.

While M'Jingo usually ate only fruits and vegetables, he was not above eating "people food", too. One night I had planned to have a T-Bone steak supper for the family after the show. M'Jingo was brought into the living room of the

182

trailer where Bob proceeded to romp with him, while I cooked the steaks in the kitchen. Every now and then, Jingles would come into the kitchen, bipedally; then, putting his foot on a big can near the stove, he would hoist himself up to where he could look down into the frying pan and say "Um, yum, yum" in that delightful basso-profundo hum that is so characteristic of the happy gorilla. He was so cute, and we were having so much fun with him, that before the night was over he had totally wrecked my living room and had conned me out of all seven of those T-bone steaks. We laughed as we had to eat bologna sandwiches that night after we put him to bed. If you were wonderfing why we let him get away with this, it was because we were enjoying having him in the house, and watching his delightful antics. None of it was allowed through fear -- it was actually done through our adoration and admiration of that magnificent creature.

M'Jingo was a happy clown and one time at Bay Saint Louis, Mississippi, he got out of his cage while Bob was away. Someone yelled, "Hey, Mae! M'Jingo's loose!" There was a small thin patch of woodland right beside the truck, and that's where he went. I got everyone to surround the woods and to close in, screaming and yelling at him urgently. I didn't want some "big hero" to shoot him. M'Jingo took the alarm and ran, with a speed I still find hard to believe, back to the safety of his cage. It was a hairy five minutes, worrying about his safety. When he jumped into the truck he planted a cute little muddy footprint on the door. Later, I outlined the footprint and painted it in as a precious memento of the incident.

M'Jingo liked to wrestle with anyone who would play with him. Of course, this was usually nearly always men. (I was the only exception.) During this wrestling, he developed a habit that was entirely his own idea, and which finally made him unpopular with most of his "buddies." When he got in the heat of the "battle" and got the chance, he would pinch them in a "delicate spot." The resulting gymnastics always seemed to tickle him mightily.

One day Bob had M'Jingo out on a lead rope and was sitting on the ground talking to a small group of interested spectators. I walked over and started playing with M'Jingo. As he rolled me over and over I struggled in a wrestling match that was a little bit more vigorous than usual. I wear slacks all the time, and they were quite handy at this time, even though none of the others were paying any attention to us at all.

After several minutes, "Jingles" decided to touch my "mainspring" to see what would happen. He fished around for it, to my gross embarrassment, as I struggled, vainly, to escape. After what he apparently considered enough investigation, he sat back, holding me with one of his feet, and resting his hands on the ground beside him. He looked at me with obvious surprise; it was as if I could see the amazement -- and even delight -- in his eyes, and he was thinking, "I'll be darned! And all the time I've been thinking you were a boy!"

Without warning, he pushed me over on my back and landed on top of me. His actions indicated that he either remembered seeing the sex act performed in the jungles, or that simple instinct was motivating him. At any rate, I now found it easy to escape from him; he did not grip me as fiercely as before, and I was relieved beyond imagination when I saw that no one had witnessed this embarrassing bit of mischief, or if they had they were gentlemen enough to pretend they'd not seen it. After this experience, I was especially cautious around him, but, surprisingly, he never tried to repeat the performance.

This seems to be similar to the behavior of the wild gorillas that Dian Fossey is studying. She says the big males accept the presence of women -- calmly. However, when Fossey brings a male observer, the big males seem to show resentment. Also our chimps -- Snookie and Butchie -- were always gentle with women and children who went in the cage to play with them, but showed no mercy to men, unless they carefully followed our rules.

I believe M'Jingo was merely showing me -- in the only way he knew how – that he realized I was not a boy. He was, ever after, much more gentle with me than he had ever been before.

It was a shock when we discovered that M'Jingo was loaded with the same parasitic infection that had killed M'Bam and the infant Goliath. Again, there was no one we consulted who knew how to save him. We went through the whole pill business again and even tried other medicines that were prescribed.

When Snookie died we had him autopsied at Duke University in Durham, North Carolina. One of the doctors there had told us to call on him if we ever needed help. When we realized M'Jingo's medicines were doing him no good we decided to call him. I was across the street from the show in a phone booth when Bob came running over to tell me that M'Jingo had died. When we took him to Durham they gave us the same sad, frustrating news that had been given us in 1951 when Goliath was autopsied at Emory University in Atlanta. Worms!

After having suffered such terrible heartbreak we both decided "No more gorillas!" But it wasn't long before another sick little gorilla needed our love, and we gave in to becoming the "foster-parents" of the irresistable Topsy.

185

Chapter Seven

It was mid-November, 1956, and the air was getting crisp and nippy. We had carried on a long correspondence with the animal dealer-friend who was in Africa. He wrote and told us that he was soon to leave Africa, and that he was bringing a beautiful little female gorilla when he came home. We had driven up from Brunswick, Georgia, where we had the show set up to work the following week. We had stopped at Roanoke, Virginia, and rode the rest of the way to New York City and Idlewilde (now Kennedy) Airport in the car with Ruth and Palmer Herndon (Bob's sister and brother-in-law). We were a happy foursome. Bob and I, so eager to see the new baby, and Ruth and Palmer glad for the outing.

We had to wait several days past the plane's scheduled arrival. Phil had made it from Africa to Paris O.K.; but when it came time to leave Paris for New York City, it was his misfortune to plan his trip at exactly the same time that a plane-load of Paris fashions was scheduled for the same flight. Fearing the animals might ruin the priceless textiles, the owners refused to let them on the plane. Weather was getting nasty (it was November), and time was vitally important. Phil hastily employed the services of another line. When they neared London, they stopped for radio repairs. The delay was a long one – almost one and-a-half days. Meanwhile, the poor animals were kept in a cold air hangar. Another false start landed them in Ireland. After another stop for radio repairs at Iceland, they came down again at Greenland and finally, at long last, at Idlewilde.

After what had seemed an eternity we met Phil Carroll and went, together, to Henry Trefflich's Pet Store on Fulton Street to settle the business end of the deal. As we all talked, the new baby -- all twenty pounds of her – sat on Henry's desk, with my arms wrapped around her.

As soon as the "business" was finished, we were on our way back home. I had planned to hold the baby in my lap all the way. However, while Bob was taking his turn driving, she decided she wanted to go up front with him. We were on the Pennsylvania Turnpike and going pretty fast. Knowing her maneuver could be dangerous I grabbed her and pulled her back. Because the suddenness of my movement startled and angered her, she bit my thumb, quite badly. It hurt, so I forced her into the puppy box we had brought along, and closed the lid. She could ride quite comfortably in it, so I left her there while I doctored my thumb, without asking Bob to stop the car.

Ruth sighed with relief. She was in the back seat with me, and "made no bones" about the fact she was afraid of the little girl-rilla.

"Oh, Mae," she said, "I'm so glad you put her up! I couldn't have stood her odor much longer!"

Because my "smeller" has been broken ever since I can remember, I had not noticed her odor. I feel I've really missed something in life by not being able to smell the unique odor of my gorillas. Strangely, many people find the gorillas' "aroma" very pleasing. One person I met kept rubbing his hand over her back, then, putting his fingers to his nose, he would sigh, "Oh, what a wonderful smell! I can't describe it, but I love it." Also, Mrs. A. Maria Hoyt, in her book, **Toto**

187

and I mentioned the "pleasant", "earthy" odor of Toto, her big female gorilla.

Within a few hours we were back home and making our little girl-rilla comfortable. She seemed a little large to be using a baby bottle, but I used half milk and finished filling the bottle with baby food. After cutting a larger hole in the nipple and shaking it thoroughly, she drank it greedily. In fact, I got tired of feeding her with regular baby bottles (it took about five or six at a feeding) so I took a one-quart juice bottle, adapted the lid to fit a nipple (with the can opener) and fed her a pint of milk and three baby foods at a feeding. This was increased in volume as she grew; she was drinking a gallon of baby food and milk at one sitting by the time she weighed 100 pounds.

We decided to call our little girl "Topsy" because we knew she'd grow.

Later in that same November of 1956, we were showing in Waycross, Georgia and two men in business suits watched the show. After the crowd had dispersed, they came to us and asked if we would consider taking the show to Cuba. They painted a rosy picture of how rich we could make ourselves, and that it would cost us nothing for transportation over and back. They said the animals would be sent by freight barge from West Palm Beach and we would be flown in a first class flight from Miami. We were somewhat excited, since we'd never been out of the U.S. with our show. We had worked, in the forties, along the Mexican border in Texas and found there were a lot of nice people of Spanish descent. But we were afraid the language barrier might pose a serious problem, since the talk we did before each show was extremely important. If the patrons did not understand exactly what they were paying to see, the complications that could arise might cause bad repercussions. These men assured us that their interpreters were masters of their trade and that we would never have a moment's trouble. Even so, I was skeptical and hung back instinctively. I argued that it was time to go into winter quarters; that I didn't want to be away from the family for Christmas; that we had a sick orangutan we needed to 'tend to before we went anywhere; that we had to repack our house-trailer for customs inspectors -- and on and on and on. I even pleaded fear of a boat trip with the animals. What if they got seasick?

We went home to the Chimp Farm arguing all the way. I kept hanging back -- fearfully. Half wanting to go and yet ominously afraid. Had I realized a rebellion was brewing on the island I'd probably have been more adamant. But Bob is not one to take "no" for an answer, and he finally won out. By the time he had rigged up a smaller trailer and done some other necessary things, we had missed the West Palm Beach "ferry" (fortunately, as we learned later, because when we did go, we went on our own manifest). I had not wanted the animals on the high seas for three days without us with them, in the first place, so missing the ferry was -- in my opinion -- a blessing, anyway. But Bob was still determined to go and earn a "big winter bankroll." I called the Key West ferry people and was told that they had never allowed a tractor trailer (such as our Noells Ark unit was built on) on their ferry. Then I explained that it was especially built to keep our animals in. The man said for us to call him back the next day to see what he could do for us. So we did. He said it would be OK to bring the truck but we would have to pay the regular passenger's fare for each of the animals, the same as if they were people. The round-trip passage for our truck, car, trailer and animals cost us a little over $1,200.00. We agreed to do this and we were on our way. When we got to Key West, the Cuban Customs Inspectors took all our Khaki clothing away from us. They said they were "uniforms" and they had to be left behind. We were to get them when we came back. This was the first inkling I had that serious trouble was brewing in Cuba. Then Bob decided, perhaps he'd better tell these people that he had a blank gun that we used in the show. It was legal in the toughest state -- New York -- because it had a sawed-off barrel through which a bolt had been driven so that no bullet could come out of it.

The man examined it and said, "I'd better keep it until we land on the other side." He put it in his pocket. A few minutes later the man was standing a few feet away from us, talking to some other Cubans, and accidentally fired the gun off in his pocket. He yelled and danced around frantically slapping his thigh where he undoubtedly suffered powder burns. For a split second, all was angry pandemonium – then suddenly everyone except the victim was screaming with laughter. They were probably all keyed up for **bombs** and laughed in relief when they realized it was only a blank gun. We felt terrible about it, but no one blamed us.

Just before we got on the boat the Customs man wanted to put a tape over the trailer door and it was **not** to be opened until we landed on the other side. I held him back and said, "Wait, there's a baby gorilla in a cage in there! We can't leave her sealed in there for nine hours!" He waited until I took her out and he sealed the door. I had to buy a quart of milk on the ship which was the last "good" milk I was to see in eight long weeks. I had to pay almost four times the regular price for it. Because the trailer was sealed shut and she had to eat, we then had to **hold** Topsy, taking turns, for the entire trip.

Every now and then, aboard ship, we could see little groups of men talking; then one would start jumping and slapping his thigh while the others screamed with laughter. It didn't take a fertile imagination to know they were laughing about the gun episode.

While I was holding Topsy and sitting – near exhaustion – in the car, one of the men came to me, followed by a friend. He said in "broken English" that his friend wanted to see the little gorilla. When he looked at her , he laughed and clapped his hands as he said "Cara Linda! Cara Linda!" I asked what this meant and they were both laughing when the "translator" told me, "He says she has a pretty face!" I knew this was a jest, but I liked the sound of the words so I told him, "That's what I will name her – "Princess Topsy Cara Linda Noell." The Princess was because Ringling Brothers

Circus had **Toto** a female gorilla whom I admired and loved from a distance; therefore she was the "Queen." So my little baby had to be a **Princess**. Topsy was given as a name because I knew she'd "grow." And the Cara Linda was genuine admiration on my part.

When we arrived at Guanajay, the first show location, we were still working desperately on a sick little orangutan named "Red." About three or four weeks later he died. Because we had taken him through Customs, we had to bring him back -- dead or alive, so I had him frozen.

Our show was well received by the populace as long as the interpreters said what we told them to say. But some of them got "big heads" and tried to "run" the show their way, which got us a lot of complaints. Part of the contract was that we were to have **able** and cooperative translators and we were not getting them.

And, what was worse, we found it hard to give the rules to the "fighters" because some of the things we said in English were "too hard to translate," according to the lazy interpreters.

A black man named Steve joined our unit as a helper, and I used him as a guide to find my way around the island. He was a Jamaican who was very helpful and most entertaining. One night Bob paid him the usual $3.00 for the evening's work. He took it and folded it, then said, slowly, "Never pay a mon where others may see him! It might cost him his life."

"**Not** for three dollars!" Bob exclaimed.

"For thirty cents!" Steve replied in his delightful sing-song voice. "In Jamaica they pick you **alive**; in Cuba they pick you **dead**."

I gave him a flashlight and saw him walking with it turned on in broad daylight. I told him the light was lit and he replied in that sing-song tone that was so amusing, "The Bible say 'let your light shine before men.'"

When I went to the market for food, I had Steve ride with me. He was strong and could load the heavy bags and boxes.

Often as not I'd also pick up some wood shavings for the "litter" we used in the boxing arena cage. One day we had travelled all around Havana and suburbs in search of shavings. We had finally filled the huge canvas bag and, with trunk lid up because the bag was so big, we took a short cut back to the lot. We came upon an intersection where sandbags were piled high on both sides of the road we had to travel. A small opening -- barely big enough for the car to pass through, was guarded by soldiers with guns with bayonets attached. One of the soldiers stopped us as another one went to the back of the car. Through the crack at hinge-line I could see in the rear view mirror that he was jabbing the bayonet into the bag of shavings. He must have thought we were smuggling some one into a restricted area. After this examination we were allowed to proceed.

We had been told to blow the horn at every intersection because the law said "the first one to arrive at unmarked corners had the right of way."

Another time when we stopped at a cabinet shop for some shavings, I was surprised to see huge logs of different woods brought in from South America. Some of the cabinet work was so exquisite it was almost breath-taking. On the way home that day, I told Steve that I always tried to be a "professional tourist" and that one of the things I wanted to see in Havana was the fortification at the mouth of the port. We had to drive all the way around the bay. Then we rode up, up and up a long sloping drive at the end of which was a big iron gate through a high stone wall. Here again we ran into soldiers with bayonets on their guns, and they all aimed their guns at us. I eased the car over a big bump fixed in the blacktop as a deterrent to traffic. A man ran up to the car on the side I was on and screamed something at us in Spanish. Steve explained why were were there and the man raged at him. Steve explained to me that we had blundered into the wrong part of the fortress. The tourist area could be reached only by boat from the other side! And we were in a military area that was used for political prisoners! I told Steve to apologize for me, then turned the car around and left. That was one time I was really frightened, but Steve said I didn't show it.

(When I journeyed back as a tourist a couple of months later, we went to the tourists' area – by boat, and satisfied my desire to see it. I had seen the ocean breakers tossing huge white waves all the way to the top of the lighthouse itself and felt privileged to have been allowed to visit the place.)

One day I received a letter from a friend who said he was coming to Cuba to try to buy some fancy chickens there, since he was a chicken hobbyist. I met him at the airport and chauffered him around with Steve's help. First place we went to was a feed store. It was nearing closing time for the siesta hour so the man got into the car with us to show us where the friend could see some game chickens. We drove way out of town and into a yard at a farm. We all got out and the Feed Store Man (a North American) acted as interpreter. We walked back to a tiny arena where they staged cock fights. The farmer showed a rooster, then looked at me and said something in Spanish that I "caught" to mean, "What's the woman doing here?" I didn't wait for the feed store man to say anything because I could see he was "in the middle" and embarrassed. I asked him, "Am I not supposed to be here? Is that what he said?" His face reddened as he replied, "Yes, I'm afraid I forgot. Women are not supposed to come into the arena."

"So," I said, "I'll wait in the car."

He sighed, "Oh, thanks! That's fine."

I didn't want to cause any friction over their customs. And they didn't buy any chickens there, anyway. The arena was crudely built of rough sawn timbers – palm logs – and had a palm thatched roof. The area for the fights was no more than eight or ten feet in diameter and the seats were built "grandstand" style and stacked, very steep, about eight planks high. The whole arena was probably twenty-five feet in diameter. I guess they are right for not letting women in because all I could think of as I waited in the car was, "Poor

American Palisades Park

(Con sus) HAVANA - REGLA - JARUCO - BATABANO - SANTOS SUAREZ - DEC 1956 TO FEB 57
MATANZAS - QUIVICAN - GUANABAY -

¡AQUI ESTA!

HERE *IT IS!*

El mejor y mayor Parque de Diversiones del Mundo
THE BEST AND LARGEST PARK OF PASTIMES OF THE WORLD

con sus máximas acciones del momento
WITH ITS GREATEST ACTS OF THE MOMENT

THIS WAS
WHEN WE
WERE IN
CUBA

"KIN GORILA"

KING *GORILA*

Monos Boxeadores que pagan al contricante un dolar por
MONKEYS BOXING WHO PAY AT THE RATE OF A DOLLAR PER
raund, un expectáculo emocionante y a la vez divertido,
ROUND, A SPECTACULAR EXCITING AND AT THE SAME TIME AMUSING,
Gorilas amaestrados que conocen todas las reglas del
GORILLAS ? WHO KNOW ALL THE RULES OF THE

BOXEO Y LUCHA LIBRE

BOXING AND WRESTLING (GAME?)

DIVIERTASE Y A LA VEZ GANE DINERO

ENJOY YOURSELF AND AT THE SAME TIME MAKE MONEY

EL SHOW más comentado hasta el momento por la
THE SHOW MOST TALKED ABOUT UNTIL THE MOMENT THROUGH
Prensa y Televisión, algo increible digno de ver. *THE*
PRESS AND T.V. SOME INCREDIBLY DIGNIFIED TO SEE

No se pierda de KIN GORILA

DON'T MISS THE KING GORILA,

ADVERTIZING USED IN CUBA
1956-57 WINTER

194

little chickens!"

Bob and I virtually never went off the show lot at night. Our business was to be on the lot no later than 5:00 or 5:30 P.M. and get ready to put on the show. Since the show ran from 7:00 or 8:00 P.M. until around 10:00 or 11:00, we were usually pretty tired by time we storm-rolled the canvas and cleaned up.

But while in Cuba, we noticed the Cubans stayed up almost all night and it was like a twenty-four hour party. So we decided, (only this one night) to walk up the street and get a "midnight snack." Along the street were vendors selling fish sandwiches and hot dogs and other native delicacies from their little hand-carts. Bob liked fish so he bought a sandwich and ate it as we walked up the street.

At a "square" we saw groups of men sitting around small tables playing dominoes. We stopped and marvelled at all the people walking around. It reminded me of New York City's Times Square when I was a kid. Everybody going somewhere, and everybody seemed to be happy.

As we stood, about ready to go back to the lot, a group of men walked up to us and one of them spoke in a friendly "broken English." He introduced a short powerfully-built man and said, "Dis man. He wants to fight wid your ape." So we walked over to an open air Cafe with counter-stools on the sidewalk where Bob and the man sat down to talk. Through his interpreter, the man "drove a hard bargain" by demanding 25% of the gate proceeds instead of the usual $5.00 or $10.00 "minimum fee." Bob surprised me by agreeing to the man's terms. When the interpreter relayed the information a big cheer went up from the ever-growing crowd. We stood on the sidewalk and the Challenger walked across the street with the crowd chanting and clapping their hands. We didn't understand what they were saying, but the challenger stopped on the other side of the street, turned around, smiled, and then holding both fists high, he flexed his muscles. It was typical of the behavior of so many of our North American challengers that we smiled back at him. He strutted a little more, and as he did, a paper bag of flour came from somewhere in the crowd and hit him in the face. Flour cascaded from his forehead to his shoes. We stood in open-mouthed shock at the sight. Then when we turned to see where it had come from, we saw the crowd dispersing wildly and laughing uproariously as they fled.

The man stood with anger blazing from his eyes and looked at us. Our amazement and sympathy must have been eloquent in its silence. We had never seen anyone do such a trick to their own and we were stunned.

He walked back over to the counter and accused the waiter who denied any knowledge of where it had come from. We went back to the lot right away, convinced that our lifetime rule of staying on the lot at night should not be broken again.

We never saw the challenger again. We don't know if he was too humiliated to show up or just what did happen.

We were getting more and more fed up with our connections on the show. The trailer I was living in was totally inadequate for even the most primitive necessities of life and the interpreters were getting progressively less competent. In addition we were having more and more trouble with the crowds. Back in 1940, when we were working to Spanish speaking people in Southern Texas, we were charging 10¢ for kids and 25¢ for adults. Many of the adults would drive me to distraction by trying to hand me 5¢ and saying "nickel, nickel, nickel," as if I would bargain with them. Of course there was no way I could bargain with them. One price had to be charged to all.

In Cuba, in '56 and '57 Winter, we found the most they would pay was only 25¢, after trying for 50¢, then 40¢, unsuccessfully. And we were giving exactly the same show we charged $1.00 and $2.00 for in the States. Sad to relate, very few of the shows we gave were what the Cuban people wanted. They were almost always wanting their money back because the man or the animal was neither bleeding nor killed. Our interpreters failed to make it clear that it was

196

merely a contest of strength and not a fight to the death. Finally, at Matanzas we had a near riot over the way the translators were mishandling our business. We would tell them what to say, and even with my limited knowledge of the language I knew they were **not** saying what we told them to say. At last, one of them told the audience we'd give their money back if they didn't like the show. In the states we were charging one dollar to see the same show we were putting on by then for 25¢ in Cuba. And the crowd threatened violence if we didn't refund. Rocks were thrown at one time and Steve asked later, "Who fired the gun?" It was not a gun – a rock had hit the truck right beside where I stood and had made the noise he took for a gun shot. I folded my arms and remained on stage. To have gone off would have opened the way for more violence. My stance backed them down -- but I was quaking inside. Bob was inside the cage shouting at the people to tell them what bum sports they were. This was not helping the situation and that night, when it was all over, I told him he could go on deeper into the island if he wanted to – but I was **going home.** He agreed that it was a hopeless mess trying to make the people understand our show when the language barrier was so impossible to hurdle.

It was Saturday night, and while we slept, some of the disgruntled patrons strung tangled barb-wire all across the area we would have had to use if we had tried to leave during the night. We were not aware of this, so we found it the next morning and removed it before pulling out. It would have ruined our tires and would have maimed us if we had walked or run into it. I believe they planned to try to scare us into running into it with our trucks or our bodies. During the night a lot of the show equipment pulled out for the next town, which was the usual procedure for them. It was fortunate that we usually pulled out at daylight on Sunday mornings.

The rest of the show headed South and we went North, back to Havana, to the boat dock. Steve pleaded with us to

197

take him with us to the States. I made a lot of phone calls, but found that it was almost impossible to bring anyone out of Cuba! Steve was heartbroken. He wanted so much to come to the U.S.A. but there was nothing we could do.

We got to the dock too early and the people at the dock would not let us park on their property overnight for fear the dock might be bombed. The situation had worsened while we were there. At a Havana suburb where we were showing two bombs had gone off within two blocks of the show, one night, destroying the front of a grocery store. At other times, three circuses had been burned to the ground and Batista had replaced the shows and equipment for the owners. In a women's room at a big department store, a woman carrying a bomb lost an arm when her bomb exploded prematurely. And I'm sure there had been other similar events about which we heard nothing.

We parked a couple of blocks away from the dock and slept. But not for long. A light was flashed in my face as I slept in the front seat of our car. I woke up to find the night watchman checking us out.

I had taken a ten weeks' course in conversational Spanish at the Clearwater, Florida, High School during the 1955-56 Winter and after the eight weeks on the island I had a pretty good smattering of Spanish. The watchman could speak no English, so I had to struggle along with what little Spanish I had and was elated at how far I had progressed with the language up to that time. We talked for more than an hour and I thoroughly enjoyed the conversation. I had to ask him to speak more slowly, several times, but otherwise we did faily well. (It is distressing, however, to realize that by not using the language I have practically totally lost it, since!)

Next morning we were at the dock and ready to leave. The show's manager came to try to keep us from leaving. He was angry, but we had had enough and our minds were made up. Steve came to me and said the show manager had told the manager of the boat that we should not be allowed to leave and that we hated the Cubans. The boat manager was behind

198

the counter and I told Steve, "You tell this man that's a lie! I have no quarrel with any Cubans! It's my own people I'm mad at! I haven't met a single Cuban person I didn't like. I even intend to come back as a tourist as soon as I can!"

Steve relayed the message, dutifully. A few minutes later I was walking around inside the office and waiting room, carrying Topsy while the papers were being checked on the animals and equipment. We know now that the delay was being caused by the showman who didn't want us to leave.

When the moment arrived for the ship to leave, our truck was still not on board. The boat manager came up behind me, and, in perfect English said, "You had better get that truck on the boat! Now!" I gasped, "I didn't know you spoke English!" He said, "Sh! Get that truck on the boat. Now!" I ran out and said, "Bob, the man says get the stuff on the boat -- now." We got in our vehicles and pulled onto the boat. Steve said -- "Can I go? Please?" -- and I had to tell him, "You'd be caught and put in jail." Standing with his toes on the boat and heels on the dock, he let the boat pull out from under his toes, as we all waved sadly at each other as long as we could see him before the big metal doors of the ferry clanged shut between us all.

When we got home we checked our money out and found that the eight weeks we had spent in Cuba had **shrunk** our bankroll by twenty-five dollars! We had almost made a "living wage," but not quite. However, it was a priceless experience because we learned that we would never -- **ever** -- leave the U.S. with our precious cargo again.

I have a diary in which I listed the towns we played in Cuba. They were Guanahay, Quivican, Batabano, Jaruco, Matanzas, Santos Suarez, Lawton, and Regla. A **beautiful**, scenic country.

Almost exactly a year after we got Topsy I found myself flying back to New York City for another little gorilla. I had never travelled by air before and the experience was one long to be remembered. We were high above the clouds that looked to me like a sea of foam, or cotton beneath us. Now and then we passed over a huge break and could see the gorgeous patchwork of man's labors below. The tops of the clouds -- as they closed in -- made me think of an illustration of the castle atop the clouds in a children's book I once owned, "Jack in the Beanstalk." It had a real fairy tale atmosphere. All too soon I was getting off the plane. We told no one I was coming so there was no one waiting to meet me.

I went right to the airline office and was told that Phil's plane was not due 'til that night. "They'd had some sort of delay," I was told. I had all day, so went over to Manhattan and took in the U.N. Building. On the way back I stopped by a fruit stand and got a big load of fruit -- grapes, apples, oranges -- quite a lot. When I got back to Idlewild, I put it all in one of the lockers, so we would have food for the animals when they got there. Instead of a few hours, I spent two full days and two nights waiting for that plane! And every minute was spent in the waiting rooms, because the plane was expected "any minute" for two days! I finally curled up, exhausted, on the benches and slept. Someone walked by singing "Goodnight little Suzie" and woke me up. I went to the desk and asked if they had any news and they told me that I had only about twenty minutes more to wait. I hailed a cabbie and had him take me over to the freight hangar where "our" plane was due to arrive. I told the man at the door who I was expecting and he said, "Yes, we got notice they will be here within two or three hours." I then had the cabbie run me back to the main building to pick up the suitcase and fruit and bring me back, then waited the rest of the two or three hours there. I was sorry I had not come over sooner. They had a small alcove with a couch in it and I flopped, and, secure in the knowledge that I could not "miss" Phil when he arrived, I "died." Two days and nights without sleep, had "done me in." When Phil got in, he rushed in to the alcove and splashed something full of alcohol all over my face and in my eyes. He told me later it was Parisian perfume. It nearly took my breath. But it certainly woke me up. What a way to wake up! Ugh! It sure put the damper on my pleasure at seeing him. Since it was about 2:30 or 3:00 A.M., we had to stay there until business houses opened up, after nine, at which time he called in to Manhattan and hired a truck to take the animals to the headquarters of the Louis Ruhe Animal Company on Long Island. This was a Compound that had existed through a couple of generations -- or more.

The gorillas were all unloaded into a cage where they could stretch their legs, and relax. And there were three beautiful babies, together, which were headed for Japan. Phil asked me if I would like to fly with them over to Japan. I guess I missed the chance of a lifetime to make the trip, but I was eager to get back to my family and Topsy. The plane that I was to take to Tampa was not to leave before 1:00 A.M. the following morning. So I had quite a visit at the place. I sat and watched for almost an hour while a man came in and sat, immobile, before a huge stack of canary cages fastened to the wall. Every now and then he would stand up to make a mark on a cage. As he prepared to leave, I asked him what he had been doing. He showed me the marks and said, "This bird is a singer we can guarantee. See how many marks? This means that he was singing that many nights, when I came here. See? There are more like this." I was surprised and delighted. The patience he displayed on this job was most interesting. I then walked into another area and was surprised to see an animal loose on top of a cage. It's funny, but I have forgotten what kind of an animal it was! When I told them about it, no one paid me much attention. "Because," said one of the employees, "he stays loose all the time. Comes down off that cage only to eat and drink."

Later that evening, I began to worry about getting the gorilla box on the plane. But we were invited to go to Chinatown to get a Chinese supper. Dr. and Mrs. Fred Roth (the veterinarian) had found a nice place to eat and took us there. We were lucky; when we hailed a cab, it was a Checker, one with a wide back door. Phil asked the driver if he would come back at about twelve and pick up a box. The cabbie was glad to comply with the request. So Phil said goodbye and went to get some much-needed sleep when we returned from Chinatown. I sat with the Roths for maybe an hour before my cab was due. During this time we let Tommy loose on the floor. He was only about eight months old and weighed a tiny thirteen pounds. The Roths were pleased with him and took a couple of pictures. He was a bit cross, but then I figured it was because he was tired.

We sat and talked for a while before putting him back in his box. I admired the property and was told that there were five acres in the place! Extremely hard to care for in the heart of so complex a city as New York, especially since it was a privately owned animal trader's compound.

I was told that a group of young hoods had climbed up on the roof of one of the buildings and threw huge balls of ignited newspapers into the pens with valuable Zebras and giraffes. One of the animals ran against a wall and broke its neck. The others had to be destroyed because of the injuries they sustained. The night watchman ran after the hoods, caught one of them, and slapped him around angrily. (He should have taken him to the police – in spite of the fact he was a juvenile.)

A night or two later the front bell rang, and when the watchman opened the gate, the boy's father stood before him with a huge club in his hand. The watchman woke up in the hospital. This explained why they had a "peephole" cut in the outside door through which they "checked" before opening the door!

Dr. Roth who had been to many interesting places told me that there were areas in Africa that were ideal places to live. Only thing was that one had to become accustomed to the weird noises of the night. He said, "You know that there is nothing in the area that will harm you, but the sounds are so foreign to your ear, you can't go to sleep." He went on to say, "There is a small lizard that lives in the house. It eats insects, and especially flies and mosquitoes. It has suction cups on its feet that enable it to walk and run on the ceiling. And when it prepares to attack its prey, it screams, then makes a dash and grabs whatever it is after. Sometimes the suction cups fail and the little fellows fall, screaming, on top of you while you sleep -- maybe even into your face. I'll admit, it does take a while to get used to that!"

When the cab arrived, I thanked them for their hospitality and went out to Idlewild. Since I was a couple of hours ahead of time, I got on the phone to see if I could get myself and the animal insured. It was then I learned that I could not travel via regular passenger plane. I was being shipped as live cargo! This was the only way I could legally ride on the same plane with my animal! The plane I was supposed to take was broken down. I found I could not get insurance on anything that went on one of these planes! I must have shown my consternation at the desk, because one of the men behind the desk started kidding me, "What will you do if you get

203

airsick? You know that plane will not be pressurized! It's no place for a woman!" – etc., etc., etc. I said, "Alright, if that's how you feel about it, put me and my animal on a regular plane!" – "Can't do it." So I said, "Well, if the pilot can do it, so can I."

I went back to where Tommy's crate sat and gave him his bottle. I felt he was becoming attached to me even faster than I had dared hope he might.

After we had been there two or three hours, a handsome pilot came to me and said, "Has anyone told you we won't leave here 'till three hours from now?"

"No," I replied.

"Well, you see, our plane broke down and won't go out today. So we are taking the second flight. Instead of non-stop to Atlanta, and then Tampa, we are taking all the air-mail for points between. Do you have someone waiting for you at the other end?"

"Yes! My poor husband expects me there at 8:00 A.M."

"If you can reach him by phone or wire, better tell him you won't be there 'till one or two P.M." As he started to leave, he turned back and said, "Did you pack a lunch?" I said, "No." – "Well, then, you'd better buy some of those chocolates or cakes out of that machine. You'll get pretty hungry before we get there!"

(I was shipped from Phil Carroll of St. Louis, Missouri, to Bob Noell at Tampa, Florida. They weighed the packages, and then weighed me! I paid for my passage as "Attendant" to the gorilla.)

I thanked him and went straight to the machine and loaded up. I began to get a little nervous, now, and thought, "Gee, maybe that guy wasn't kidding about the airsick bit." I went into the office and saw the same kind pilot behind the desk. I said, "Say! I've never flown but once before! Do you have any pills in case I get airsick?"

He spread his hands on the desk in a hopeless gesture and leaned back and said, "Now, look! If you're gonna go getting airsick on us....!"

I protested, "Now, wait a minute. I don't know that I will, I just wondered. Never mind." And I retreated, sheepishly. I wished there was a drugstore near, where I could get some Dramamine, but the only place one could spend any money was at the vending machines for coffee and cakes. And I was not hungry.

I put on a pair of dungarees and it was well that I did. The only way up into that ship was through the baggage doors and up a step-ladder! I thought, as I climbed, "This will be quite a wonderful experience for old greenhorn Mae." And it really was. I stood back, out of the way, and watched the most marvelous job of packing and tying I had ever witnessed! If the load had not been tied down, it could have shifted and caused the plane to go out of control. The system was one from which anyone could learn. Beautiful! I was there to see that my Tommy did not wind up on the bottom of that pile!

I don't think I've ever met kinder, more considerate people anywhere in all my travels than the people who were connected with that trip!

As the motors were warming up, a man climbed up the ladder in preparation to closing the big door. He shouted above the roar of the motors, "Lady, if you get tired and want to sleep, there's a hammock over there in the tail section. And near the hammock is a bucket and a roll of toilet paper." He then slammed the door shut, and I smiled as I ran for the front end of the plane. (I've often wondered, since, if that hammock and bucket were put in especially for me -- because I had asked about becoming airsick -- or if it was "standard equipment.") The pilot stood up and fastened the door, then told me to sit in the navigator's seat and to fasten the seat belt. I did this as quickly as possible. Inside of five minutes we were racing down the runway and were soon up in the air. When we got 'way up high, they tilted the plane and flew in a couple of circles. I asked, "What is that for?" "Look down there," the co-pilot said. "Did you ever see anything more beautiful? We never leave without taking a last look. It's more beautiful than a huge Christmas tree."

I thought I had seen a tremendous "cross section" of "little old New York" in my lifetime. but that one breathtaking view is one I shall never forget. I was actually speechless! The lights! -- even at that early morning hour!

After we levelled off I began asking questions about the instrument panel. (But, first I asked if these questions would annoy them.) They explained the instruments and I found myself watching them as much as they did. Then they set it on "automatic" and it kept an even keel, while one man relaxed, the other kept an eye on things. The noise was terrific, so one of the men told me to reach overhead and put the earphones on and I could listen to radio music. That filled the gap for awhile.

But then, my long days and nights without sleep caught up with me and I snuggled down in my seat and went to sleep. After what seemed only a few minutes, one of them tapped my shoulder and said, "Better fasten your seat belt, we're going down."

I sat up and fixed the belt. Landing was the experience I most dreaded. I don't like elevators in buildings because I "leave" my solar plexis "upstairs" when they descend too rapidly. But it wasn't that way, at all, on the plane. Nevertheless, I held to the edge of my seat, knuckles white with the almost frantic grip.

We hit a wind-pocket. The wheels hit the pavement **hard**. We bounced thirty or forty feet into the air, then hit again, wingtip barely missing the ground. Both men struggled grimly and silently with the controls. After we were taxying into the hangar the pilot waggled a forefinger and said, "Shame on you!" to the co-pilot. He said, "Yeah! But it was a cross-wind! I couldn't help it!"

I figured to "break the ice," and said, "Gee, fellers, you'd better tell them to fix that hole in that runway!" -- And, by the relieved way they both laughed, I knew I was "in."

We had to go down five or six times to unload the air mail. They must have radioed ahead that I was aboard, because at Orlando I was met and welcomed to use a house trailer to wash up. I had not slept nearly enough -- even yet. I even got a cup of hot coffee there! The pilots had their lunch along and while we were aloft, I slept and they ate. I woke up and saw them eating, and knew it would embarrass them if they knew I was awake so I turned my back to them and went back to sleep.

At Orlando, when I came back to the plane, there was a long ladder in front of it and a man was fixing something on the side near an engine. I said, "Who discovered that?" The pilot said solemnly, "I did. One of my best friends lost his life because of a little thing like that." And I remembered the remark the man at the desk in N.Y. had made, – "No place for a woman – put together with baling wires." Just as this thought went through my head, the man on the ladder called down to me, "Anybody got a Bobbie pin? I need one up here!"

Realizing I was being kidded, I said "Sorry! I don't use them," and climbed back in the plane.

We arrived in Tampa at about 1:30 P.M. and Bob was exhausted. When I took Tommy out of the box to show him to Bob, he was disappointed.

"Why did Phil send me such a tiny baby?" he asked. Then I told him that Phil insisted the male should be **much** smaller than the female for them to make a congenial pair.

A newspaper man was there and they ran pictures of me with little thirteen-pound Tommy in my arms in the newspapers.

When we got ready to leave, I shook hands with the pilots and thanked them for their patience with me, and we watched them head for their home – one more trip up and down – to Miami.

We built a bigger cage for Topsy and put tiny Tommy in her old cage. All the cages we built for our gorillas and orangutans always had a six-inch by six-inch feed door, plus the larger door for the animal to go in or come out. The feed door kept the babies from suffering unnecessary frustration.

They enjoyed coming out of their cages for their romps and outings. So when we opened the big doors, they expected to come out. If -- for any reason -- the big door was opened and then closed without letting the baby out -- pandemonium ensued! So the feed door served an important function. There simply was no frustration involved, when the tiny door was used.

Once, Tommy hurt my arm -- when he weighed a tiny fifteen pounds! I reached through the feed door to feed him, and he decided he wanted me to come in the cage with him -- or for me to take him out. He got a fierce grip with all four of his hands, and, pressing his head against the top of the cage, pulled on my arm with a strength that I found amazing! In fact, during the two or three minutes that he screamed and held me so fiercely, I actually feared that the flesh would be stripped from my arm! And what made it so frightening was the fact that I was completely helpless and at his mercy! Only when he decided he could not pull me through, did he stop. I figured then that it might actually have been a good thing that it happened, because, as Bob says, "They never forget anything," and it just might prevent a more serious effort later on.

Topsy had been with us almost exactly one year when we got Tommy. She was established as one of the family, looking upon us as her parents. She accepted Tommy most graciously, and was gentle and kind to him even though he was a "newcomer". However, because there was so much difference in their sizes, we kept them in separate cages, for Tommy's protection for a time -- just "in case." As I look back, now, I know that it was not within any area of possibility for Topsy to be mean to anything. Much later, when they had been together for about three or four years, Bob decided to "wrestle" with Tommy, who weighed about a hundred pounds at the time. When he did, Topsy walked toward them and grunted a warning. I was in the cage, too, and said to Bob, in the usual "baby talk" voice, "Careful, Daddy, Topsy said cut it out -- I don't know how she means

208

that. Be careful!"

Bob stopped -- then tried again.

Once more Topsy said "stop!"

After several trips in the cage, Bob decided to go ahead and see just what she would do. We were both surprised when she walked over to Tommy and made him, "Leave her Daddy alone." Using this natural behavior, then, Bob "wrestled" with Tommy while Topsy acted as an unorthodox referee. This was one of the funniest things we ever did with any of our animals, because it was so completely natural, and the animals were thoroughly enjoying themselves. Greater "hams" never lived than those two when they were "in the groove." The audiences loved Topsy's referee act after we explained what was happening.

One of the most hectic days we ever spent with Topsy and Tommy was through no fault of theirs. We went to Pittsburgh with their cage truck to have them on **B'wana Don's "Kiddie" show** on KDKA T.V. I had made arrangements with an executive and had warned him that the "babies" were not house-broken and requested that they be **only** on tile floors. I stressed the need to keep them off of plush carpets.

He told us we were to pull the truck up beside the building and no one would bother us. We were close to the side door there. When we arrived I left the animals in the cage until I could check things out. The executive came down with me and we got the babies out and went inside. Topsy, who weighed about 300 pounds, was on a lead and Bob took her in. Tommy weighed about 30 pounds -- so I carried him in. We went straight to a thickly carpeted stairway and went upstairs. I was wailing my protests all the way up -- fearful that Topsy might have one of her massive accidents on that lush rug. But the man laughed and said, "It can be cleaned -- don't worry about it."

When we got to the top of the stairs we were in an office complex, with no studio in sight. It was then we were told that we were not to go on the air for another hour or more!

209

A T.V. convention was in full swing and the executive, being an opportunist, had had a sign painted that read, "We intend to make monkeys out of the opposition," and had it hung on the wall behind his desk. He then had Topsy sit in his chair at the desk and planned to pull this as a joke on one of his friends. He said, "I want her to be in the chair when this fellow opens the door, but I'd like for Bob to be out of sight." So every time the door opened, Bob – still holding Topsy's lead chain -- would duck under the desk. I had tried to get him to wear a summer suit, but' he wore his black woolen suit and it was warm in that office. The door opened some ten or fifteen times before the right man came in – and the perspiring Bob ducked under the desk every time.

Meantime, I was having no better luck with Tommy in the next room. I was "hiding" in the adjoining office and trying to keep the unhappy Tommy quiet. He did not want to be separated from Topsy and in his fright and anxiety he had an "accident" on my clothes from my waist down. Worst part of it was I was to go on the air very soon and the color of the accident did not match my clothes. Still worse, some of it managed to get on the plush carpet. The three ladies at the desks were very sympathetic and cooperative. They brought me paper towels and toilet paper and we soon had their waste baskets full of the stuff. A few minutes later the executive came in and laughingly said, "You know something? This office **stinks!**" He was thoroughly enjoying himself, but I was mortified.

Meantime, our son, who was guarding the truck, was having no better time of it. A policeman came by and made him move. Having no place to park in that area, he started driving around the block slowly -- waiting for us to come out.

When finally we did get on the air 'B'wana Don" very graciously had me sit at a table and no one was the wiser about Tommy's accident on my clothes. All went well in the studio, but when we walked out onto the sidewalk in downtown Pittsburgh, with two gorillas, we had no cage to put them in for about ten minutes, until Bobby got back with the truck. He was nearly frantic because the truck was almost out of gas! What an experience!

All through their lives together Topsy was the "Boss" over Tommy. It is an interesting thing, and something we noticed about the apes – years ago. One ape **must** be "the boss" over the others. One animal asserts himself and the others take it for granted that he (or she) is the boss.

In the case of Topsy and Tommy, Phil warned us that the female should be purchased first, so she would have control of the male. The male should be smaller, because in time he would pass her in size, and her maternal instincts would make her a gentle boss, whereas if the situation was reversed, the male might kill a small female -- just playing with her. And, because we had her a year before we got Tommy, Topsy was decidedly bigger and very much the boss.

Many's the time she "beat him up." I would run into the truck and break it up. Then, because Tommy had been on the bottom, I would examine him and only once or twice did he ever have even as much as a scratch! And to hear the screaming that went on, you'd have thought she was eating him alive!

Topsy took priority on foods, too. She was the one who always got the first choice on everything. She sat at the feed door and made her selections, and Tommy got the "leavings". Sometimes he would stand and gaze directly into her mouth, from inches away, as she ate and ignored him. I got the feeling he was telling her, in "gorilla", that he loved her, because he'd glance at identical food, that was offered to him, as if to refuse politely – then continue to gaze until she pushed him away, impatiently.

After Topsy died, Bob continued to play with Tommy before the audiences. Tommy was a big ham and loved to clown around with Bob, even after he became a fully grown adult!

We were anxious to learn all we possibly could about apes when we got Snookie. When a New Orleans newspaper advertised a live gorilla on stage, we simply had to see the show. It took us almost an hour to find the little theater back on a side street. We took our seats at about the center of the theater when we went in, because the movie was in progress.

When the lights came up, a man in a pith helmet, Khaki shirt and riding pants, wrapped legs, with a gun in one hand and a whip in the other, walked into the spotlight and made an announcement, "Ladies and Gentlemen," he said, "These footlights will hide your presence from the gorilla. Please be as quiet as possible and do not let him know you are out there. This gorilla was just caught recently and he is not trained, yet. He likes girls, so, please girls -- don't make any noise out there." About this time a big hand covered with red hair reached out from behind the front curtain and pulled on it. Immediately, I nudged Bob and whispered, "That's no gorilla! Gorillas are black! It's a fake!" The announcer turned toward the hand and said, "Don't bring him out, yet, I'm not finished with the announcement!" Then there was more action "backstage." Then, "Oh, alright, if he won't behave back there, give me his chain!" Someone handed a chain out from the wings. He took it with his gun hand and a "big red gorilla" came out on stage with a ring in his nose! Bob and I laughed softly, not wishing to interrupt the show. We looked around at the audience. Every single person was sitting -- at the ready -- on the edge of their seats. I whispered, "My Gosh, Bob -- these people are ready to panic!"

The huge muscular man in the ape suit was a marvelous performer. The illusion was remarkably good. The red hair and the ring in the nose spoiled the effect for us, but the audience was buying every word and every movement. The announcer was interrupting himself often with, "Sit still!" or "Don't do that!" or "Come back here!" as the restless 'gorilla' jumped around fitfully. The announcer said that as part of the training for big time theaters later, they were trying to introduce the gorilla to a young lady. The last lady had been hurt so they had a new young girl who wanted to become famous as the gorilla trainer. He called her on stage.

212

She came on – hesitantly – from the side of the stage opposite to where the 'gorilla' had entered. She wore a very revealing leopard skin, fastened over one shoulder and wore no shoes. Her long blond hair reached to her hips. She acted as if she were ready to run at the slightest provocation. Suddenly things happened fast and within five seconds they had passed the climactic ending of their 'performance.' First the 'gorilla' shoved the man over backwards. As he fell he released the end of the chain and fired the blank gun three or four times. As he was falling and the startling reports of the gun were going off, the 'gorilla' grabbed the girl and throwing her over his shoulder, he stepped over the footlights as the house lights went out and the movie began. We were fortunate that we had selected middle seats. We were the only people who remained seated. Pandemonium, such as I had never seen before, took over and the panicked audience nearly destroyed each other in their mad scramble for a safer place. If the theater had been filled to capacity it would have been a real disaster. As it was – with less than a half a house, several people were trampled in the wild rush of the patrons who were insane with fright. I don't know how such an act could have survived for long – hurting people that way! But I learned a valuable lesson from that show, and used the knowledge every time Bob went in the cage to wrestle our big gorilla, Tommy. My "lecture" went something like this:

"Ladies and Gentlemen, please listen to every word that I am going to tell you. In a couple of minutes Bob will open that door and Tommy will walk into this cage. When he does, the first impulse of every person in this audience is going to be to gasp at his size. Don't. We don't want anyone to make any unusual noises while Tommy is in this cage. This arena was not built to hold a six hundred-pound gorilla. As you can see, it is chain-link and was originally designed for the chimps' boxing and wrestling matches. Tommy is happy in this cage. He doesn't know he could get out if he put it to a serious test. Let's keep him happy in this cage. Oh, you lady, over there with the youngster in your arms! Tommy loves

Photo by Flash Jarocki taken after Tommy playfully tore Bob's shirt. Here he is running away, impishly. This was part of the fun we presented in the arena when we were on the road.

children. If the child should cry, please take him out as quickly as you can. Tommy may take the attitude that you are hurting the child and may want to come out to help him. Tommy doesn't know it, but he could put one hand on each side of this cage and pull these wire walls in. Let's don't let him know he could. Now! So that you won't gasp when he walks in, I'll show you how high his head will be when he comes through that door." With that I would put my hand about chest high on the door and say, "And remember, this is on 'all fours' – he will not be walking erect." Eyes would widen and mouths fly open. Later when Tommy actually did walk in, most would be wide-eyed and holding both hands over their mouths. Twice, that I can remember, Tommy walked in and hit the metal ceiling with his fist, making an explosive sound and someone in the audience fainted. But we got the proper cooperation and we had a featured attraction with Tommy that has probably never been duplicated in the history of the world: "A 200-pound man 'wrestling' and playing with an adult male gorilla."

We were able to handle Topsy and Tommy, successfully, on lead ropes, well into adulthood. Topsy weighed a hefty 300 pounds or more when she died, and we continued to handle Tommy until he was a huge 550 to 600 pounds. We never had him on a scale, but we were told many times that we were underestimating his size.

When Bob tied him out, we could play with him, without fear. He was a "big baby" until one day about 1973 when Bob lost his temper with him.

I never allowed anyone to play rough with my baby apes and especially not with the gorillas. I realized that when the gorillas were grown, they would have hands the size of Virginia hams and I had no intention of being walloped by one, later. The gorillas could be – and were – controlled by voice inflection. I could show displeasure vocally and they would be crushed and apologetic in the extreme.

But, one fateful day after Bob tied Tommy out in the back yard, he took a watering can to give Tommy a drink. I had always given him his water in a paper container so he could play with it after it was empty. Tommy felt he had a right to take the watering can, and Bob thought otherwise. It was the first real confrontation any of us had ever had with Tommy and it ended unwisely, in my opinion.

Bob pulled the can and Tommy pulled it back. The tug-of-war ended with Bob first slapping Tommy, angrily, with his hand, then with a tiny stick. The slap and the stick would have meant little to Tommy because we had used a fly swatter, tapping him with it to correct him, many times in the past. However, Bob's tone of voice is what made the incident a dangerous one. I happened to be walking by at the other end of the zoo when the conflict started and I warned Bob that he should, "Lay off!" -- I told him, "You will be moving him back into the cage within the hour and he's not going to forget this -- you'd better cut it out!"

Defiantly he argued, "If he doesn't obey me I don't want him!"

I realized this was a temper-tantrum over which I would have no control and ran, weeping, into the trailer to get Tommy's treat bag ready. I figured if I got out of sight it might break up the contest quicker.

Our usual ritual for putting Tommy back in his cage was simple enough: When he had to walk from the back of the lot to the front, I would sit on a chair at the half-way point, with a "goodie bag" on my lap. When Tommy came alongside, I would take a banana out of the bag -- peel it and "hand feed" it to him. Then, twisting the top shut I would hand the bag to Tommy who would then be extra-anxious to get into his cage to see what goodies it contained.

But, this day Bob was too fast for me and I sat on the chair with the bananas on my lap -- with no bag. Bob foolishly tied the lead rope around his own waist-line. When Tommy suddenly bolted past me ignoring the protesting Bob whom he had "in tow", I was paralyzed with fright for Bob's safety, and when Tommy started to vault over the seven-foot-high driveway gate, I instinctively grunted

216

Tommy's "cuss-word" twice -- loudly. He dropped from the gate and made straight for me, and I thought "Oh dear God, this is where I get myself killed." But as soon as his feet had hit the ground I had started talking "baby talk" to him. He ran right up to me and stared into my eyes at close range, as if he were saying, "Did you mean what you said, you so-and-so?" I said, encouragingly, "I got you some!" And as I reached for a banana he grunted an angry warning. Bob said, angrily, "He'll bite your arm off!" Leaning back -- still "baby talking" I said, "If that's the way you feel about it, Tommy, peel yer **own** bananas!" Whereupon he picked up a banana, belligerantly, bit it in two as if to say, "This is what I'd **like** to do to you!" discarded half of it, then walked stiff-legged (a clear indication that he now considered **himself** master of the situation) into his cage without accepting the other bananas. Once in the cage I said to Bob, "You have ruined him. That should never have happened! Leave him there now." Bob did take him out several times after that, but he was not the "cute little" gorilla anymore, and we have not dared to take him out because of his tremendous strength and formidable size, and the danger that someone might cross him up and get hurt.

Years before, Bob had discovered that Snookie reacted exactly the way a person does when spoken to: A gentle shove with a rough word creates antagonism, whereas a hearty--even hurtful--slap on the back or punch on the arm is not resented if done in a friendly manner. This is the exact parallel to Tommy's reaction over the water-can episode. The slap and the stick had meant little -- if anything to Tommy because Bob had often used a fly-swatter that was much bigger than the stick -- but always in a half-jocular manner. It was the fact that Bob had shown a temper that created this dangerous episode, and again, it was a case of the animal showing better judgment than "his human pets" had shown.

When Tommy was a baby, I used to tickle him -- and then when I got close enough I would blow on his tummy. The hairs would flutter and tickle him when we had these little romps and he would laugh hysterically. Because of these games, he would often "play-bite" us. Some of the greatest photographs that were made of Bob and Tommy were of Tommy's mouth, wide open, with his full complement of teeth. And even after this agitating water-can episode, gentle Tommy wisely elected **not** to use his teeth!

And, even now, he gives us gorilla kisses through the bars when we ask him to! He still wears his chain bracelet (instead of a collar) in case we might ever have to take him out again.

Chapter Nine

A sweeter disposition than Topsy had (our adorable little girl-rilla) would be impossible to imagine. She was a precious baby and she knew it. Everything I did around our Chimp Farm Winterquarters (at Tarpon Springs, Florida) had been done with Topsy riding on my back. Sometimes, when no one else was around to kid me or poke fun at me about it, I would turn the record player on with the volume loud enough to hear it outside, and I'd hold her in my arms and waltz her around the lot, the way I did with my two (natural) children when they were small. Her beautifully serene facial expression was my reward. I loved her dearly and knew it was mutual.

Somewhere I've read that children who are handled a lot as babies turn out to be super intelligent. Both my natural children were treated this way, and Topsy was carried around a lot, too. I truly believe all three were above average (for their respective species) intellectually.

One day, in Winterquarters, I needed the shovel. Topsy's twenty odd pounds, as usual, was perched on my back with her feet firmly planted on my hips and both arms around my neck. I remembered that the shovel had been taken across the railroad tracks the day before.

"I'll bet those boys left that derned shovel over there yesterday!" I muttered to myself. "Never put anything away! Hope no one has taken it! Better go get it." And off I went.

Always the perfect passenger, Topsy balanced and watched over my shoulder as I stepped cautiously through knee-high weeds. Arriving on the tracks, I walked on the cross-ties to the spot where I felt the shovel might be. Leaving the tracks, I walked cautiously again, because there are rattlesnakes in our territory, and I have a most healthy respect for them.

Sure enough! There stood the shovel, stuck into the ground, right where they'd finished working the day before. I walked toward it – then stopped. I felt Topsy go tense at about the same time that I saw what I thought was a length of black water hose, beside the shovel.

"Now what the heck did they bring a water hose over here for?" I wondered. Then, on closer scrutiny, I thought I saw a pattern of scales. "A black snake?" I wondered. We don't bother any wildlife if we can avoid doing so. I already had my hand on the shovel, so decided to tap the ground near the object to see if it was a snake. When the shovel hit the ground, about three feet of startled black snake rose swiftly out of the grass. Topsy and I screamed together. I ran backwards and the snake followed, with about eighteen inches or so still in the air -- mouth open. After I'd run backwards some ten or twelve feet, the snake disappeared into a hole where I had been standing. Apparently, his only aim was to get back into the hole and safety. Only then did I realize I was being "choked to death" by a frightened little girl–rilla.

Somehow, experiences like this had sealed a bond between us that was impossible to explain to people who knew nothing about these so-called "sub-humans." May God forgive me if I am wrong, but there have been many times when I felt they were actually superior, in some ways, to some of the egotistical primates known as homo sapiens that

220

I have met. Topsy would never have maimed or killed anyone to take anything away from them. I've even seen her share what she had to eat, many times.

Our son was born in 1934. I was most anxious to be a model Mother when my baby came, so went to a clinic-type "school" for expectant mothers. This was in Savannah, Georgia, where we were showing for a few weeks. As part of the instruction, we were given the address of the Government Printing office, and I bought the books they put out on "Prenatal Care," "The Child from One to Six", and so on. These books contained some of the finest information available for a new mother, and I read them from cover to cover.

One of the things that made life livable for us and the children on the road was the lesson on how to keep them from being spoiled. Never pick a baby up when he's crying for attention. Check him out carefully. See to it there is no cause for tears, then put him back in his bed and let him cry! Crying is good exercise for the lungs. So, let him cry! After the crying fit is over and forgotten, pick him up when he is quiet. This trains the child that screaming will be useless and that it actually pays to be good! This worked with our two children, and, when the gorillas came on the scene, it worked with them, too!

I had to put Topsy in her cage, one day, in great haste. It was quite a struggle getting her in. She screamed and fought valiantly. But – after several tense moments – I got the box closed. I could not let her win that battle. She rolled and tumbled and screamed. I let her wear her tantrum out, while I attended to whatever it was I was trying to do. After several minutes -- when she realized it was useless to continue, she stopped crying. And -- when the task at hand was completed. I took her out (while she was quiet) and played with her and loved her. This one lesson seemed to be all that was needed for the rest of her life. She seemed to understand that I loved her -- but that I was to be boss. I am proud of the fact that I never, once, laid a "heavy hand" on that precious friend. It was not necessary! Her greatest ambition in life seemed to be a keen desire to do what pleased me. We had such a mutual love and respect for each other, that it is impossible to explain it to anyone who did not actually know Topsy. I feel that I was privileged to have a friend in her such as only one person in billions has ever had! I tried to share her boundless love for people with everyone who would take heed. Some were afraid and lacked faith in what I told them. But the ones who took me at my word were people who will cherish their brief friendship with Topsy for their entire lifetimes.

One was Don Riggs, who had a "kiddie" show on KDKA T.V. in Pittsburgh, Pennsylvania, when we were showing in that area. He came out to the show lot, in Butler, Pennsylvania, and brought a photographer. They made up a lot of film footage about the animals. Don sat in a chair, and Topsy came over and sat beside him, and actually kissed him!

As long as Don shall live, it is certain that he will never forget this!

Another one was Mrs. Lorayne Carlson, of Tarpon Springs, Florida, who, as a newspaper reporter, came to "interview" Topsy. Because she was a little bit afraid, Topsy sat off from her, a little distance. But Topsy loved people so dearly, that she had to put her hand in Lorayne's lap. Mrs. Fran Brush was with her, and snapped a classic photo which was used by the paper.

Still another one was professional photographer Chaffee (in 1961), who was the newspaper reporter for an Indianapolis paper. He posed for photos as he "interviewed" her, and his paper ran four pictures of the two of them, on the top of their front page.

And there was Patsy Condella of Penn Yan, New York, whose picture was run in a number of papers as he "signed her up" for the Fair.

There were many other newspaper reporters in other papers who shook hands with her and were photographed with her because she was so friendly and good. One who really learned to actually love her was Fran Fry, Junior, of Franklin,

Pennsylvania. In his "The Frying Pan" column in the Erie-Pa. Times-News, Sunday, April 24, 1977, he says:

Chances are most of us have some special friends. You know the kind I'm talking about, you might not see them very often or visit back and forth, but they along with fond memories occupy a special place in your heart.

This is the case with our friends Bob and Mae Noell in Tarpon Springs, Fla. You might remember their names as being the owners and trainers of "Joe the Boxing Chimp," who was featured in "The Frying Pan" a few weeks ago.

The Noells worked the south with a medicine show in their early years in show business and then graduated to the expanded carnival circuit. They have been and still are animal trainers and breeders and above all animal lovers. Their animals, and they number well over 70, always have and always will come first.

The Noells have to be the only people in the country who send out cards at Christmas time with pictures of gorillas on them.

When the middle of December rolls around I look forward to the arrival of their card and Mae's chatty newsletter almost as much as I do Christmas morning and all the presents. My family plays a little game to see who gets to open the "gorilla card" first this year. It's sort of like getting the prize out of the box of candy-coated popcorn at the circus.

I was attracted to the Noells over a dozen years ago almost like steel to a magnet. Their "Noell's Ark Boxing Chimps and Gorilla Show" was playing with a little carnival in the area. The show sounded like a good subject for a picture-feature for the Sunday magazine.

One bright sunny afternoon I walked onto the carnival lot and asked where the boxing chimp show was located. I must have looked like a constable or someone who was trying to serve some sort of a legal paper because at first the carnies sort of played dumb. After I explained I was a reporter they quickly ushered me to the back of the lot where "Noell's Ark" was set up.

Bob and Mae Noell were brought out and we met for the first time. This is when I learned that Mae was the spokesperson for the family. After about an hour of conversation she asked me if I wanted to see their two gorillas. She went on to claim that the smaller one was "perfectly tame" and might make a better magazine feature than the fighting chimps.

Both Bob and Mae went into a heavy steel cage and started to play with a large gorilla named "Thomas John Henry." I just couldn't believe my eyes the way they could maneuver that huge animal around.

As if that wasn't enough, then the real treat came. Mae left the cage and then asked me if I wanted to meet "Topsy." That was the beginning of a long love-affair. She told me not to be afraid and not to run. The next I knew Mae came out of their house-trailer and had a smaller gorilla by the hand, she weighed about 150 pounds.

She introduced us and I must admit I felt a little bit silly at the time, but I said hello and shook hands with my first gorilla. She had big dark eyes and liked to stare newcomers down.

The Noells put "Topsy" through paces and I never knew a gorilla could be so gentle. Mae, being a real showperson and appealing to my vanity, suggested that I come back another day. She further added that I bring along a second person to take photographs and do a feature on me interviewing the gorilla.

I couldn't drive fast enough back to the office to discuss the possible assignment with Bob Sutherland, then Sunday Editor of the **Times-News**. He cautioned me that he felt those animals I saw weren't gorillas, but large chimps. He finally agreed to the story and as soon as he saw the pictures he quickly changed his mind.

My return visit to the carnival was something I will never forget. We got pictures of "Topsy" and I feeling the hair on each others face. Then she tried to eat my notebook, play with the camera, share cottoncandy, ride the carnival rides and a whole series of child-like things.

I still wasn't sure about a couple of people who would keep a growing gorilla in their trailer. Mae explained her secret of success with "Topsy" was they got her as a baby and from the start treated her like they were raising a child and not a gorilla.

If people like Cleveland Amory and his Fund for Animals and the Society for the Prevention of Cruelty to Animals ever give an award for humane treatment to animals it should go to the Noells.

Bob and Mae hung up their traveling life in 1971 when they retired to operate their animal farm fulltime. At last count they had four gorillas, 27 chimpanzees, three orangutans, a mandrill, family of monkeys, an alligator, a bear and a variety of domestic animals.

Mae explained they bought their first chimp back in 1940 for only $300. Since that time they have had 45 young apes born in their collection. She added that a baby chimp now days sells for between $2,500 and $3,000.

Mae said their animal farm has become a dumping ground for adult chimps that people no longer want. As she was making this statement she went on to say she was nursing a broken wrist when one of the recently acquired chimps got a little too playful.

"Everytime I hear about someone at a zoo or show folks who are going to destroy an adult chimp because they can't handle it, I send Bob out in the truck and we have another addition at the farm," Mae said.

"Chimps play with you and make you believe, but you don't have to worry about them eating you."

As if the animals weren't enough to keep her busy, Mae is now into collecting books. In our telephone conversation she reported now having over 2,200 books on the shelves and classified by title and author. She said books are her second love and she has filled a barn, large

225

truck body and a trailer.

Needless to say, the Noells themselves would make a great book someday.

Leaving all these -- and all the people who shook their heads in disbelief when they saw me sitting in the cage with Topsy and Tommy -- we come to two little fellows, who, though they said very little about it when she died, must have felt it most keenly of any of her many friends: our two grandsons, Robert and Chris Noell (Robert E. Noell, Jr. and Christopher E. Noell).

They came up from their home in Clearwater, Florida to visit Topsy and to romp and wrestle with her. These two she loved especially well. Amazingly, she knew she was too heavy to lean on them, and handled them with affectionate caution. She held an arm with all four of her "hands" and "chewed" on it, tenderly. She would go into "blind hysteria" whenever the boys played with her. (See photographs in the album section of this book.)

It is my firm belief that Topsy would have remained a gentle and careful friend, throughout her life – no matter how long she had lived!

Back in the thirties we travelled with several circuses and made a lot of friends in the circus world. After we went back to our independent show, we never missed an opportunity to visit a circus that appeared close to where we were showing, because there was almost always someone we knew on one or the other of them.

When Topsy was small we took her with us on these jaunts, and I had as much fun watching her as anything else I did.

The first show she saw actually frightened her. The booming of the drums in the band seemed to distress her. I clapped my hands and smiled at her to relax her a little. Then as the show progressed, she got more and more in the spirit of the thing. When the kids in the audience applauded, she looked up on the high seats at them and clapped her little hands too. At last she was acting like any human child who is seeing its first circus.

When we left we met a couple of friends and I reached for my driver's license, out of habit, and discovered my pocket was totally empty! Money, license and all, **gone**! I said, "Bob! Hold Topsy! I'll be right back!" He took her and I raced back to where I had been sitting. The show was still in progress so no one had noticed my things on the ground. Expert pick-pocket that she was, Topsy had taken my things when she got bored and had taken them all apart and dumped them on the ground! Rascal!

Often as not, when I entered the cage with Topsy and Tommy, I had to be careful because Tommy's way of showing affection was to playfully charge and slam his body against me. After seeing my discomfort and displeasure at this, a few times, always thereafter, Topsy would step between us and take the bump, which never fazed her. Those affectionate onslaughts could have broken my bones.

Chapter Ten

Many times people who visit our place express a certain amount of concern because the animals are in cages. One day a young girl came running out of the place, sobbing. I went to the car with her and asked her why she was crying. She said, "Why are those poor animals in jail?"

Realizing she was sincere, I explained that most of these animals were raised in cages much smaller than the ones we have them in. And the animals regard the cages as havens. In fact, most of them would be totally lost if they got out, and would even want to get back in as fast as they could. The cage is "home" and represents security.

A lot of these animals were truly "orphans." Some were pets and others were trained animals who had outgrown their usefulness – and some we bought.

Sad to say -- if there were no zoos where endangered species were being reproduced — many species would now be extinct.

Many of the animals we took in were already sick before we got them. It seemed like a losing fight from the first day with the gorillas. The first one was Goliath, renamed "Golly Gal" in a letter I received from the late Dr. Robert M. Yerkes. She was very sick for the entire time we had her -- which was almost exactly a year. She was autopsied at Emory University in Atlanta, Georgia. She died of an intestinal parasite, even though she had been treated for worms by caring veterinarians.

Then, along came M'Bam who died the same way, after only one year. It was hard, sometimes, to get them to take the pills.

M'Bam loved chocolate milk so I brought the pill to him and he put it in his mouth. Just as I started to give him the milk, he spit the pill out in a sneaky way. I stepped back and said, "Oh, no you don't! If you don't take the pill you don't get the milk!" He scrambled around frantically, as he whimpered pitifully, and actually found the pill in the wood shavings on the floor – put it back in his mouth and I then gave him the milk. But the pills did no good (they were the enteric-coated gentian-violet pills).

We needed more cage space at our winterquarters and Bob heard that the old gorilla wagon on the Ringling Brothers' Circus was for sale. Knowing it had been a well built outfit, we took the money out of the bank and Bob went down to Venice to buy it. When he got there someone else had already bought it. On the way home he stopped in to see Frank M. Thompson – an old friend of ours. Frank was an animal dealer at that time, and he had a very sick little gorilla on hand, named Otto. When Bob saw Otto he fell in love with him. And, indeed, Otto was a beautiful speciman. However, he had an extremely bad case of what the doctors called "Septic Arthritis," and Frank was working hard at trying to make him well. When Bob came on the scene, Frank explained about Otto's affliction and Bob bought Otto at an extremely low price because he was so sick. Bob figured we could pull him out of it with the help of the doctors. We took Otto with us in 1971 (our last year on the road). I medicated him faithfully and watched him grow progressively worse. Finally, I stopped giving him the cortico stearoid medication and put him on baby aspirin pills. I saw a slight improvement, but certainly not as much as I'd have liked. When we got home that fall Frank called us up to ask how Otto was getting along. When I told him "not·so hot", he brought two doctors to the chimp farm. They tranquilized Otto and checked him out thoroughly. They came up with a much different medication than had been given to Frank for Otto, and the animal began to improve almost at once. Today, Otto is a magnificent animal, and if Frank Thompson had not been the honest, caring, man that he is, Otto might not be alive today.

MARCH 18

OTTO: STILL HAVING SOME PROBLEMS WITH HIM, TRIED TAKING HIM OFF
MEDICINE BUT NOW HE HAS TROUBLE WITH LEGS AND WALKS BAD.
HAVE OFFER 2000 CASH IMMEDIATE SALE. I SUGGEST YOU ACCEPT IT AND
I CHARGE NO COMMISSION ON THIS SALE JUST TO GET HIM GOOD HOME
WITH PRIVATE FAMILY. (WE ALREADY HAVE OVER 800 DOLLARS IN
VETERINARY CARE FOOD ETC) PLS REQUEST ANSWER FROM FRANS VIA TELEX
SOONEST

REGARDS FRANK

1971

Otto's case was a puzzler and had stumped the doctors at a big midwestern zoo where he had been before he was sent back to Frank for a refund.

I had not taken Otto to our doctor because I had thought the only thing that could help him was that cortico stearoid since that was what the first doctor had told Frank to use on him.

A woman came to our place and took a photograph of our female orangutan who was sunning herself in a window of her cage. She was a member of some "society" that was lobbying in Washington, D.C. to close all zoos and to pass laws that would prevent anyone from having exotic pets. Sadly -- these people were not above abusing truthfulness in order to gain their ends. The caption under the photo of our orangutan misrepresented the facts in thousands of brochures circulated world-wide in an effort to raise funds. The window frame was barely higher than her head and her body filled the framework. The caption said this beautiful orangutan was being kept in a cage so small she could neither stand up nor lie down! And close examination of the photo showed the male's head some four or five feet behind her! This false testimony was even put into the Congressional Record! The orangutans had **two** large cages – one was up high because they like to climb. I wrote to the congressmen who were on the committee who heard this false testimony and received letters from them that indicated that they were shocked to learn that anyone would falsify their testimony in that way.

I then requested letters from everyone I could think of who might be able to shed truthful light on the matter. However, the laws had already been passed on the strength of these underhanded tactics.

All this was done without giving any of the accused a chance to answer the accusations. If it had not been for a showman named Hal Haviland, we'd never have known these lies had been told on us. He was living in Washington at the time and was checking the Congressional Record about animal laws. He very kindly wrote to us and sent us a photo-copy of the false testimony. But by time we learned about it the statute of

231

limitations had expired and we could not sue.

Another woman had been to our place before all this came up and represented herself as a college student. Always willing -- even anxious -- to help anyone I can, I spent almost three hours with her one afternoon, answering questions on a tape recorder and showing her some of my ape books. When she got ready to leave she stunned me by saying, "Well. I guess I've wasted my time! I was told I'd be given a scholarship if I could get a roadside zoo in trouble. You're clean. I guess I'll go up north of here. I've been told there's a pretty bad place up there."

I was stunned speechless. These were the tactics that were used by the lobbyists to get the laws they wanted passed, and to raise many thousands of dollars. They even lied to a prominant columnist who put one of their "stories" about us in his national column, without checking to see if it was true!

It's nice to have friends and our friends did not have to stretch the truth in order to "give the lie to" the lobbyists' testimony.

Here is the body of one of the letters I received:

"I can thoroughly appreciate your concern and your desire to clear the record of the charges made against your primate establishment.

"....witnesses...are not required to swear under oath that the evidence they are giving is the truth...I am sure your concern is...the fact that the statements remain in the hearing record unchallenged."

Another letter -- the kindest one from one of the legislators:

"I am very much disturbed that a witness...would distort the true facts concerning your Noell's Ark...and I am asking the Committee to include your letter as part of the file on the hearing concerning this bill."

232

A letter from one of our veterinarians:

"It is indeed a shame that through misinformation by people who know nothing about exotic animals or the problems of their care can cast...reflection of doubt on a person such as yourself whose concern for humane care of animals has been demonstrated many times over and is indeed beyond question."

Another veterinarian:

"If I had even suspected you might ever have been inhumane with your animals in any way, I would have refused to help you with them and would have worked against you in every way possible.

I can sympathize with your distress over the false accusations which have been made by people who apparently know nothing about the needs of individual exotic animals in the hands of people, such as yourselves, who have an enviable breeding record."

This was a time of anxiety for us because we were battling Otto's affliction, and our caretaker -- an old magician and buddy, Clifford L. Faust -- had died. We did not go on the road in 1972. Then, because of all the "complications" (1. Death of our caretaker; 2. New, arbitrary legislation about transporting animals that we did not even understand; 3. Illness of poor little Otto and last but not least; 4. The way the dope and drunk problems were worsening at show time) we decided to retire, much sooner than we had intended.

Chapter Eleven

The orangutan is the only great ape with red hair and is also probably one of the most interesting of all wild animals. Much research has been done on its existence in pre-history, and huge fossil remains have been found as far north as Peking, China. Such remains may have started the "Yeti" or "Abominable Snowman" legends. The word "orangutan" is said to mean "Forest Man" or "Man of the woods" in Bornean. From a distance the great apes **do** look like big hairy men, and the orang does, especially. Unfortunately for the species, they have been killed off by humans until their natural habitat is now based only on the islands of Borneo and Sumatra in southeast Asian waters.

I have always found it interesting that gorillas and chimps, who have black hair come from Africa, where black humans originate and Orangutans, who have oriental-looking eyes, mandarin-type beards, are stoic and have red hair come from Asia where the people have almond-shaped eyes and yellow skin. This intrigues me but I've never known of a scientific study that attempts to explain the reason for this. Since one train of thought puts man's origins somehwere in Africa, it is even more interesting to notice that some chimpanzees have white skin under the black hair. Climate may have been the governing factor in these differences. At any rate it is interesting.

Like their unfortunate cousins (the gorillas), the orangutans were easy prey for protein-starved humans from prehistoric times until today! It has been said that diggings have produced evidence in the ancient caves of Western Borneo that as far back as thirty or forty thousand years ago the natives were eating orangutans. The big males were too strong for primitive man to catch, so the females and their young were usually the victims. I wonder if this could have started them into their present day life-style of "every man for himself?" In other words, could the males have learned to become loners as a means of avoiding confrontation with spear-armed humans? From some of the evidence in the caves the natives may even have raised orangutans, the same way we raise cows and hogs, to use them for food! An amusing and often-told story taken from ancient folklore is that the great apes were actually deformed humans who got lazy and went to live out in the wilds to avoid the responsibilities of civilized life. This story goes on to say they even refused to learn to talk because they are not willing to go to work or to have to pay taxes. The natives even thought that because they were so grotesque that they were cursed by God and that this gave them the right or the duty to hate them and to hunt them down and kill them in savage, cruel and inhumane ways.

Orangutans are probably stronger than chimps or gorillas because they are true tree-dwellers. They nearly never come down to the ground, and when they do they use their arms like crutches and travel faster than a man can run. However they travel even faster in the treetops, where they are more at home, by swinging gracefully from limb to limb.

Wild stories were told about the fierceness of the orangutan, just as such stories had been told about the gorilla. But, as with most wild animals, the orangutan will try to hide from humans, or better yet, will rapidly put space behind him when he sights man.

In recent years baby orangutans brought high prices and natives were bringing babies in, claiming they had fallen out of trees. Naturally this story was doubted until a white hunter shot at another type of animal to use for food. The woods were silent until the gun went off. Not far from where he stood a baby orangutan fell out of a tree. Evidently the report of the gun startled the mother who must have dropped the baby accidentally. Accordingly it was then thought that some of the natives had told the truth.

The "population explosion" presently being experienced by humanity is shrinking the land area of the world to the extent that the great apes are rapidly disappearing from their native habitats. And the destruction of the rain forests where the apes live is said to be seriously changing the weather patterns throughout the world.

When we were members of the American Association of Zoological Parks and Aquariums in 1968, we signed the pledge that we would not buy any more organutans because they had become an "endangered species." That pledge was signed in good faith by many people as a hopeful and valiant attempt to insure the safety of the fewer than 2500 individuals then living throughout the world. But almost before the ink had dried, it was said that poachers -- not to be outdone by losing the sale of **live** orangs -- began shipping **skeletons** to scientists and medical schools. A later survey then put the **world population** at fewer than two thousand. Now there are nearly none in the wilds and practically all orangutan births are happening in captivity. We were fortunate in that the two orangs we bought in 1959 presented us with a daughter, Jewel, in 1968 and Gem in 1971, a son.

When we got Pinky and Skinny (the parents of Jewel and Gem), they were "damaged" orangutans that Henry Trefflich was trying to sell. No one seemed to want them because Pinky had a finger missing, and "Skinny" was awfully thin and had a hideous scar on her arm. I heard Henry ask a famous Zoo Director if he wanted to buy them and the Director said, "No

236

thanks! My keepers would be driven to distraction by the public asking "How'd he lose his finger?" or "How'd she hurt her arm?" No – I couldn't subject my men to that."

Poor Henry was afraid he wasn't going to sell them. When he came to us, I told Bob we should get them because we had chimps and gorillas and these poor kids would make the complete group of anthropoid apes. We bought them because Henry sold them to us at a very reasonable figure, as damaged animals. Orangs were selling for $2,500.00 to $3,000.00 each at that time and Henry sold these two to us at about half-price. Skinny had a lovely little girl in 1968 and in '71 she had a precious little boy. Then in '76 she had another girl but both mother and baby died. We still have the brother and sister, Jewel and Gem, but Pinky, their father died in '79.

Pinky was a tiny, pink, ball of fluff and Skinny was about three times his size. It took a lot of years, it seemed, for them to grow up.

Pinky was a cute little Orangutan and very spoiled. He had been cared for by a lady who loved him very much. Since she bathed him and dressed him regularly, he constantly looked for affection, and for some time he got it. But some male orangutans have several nasty habits that make them quite unpopular with the people who must take care of them. One of these is the habit of spitting on spectators. Or – if you are unwary enough, he might even "sprinkle" you with Eau de Orangutan! For this reason, I was not too crazy about Pinky. He victimized me every chance he got. However, when he was about half grown, I broke him of this nasty habit, by going into the cage and spanking him. I'm sure the spanking did not hurt him, but my angry attitude probably gave him food for thought, and he never "sprinkled" me again, even though I'm sure they do these things only to get attention.

A cute write-up in the Charleston, S.C. newspaper "News & Courier" was written because of the following incident:

We were parked at Islandton, S.C. with some of Bob's in-laws. We used to stop there from time to time to visit on our way North in the Spring or on our way South in Fall. We had just bought the Orangutans and Bob let them out, in the yard. There were several huge "live oak" trees (a southern evergreen oak) in the yard and Miss "Skinny Winnie" went aloft. It was late in the afternoon and we knew she (being a wild-bred youngster) would be hard to bring down. She stayed up there all night, while Bob sat under the tree with a bright light beamed on her. About three A.M. he got me up and I sat and watched till dawn. Then I woke him and said, "If you had listened to me she'd never have been turned loose to do this so you go back and watch!" He gets by on lots less sleep than it takes for me, for some reason. It was getting late in the afternoon again, and as we sat watching her, we heard a weather forecast that **did** cause us anguish! "Clear and much colder tonight." Seeming to understand the forecast, Skinny came down rapidly and went, willingly, back into her cage. The newspaper ran the story, and even though we were not looking for publicity at that time, we have it in the scrap book. Skinny ate acorns and built several beautiful nests -- some of which could still be seen, many months later! But I believe she simply got thirsty and hungry enough that she thought it best to come down.

If that clump of trees had not been surrounded by open fields as it was we would proably have lost our pretty little girl-orang. But as it turned out, she grew up to be the mother of two lovely children -- Jewel and Gem.

But Pinky almost didn't grow up. He loved to crawl into potato bags or to wrap up in old rags. Bob put a bag in the cage with the orangs and Pinky got inside the bag. Skinny poked the top of the bag through the iron mesh between their cage and Tommy's cage. Tommy grabbed the bag and pulled. Skinny then started spinning the bag round and round, as Tommy continued to pull. I heard Pinky squeeking and went into the truck to see what he was crying about. Between Tommy's and Skinny's efforts, Pinky was almost a squashed orangutan. He was very grateful to be rescued.

And Pinky was inquisitive to a fault. There was a peephole in the solid wall between his cage and that of one of the adult chimps. Pinky poked his thumb in and got the tip of it bitten off for his pains. The finger had just barely healed when he stuck his tongue in the hole and got it split open. Then he poked a delicate part of his anatomy in the hole and got the tip of **that** nipped off! He finally gave up "exploring" the peephole.

In his book, **Almost Human,** Dr. Robert M. Yerkes says that intelligence tests done with great apes have demonstrated that they often use "tools" effectively in order to get the things that they want. We have witnessed many such spontaneous and natural demonstrations in our long years of close contact with our furred friends. I must tell you what our five-year-old (at that time) "girl-orang" did, because it was a remarkable demonstration of intelligent problem-solving.

Jewel was tied to a pine tree from which she had access to the top of our seven foot high cement wall. We tied the chain to a wrist or an ankle because we feared strangulation from a collar on the neck. When she tried to come over the wall, she held the chain with both feet, and her hands just barely reached the ground, as she suspended herself upside-down.

She had, as her favorite toy, a stainless steel milk-shaker tumbler of the type used by soda fountains. One day, as I was walking by, I saw her drop the tumbler -- out of reach. I started to go over the guard rail to get it for her, but stopped when I saw her rapid movements. I realized she had the idea she could get it herself, so I decided to stand by and see what she would do. That was when I learned we can sometimes be too helpful, and I was deeply impressed with her native ingenuity!

First she tried to reach for the cup, stretching as far as she could. But it was just out of her reach. She went to the top of the wall, looked at the cup and then seemed to be in a deep concentration for a mere ten or twelve seconds. She quickly disappeared over the wall, coming back in a twinkling with an empty citrus fruit bag in her hand. Stretching out again, she flipped the bag on the cup, but the cup was too heavy to move with so light a tool. After four or five "flips," she quickly disappeared over the wall again and in a flash returned. This time she put an orange inside the bag, which gave it more weight. When she flipped the bag and orange, the cup moved. However, since it was big at the top and small at the bottom it rolled in an arc instead of toward her. As soon as the open end faced her, she disappeared over the top again to put the bag in a safe place. Then, back over the wall again, she broke a switch some two feet long from a nearby shrub and inserted the end in the cup, and then lifted it, successfully, into her left hand. It takes longer to tell about this episode than it took for her to accomplish the entire act. I was glad I decided not to help her that time. She had demonstrated mental ingenuity far beyond her tiny five years of age! The rapidity of her movements showed she had worked it all out, mentally, before she "performed." Or perhaps she had done this before when no one was watching. However that may be, it was all done almost before I could have climbed over the fence!

In the same book, **Almost Human,** Yerkes expressed the opinion that apes may learn "ideationally with insight," when they solve problems suddenly as Jewel did, in this case. He says that insight is something that happens suddenly in the mind and not something that takes a lot of thinking – this is what he classes as "ideational behavior." Such behavior had always been thought to be exclusively humanoid in nature. Recently it has been found that this is not always the case, and Yerkes was one of the earliest pioneers in searching out and proving this truth.

The apes are pretty smart, too, in figuring out ways to make us understand what they are trying to say to us. Take, for instance, one time when Gem, our precious little boy-orang was put into a chair beside the recliner. He made a cozy nest and I pushed the recliner back and we both went to sleep for the night. Within minutes, he raised up and very gently "kissed" me on the cheek. I thought he wanted to come into my lap, but he refused my open arms. This went on three or four times. Every time I fell asleep he woke me by kissing me gently. Finally, about the fourth or fifth time, I woke up when he placed his little hand -- ever so gently -- over my mouth. I assumed, from this, I had been snoring and keeping him awake!

Both of these "kids" have picked up the habit of spitting at people to get their attention. Gem can squirt a mouthful of water a full ten or twelve feet beyond his high perch in the cage! Annoying.

It was not noon, yet, and already I had had a busy day! About nine A.M. I went outside with Gem to tie him out for the day. Instead of going straight to his tie out, I carried the little thirty-five or forty pound fellow out to the car to get him some apples -- and met Jewel headed South on the parking lawn! When she realized she had been discovered she retraced her path and went back over the wall. I saw that Bob's car was gone, so I knew I would have no help. I got Gem's apples and some for Jewel and raced back to the tie out and tied Gem as I kept up a patter of nonsensical baby talk to him for Jewel's benefit. I then went after her and she let me take her hand, but refused to go to the tie out with me. I am always afraid of being bitten, but it was unthinkable to let her go -- I feared for her safety.

Although neither Joey, Joe, nor Herman would be able (or want) to control her, I called to them, "Jewel is not cooperating with me -- I may need some help."

All three came toward me and I said, "Don't come any closer, but command her in a rough voice." Joe shouted, "You'd better behave yourself Jewel!" And she -- as was usually the case -- gave up and did what I wanted her to do, because she felt she was "outnumbered." I got her tied out and we went to her nesting box and found she had literally kicked it apart. It's fortunate she never goes far because we had no idea how long she had been out.

It didn't seem like more than five or ten minutes since I had stretched my weary body out on the couch to take a much-needed nap, when Bob popped into the trailer and said, excitedly, "Jewel is loose and I can't find her," then popped outside again.

I jumped up, terrified for her safety. She is very intelligent but would have no way of knowing the dangers of the highway out front, or the railroad track out back. I worried, too, about snakes. We simply **had** to find her, quickly. I became even more concerned, when I remembered how carefully I had tightened the link for her safety. I reasoned, "There's no way she could have freed herself. **No way!**"

Hearts pounding with fear, we ran all over the place hunting and calling. As was usual, when she performed these "escape acts," we found her near one of the vehicles on the property. She had demolished one of the kids' toys (a glass staining paint set), broken up a hen's nest, and gotten into several other bits of destructive mischief, but that had been the least of my worries. All I cared for was that she was safe.

After she was securely fastened back on her chain I went into the house to fix her a jelly sandwich as a reward for coming to me so nicely when I called her. When I came around the corner of the building, she didn't see me for several minutes, so I stood and watched in amazement until she discovered me. The little rascal had two big pieces of scrap cement she was using as tools. One piece was almost an oblong and flat -- about fourteen inches by nine or ten and some two or three inches thick. The other piece was an acute right triangle about seven or eight inches on the short side and some twelve or fourteen inches on the long side. The big piece was on the ground -- flat, and was her anvil. The link was positioned on the anvil and she was using the pointed end of the triangular piece as the peen of a hammer. Using both hands, she was pecking vigoriously on the link – a sure way to loosen the threads!

"So **that's** how she did it!" I thought.

She offered no resistance when I removed her primitive tools and gave her the sandwich.

A mirror is a fascinating and mysterious object to the primitive mind of an ape. The reaction, when they see

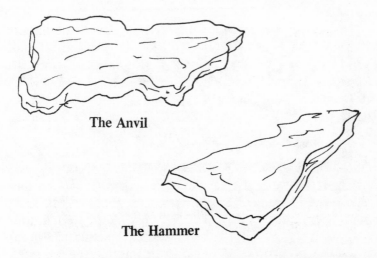

The Anvil

The Hammer

themselves for the first time, is almost always exactly the same: they see themselves, then reach behind the mirror to touch "the other monkey" who is not there. The expression of surprise is sometimes overcome by an expression of disappointment.

We had Otto, the young gorilla, in the cage with Jewel, the orangutan. I had purchased a nice shiny stainless steel serving tray to give to them as a mirror. Otto admired himself for some time as he held it before his face. Jewel saw herself in the back of the thing. Otto was sitting very still, gazing into his own eyes. Jewel advanced and when the image advanced, it scared her so she quickly backed up. When the image backed up she became bolder and advanced again. She did this six or eight times. Meanwhile Otto had decided he wanted to touch the other little gorilla and he reached behind the mirror at the exact instant that Jewel arrived close to it. Otto got a handful of hair, then eagerly looked around the mirror, and his expression of surprised disappointment was eloquent. And Jewel just knew that funny looking "red critter" in the mirror had caught her. It was a hilarious episode.

Chapter Twelve

When we retired to the Chimp Farm, we retired our animals with us. We could have sold them easily enough. But we felt they had earned their living as well as we had. Butchie and Joe died in winterquarters in 1978 within a few months of each other. The only "Athletic Ape" left is Kongo. Joe was about 46 or 48 years old -- Butch was nearing 40 and Kongo (born 2-28-48) is thirty-one as I write this.

Many of the other animals at the Chimp Farm are, in the truest sense of the word, "orphans." Most chimp trainers work only with very young animals because chimp youngsters, like human youngsters, are more tractable, energetic and teachable than adolescents of either species. Once a chimp begins to "feel his oats" he is no different than the teen-aged boy who feels a surge of rage when his father refuses to let him use the car. The big difference between the two species is the fact that the chimp has never been told that it is wrong or immoral to harm his boss. When pressed too far, a chimp can -- and sometimes does -- do horrendous damage to anyone who crosses him up. As a result of this simple fact, most trainers dispose of their chimps when they get too big to handle. Usually, a younger chimp is being trained to take the older chimp's place. This is why so many people do not realize how very big a chimp can get. When a trainer gets rid of an animal he has learned to love, he wants to place him in a good home. That is where many of our chimps came from.

A classic example of what is the least of what can happen to inexperienced people who buy an unrestrained chimp for a pet was described to us in a delightful letter by a lady from Festus, Missouri, who came to Tallahassee, Florida, to buy a chimp. Her name is Connie Braun and she says, in part:

"We were under the impression that the chimp (we had just bought) was friendlier than she really was. We did not even take a cage and as it turned out she had never had a collar or leash on so we could not control her very well. We did manage to get a chain around her waist before we started...home but as you can imagine it did not stay on very long. Well, to make a long story short it's not easy to control a frightened chimp in an automobile on a twenty-four hour ride with complete strangers....As of yet we still have not been able to get a collar or leash on her. She's very good when she's out but it's just hard to control a chimp without any restraints."

Apparently, since they do not mention being bitten or hurt, this must have been an exceptionally nice little chimp!

A goodly number have come here from misguided people who, like this lady, thought the cute little chimp would always be cute and little, only to find out to their dismay that the "cute little" fellow is already stronger than an adult human when they get him, and that he gets stronger and more head-strong as he gets older. We have taken many of these "hapless kids" into our colony. But space is limited, as are funds for this humanitarian work. When a chimp is given to us it represents more than a thousand dollars for a cage --

sometimes as much as two thousand dollars. Then the animal will be fed for the rest of its life – which runs as long as forty or more years -- and the cage must be kept clean -- it must have medical attention from time to time. Truly this is a "retirement home for aging primates." And any financial aid anyone feels he can afford to donate is accepted gratefully – in the spirit in which it is given.

Address:
Mae Noell
Chimp Farm
P. O. Box 396
Tarpon Springs,
Florida 33589

The day will come when Bob, Kongo and I will be gone, too. And that is why I felt so strongly that this book just **had** to be written. I have a keen interest in genealogy; I have found no rogues in either Bob's lines nor mine. This is a good reason to have the true story of our show on record – mainly to "give the lie" to some of the misinformation that has been dished out in the past about our show. We know we would be welcomed back any place we ever showed in if we were still trouping because we always treated our patrons with respect. We **never** called our customers "yokels" – only "towners" or "locals" – and we always gave our patrons their money's worth in entertainment.

The Photo Album

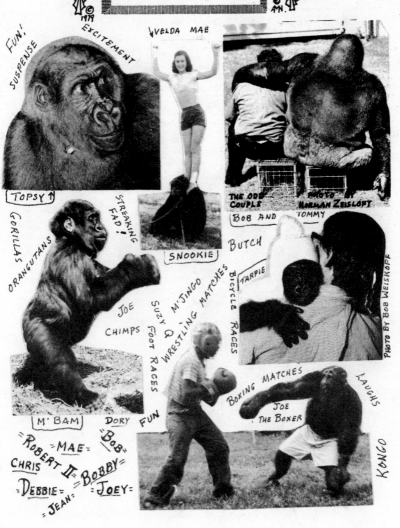

WE CAMPED ON THE LEVEE   1940

LOWER LEFT: SLIDING DOWN THE LEVEE ON DRY GRASS
LOWER RIGHT: MARDI GRAS DAY NEW ORLEANS

THIS WAS "B.C." — "BEFORE CHIMPS"

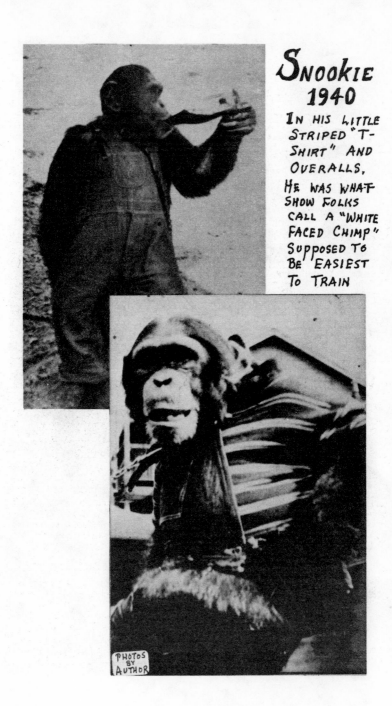

SNOOKIE
1940

IN HIS LITTLE
STRIPED "T-
SHIRT" AND
OVERALLS,
HE WAS WHAT
SHOW FOLKS
CALL A "WHITE
FACED CHIMP"
SUPPOSED TO
BE EASIEST
TO TRAIN

PHOTOS
BY
AUTHOR

SNOOKIE AND BOBBY WERE INSEPERABLE BUDDIES.
IT WASN'T SAFE FOR ANYONE TO BOTHER BOBBY
IF SNOOKIE WAS NOT LOCKED IN HIS CAGE. THESE
SNAPSHOTS WERE MADE SOON AFTER HE CAME
ON OUR OUTFIT IN LOUISIANA IN 1940.

PHOTOS
BY
AUTHOR

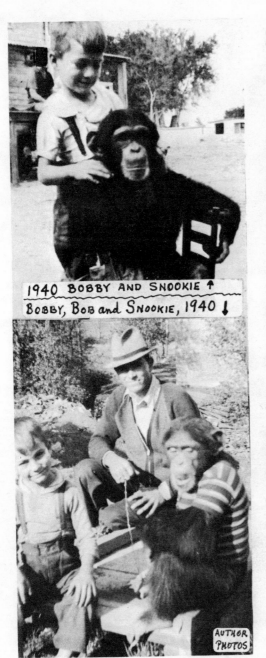

1940 BOBBY AND SNOOKIE ↑

BOBBY, BOB and SNOOKIE, 1940 ↓

SNOOKIE WAS OUTSIDE WITH THE FAMILY MORE THAN IN HIS CAGE. WE LOVED HIM AND SPENT A LOT OF TIME WITH HIM. I GOT HIM A LITTLE CHAIR WITH OCTAGON COUPONS, AND HE LOVED TO SIT ON IT. BOBBY (TOP PHOTO) IS COAXING HIM TO COME AND PLAY.

BOB, BOBBY AND SNOOKIE (LOWER PHOTO) REST ATER TAKING A WALK.

TOP PHOTO
SHOWS
WHAT
JANE
GOODALL
CALLS
THE
"PLAY
FACE."
SNOOKIE
WAS,
INDEED,
PLAYING
HERE —
LAUGHING.
ABOUT 1941

THIS IS AN
EXCELLENT
SHOT OF THE
MUZZLE.

IN THE
BOTTOM
PHOTO,
SNOOKIE
IS
EATING
AND
GIVING
THE
"FOOD
BARK."

PHOTOS
BY
AUTHOR

PROFESSIONAL WRESTLER JIMMIE RAY IN
THE ROPE ARENA WITH SNOOKIE, ABOUT
1952.

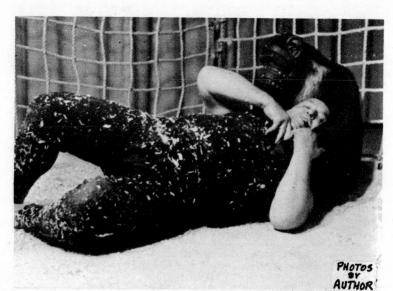

↓AFTER THE BOUT SNOOKIE SAYS "IT'S ALL IN FUN."

SUZY Q

LITTLE SUZY Q, NOELL ABOUT 1942, SMALL BUT STRONG! PHOTOS BY AUTHOR

LITTLE SUZY Q, ABOUT A YEAR LATER. A NIPPY LITTLE TYKE.

SHE WAS NAMED AFTER "THE SUZY Q" - A VIGOROUS DANCE OF THE '30's and '40's

THE CRATE IN WHICH SUZY Q ARRIVED.

LIVE STOCK

BUTCH

NORMAN ZEISLOFT PHOTO

BUTCH WAS BIG AND HUSKY BUT WAS ALWAYS GENTLE WITH WOMEN OR KIDS.

PHOTO BY AUTHOR

JOE WORE THE MUZZLE
WILLINGLY. (ABOUT
1945)

JOE THE BOXER
PHOTOS BY
THE AUTHOR

"JOE THE BOXER" HAS A FRIENDLY WORK-OUT IN MIAMI, FLORIDA - 1948

PHOTOS BY AUTHOR

JOE WORKING-OUT AT THE
TROPICAL BIRD AND MONKEY
FARM ~ MIAMI, FLA. 1948

PHOTOS
BY
AUTHOR

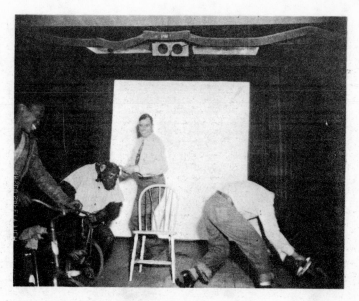

BICYCLE RACE AND A BOXING MATCH IN A PHOTO STUDIO IN NORFOLK VA ABOUT 1947

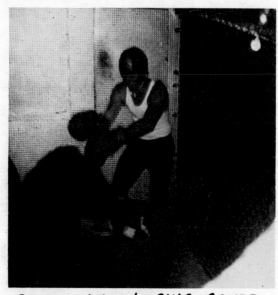

JOE
PULLS
PANTS
DOWN
AROUND
THE
MAN'S
ANKLES,

THEN---

CONTESTANT LOSING COVER-
PANTS TO JOE THE BOXER.

JUMPS
UP
IN THE
MAN'S
FACE
TO
DIS-
TRACT
HIM ---

THEN
GIVES
THE PANTS
A MIGHTY
JERK ----

SOME MEN WHO REFUSED TO PUT
THE OUTER PANTS ON ENDED
UP IN THEIR "BIRTHDAY SUITS"

THAT
PULLS
THE
MAN
COMPLETELY
OFF
HIS
FEET!

KONGO

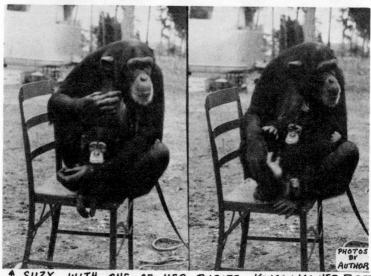

PHOTOS
BY
AUTHOR

↑ SUZY WITH ONE OF HER BABIES. KONGO WAS HER FIRST.
BORN — FEB. 28, 1948

KONGO IN HIS PLAY-
PEN. AGE ABOUT 10
OR 12 MONTHS SUZY'S
FIRST

KONGO, ABOUT 1950
IN THE ARMS OF HIS
OLD BUDDY, THE LATE
MAGICIAN CLIFF
FAUST

BELOW
KONGO, ABOUT
1949, BOB NOELL
LEFT, AND MAE
NOELL, RIGHT

BORN IN 48 IN
MIAMI, FLA., KONGO
BECAME OUR
STAR WRESTLER

KONGO LOVED
ROBERT E. NOELL
II — OUR
GRANDSON. ↑
HERE HE GAVE
THE BABY A
KISS,

EVEN LATER →
THEY WERE
BUDDIES.
HERE KONGO
WEARS A
COMIC
NOSE AND
EYEGLASSES →

ORANGUTANS

Bob
WITH OUR
MATRON
ORANGUTAN
"SKINNY
WINNIE,"

SHE WAS
SWEET
AND GENTLE
ALL
HER LIFE

(MOTHER OF
JEWEL AND
GEM)

PHOTOS
BY BOB WEISKOPF

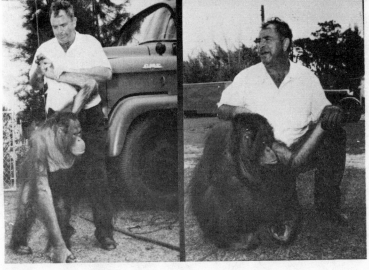

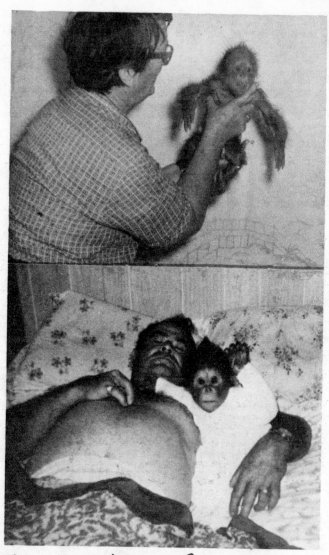

TOP PHOTO - BY LORAYNE CARLSON - SHOWS
INFANT JEWEL LESS THAN TWO HOURS OLD,
WITH MAE. LOWER PHOTO - BY AUTHOR -
SHOWS JEWEL, AGED ABOUT TWO MONTHS.
CAMERA FLASH WOKE THE BABY BUT
BOB SLEPT ON.

BECAUSE SHE WAS BORN IN 1968, JEWEL GOT
TO TRAVEL THREE SEASONS WITH THE SHOW. GEM,
HER LITTLE BROTHER, WAS BORN AFTER WE
RETIRED, IN 1971. HERE BOB HOLDS JEWEL – 1969

PHOTO BY NORM ZEISLOFT

DEBBIE DEDDO (OUR GRAND DAUGHTER) WITH JEWEL ABOUT 1970 ↑

MAE WITH LITTLE GEM ABOUT 1974 — PHOTO BY ROGER BOYD, JR.

"GEM" IN MAE'S ARMS
PHOTO BY ROGER BOYD, JR.

PHIL CARROLL

THE LATE PHIL CARROLL WAS AN ANIMAL DEALER.
HE BROUGHT MANY SPECIES OF LIVE ANIMALS OUT
OF AFRICA FOR MANY YEARS. HE WAS DISTRESSED
AND ANGRY AT THE WAY GORILLAS WERE BEING
WANTONLY SLAUGHTERED BY NATIVES WHILE HE
AND OTHER DEALERS WERE UNABLE TO GET
PERMITS FOR CAPTURING LIVE ANIMALS FOR ZOOS.
HE GAVE ME THESE PICTURES WHEN I TOLD HIM
I INTENDED TO WRITE A BOOK ABOUT THE
SHOW. PHOTO ABOVE SHOWS PHIL WITH THE PYGMIES.

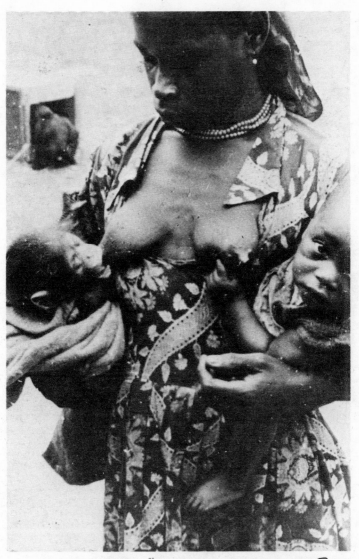

PHOTO GIVEN TO MAE BY ANIMAL COLLECTOR PHIL
CARROLL - (1958). NURSING MOTHER TAKING CARE OF
INFANT CHIMPANZEE. ON SAFARI IN THE OLD DAYS
THEY CARRIED NO REFRIGERATION. LACTATING MOTHERS
WERE HIRED TO WET-NURSE INFANTS THEY
PLANNED TO BRING BACK.

MAY 22, 1957   P.J. CARROLL
NATIVES KILL
BUT TRY TO
GET PERMIT TO
EXPORT LIVE
TO ZOOS THIS
IS ANIMAL PROTECTION   NO 15
                        SKULLS

PHOTOS GIVEN TO MAE
FOR THIS BOOK BY THE
LATE PHIL CARROLL

ON ROAD
ABONG M'BANG
MAY 6, 1957
25 GORILLA SKULLS
COLLECTED IN
98 Kelometers
P. J. CAROLL

2 GORILLAS dead
RESULT BEING SHOT
AND BRUTAL BEATING
during CAPTURE BY
ABONG ABONG PYGMIES
P. CARROLL
Yaounde Oct. 24/58

POOR LITTLE BABIES!

SAD PICTURES. AND WHAT IS EVEN WORSE — THE
SLAUGHTER STILL GOES ON. DR. ROBERT M. YERKES
GUESSED (IN 1950) THE GORILLA WOULD BE EXTINCT
IN 100 YEARS. IT MAY BE MUCH SOONER. EVEN
THAT BRAVE LADY — DIANE FOSSEY — HAS KNOWN
THE HEARTBREAK OF SEEING HER STUDY SPEC-
IMENS SLAUGHTERED — EITHER SPITEFULLY OR
RITUALISTICALLY. AN EXTREMELY SAD SITUATION.

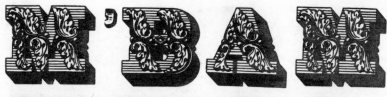

M'BAM ENJOYS A
SOFT DRINK
PHOTO BY AUTHOR

M'JINGO

M'JINGO WAS A HANDSOME AND
AFFECTIONATE FRIEND. WE GOT HIM
FROM BILL SAID OF OHIO. STUDIO PHOTO.

JEAN, BOBBY'S WIFE
WITH LAZY M'JINGO

(PHOTO BY AUTHOR)

M'JINGO HAD A
BOSTON TERRIER FOR A
PET. (PHOTO BY AUTHOR)

BOB AND M'JINGO
TAKING A NAP TOGETHER

(PHOTO BY THE AUTHOR)

PHOTOGRAPHS BY
NORMAN ZEISLOFT

"UM-YUM-YUM."
TOMMY LOVES HIS
MILK.

BOB AND TOMMY
GETTING READY
FOR THE "BANANA
TRICK." (BOB
TAKES A BIG
BITE, THEN
TRANSFERS IT
MOUTH TO MOUTH
WITH TOMMY.)
(overleaf)

TOMMY WANTS BOB TO "HURRY UP" AND GIVE THAT BANANA!

↓ BOB, (IN SHIRT TORN FROM EARLIER WRESTLING FUN) PEELS ANOTHER BANANA FOR THE "TRICK." NOTICE, TOMMY'S TUMMY IS ALREADY ↓ FULL.

PHOTOGRAPHS BY NORMAN ZEISLOFT

BOB PUTS A BIG PIECE OF THE BANANA IN HIS
MOUTH, ABOVE. THEN (BELOW) TOMMY TAKES IT —
GENTLY — AWAY FROM HIM. THIS LITTLE RITUAL WAS
ONE THE CROWDS FOUND MOST UNBELIEVABLE.

THIS REMARKABLE PHOTO (BY
NORMAN ZEISLOFT) SHOWS ADULT
TOMMY STILL GIVING PLAYFUL
SHOULDER BITES TO BOB. AT
THIS TIME HE WAS OBESE AND
WE "GUESS-TIMATED" HE WEIGHED 600

THIS IS ONE OF THE FAMOUS
PRIZE-WINNING PICTURES MADE
BY NORMAN ZEISLOFT, AT THE
CHIMP FARM, TARPON SPRINGS.
FLA. BOB NOELL and TOMMY

Gorilla suddenly attacks trainer
— crushes him to death

BOB AND TOMMY READING FALSE REPORT
ABOUT HOW THEY BOTH DIED, DON'T BE-
LIEVE EVERYTHING YOU READ!

GENTLE TOMMY PLAYING CARE-
FULLY WITH A YOUNG PUPPY
PHOTO BY NORMAN ZEISLOFT.

NORMAN ZEISLOFT PHOTOGRAPH

GOTCHA!

Bob and Tommy
Resting after a Romp
at the Tarpon Springs, Fla.
Winter Home — The Chimp. Farm.

TOMMY PLAYFULLY HUSTLES MAE ACROSS
THE LOT WITH THE "RUMP BITE,"

TWINS

We are proud of our birth record at the Chimp Farm. Forty five babies were born to our residents (chimp retirees) between 1948 and 1978. Especially rewarding was the birth of Pete and Donna — fraternal twins — born to Sweet Little JoAnn Register, May 21, 1967. (Photos by Bob Weiskopf)

"PETE" WAS NAMED AFTER PETER THORNTON OF KDKA-T-V, AND DONNA WAS NAMED AFTER DON RIGGS ("B'WANA DON") BOTH OF PITTSBURGH, PENN. = PHOTO BELOW SHOWS OUR GRANDSON, JOEY DEDDO HOLDING PETE, AND DEBBIE DEDDO (JOEY'S SISTER) IS HOLDING DONNA.

TOP PHOTO BY NORMAN
ZEISLOFT, SHOWS TARPIE ALMOST
GROWN - LAUGHING WHEN TICKLED.
.... FLA 1970

LOWER PHOTO BY BOB
WEISKOPF SHOWS TARPIE AS
A VERY SICK INFANT IN
MAE'S ARMS.   1965

This beautifully eloquent photo was made at Cayce, South Carolina (near Columbia) by Dave Underwood. Tarpie is asking our grand-daughter, Debbie Deddo, to pick her up.

TARPIE COULD GET
ONLY HER HEAD AND
ONE ARM OUT OF
THE TINY FEED DOOR
IN HER CAGE. ONE
NIGHT, AS I WAS
GOING OUT TO PUT
ON THE SHOW – SHE
WOULD NOT LET ME
CLOSE THE FEED
DOOR. IT TOOK
SOME FOUR OR FIVE
HOURS TO DO ONE
NIGHT'S WORK.
WHILE I WAS GONE, –

—MY LITTLE HOUSE-WRECKING IMP AMUSED HER-
SELF BY COMPLETELY WRECKING THE FRONT ROOM OF
OUR TRAILER! USING A HUGE BEACH TOWEL I HAD
GIVEN HER TO USE AS A BLANKET, SHE LASSOED
EVERYTHING THAT WAS WITHIN SIX FEET OF HER CAGE
AND EITHER DESTROYED WHATEVER IT WAS — OR

HAD IT IN THE
CAGE WITH HER.
WHAT A
CLEVER LITTLE
RASCAL! AND
THIS WHEN SHE
WEIGHED LESS
THAN FIFTEEN
POUNDS!

PHOTOS
BY
AUTHOR

IN HER BOOK
"TOTO AND I"
A. MARIA HOYT
TOLD HOW TOTO
SELECTED A
WHITE CAT FOR
A PET. OUR
TARPLE PICKED
THIS WHITE
PUPPY — JUST
LIKE TOPSY
DID — YEARS
BEFORE.

THE PUPPY
MUST HAVE
ENJOYED IT,
BECAUSE IT
ALWAYS CAME
BACK FOR
MORE LOVING

PHOTOS
BY
NORMAN
ZEISLOFT

TOP LEFT: " OH, BOY ! THE BOSS
IS BUYING WATERMELONS !
WONDER IF I GET SOME ?"

"AH ! THIS IS GREAT ! HE DIDN'T
FORGET TO GIVE ME SOME !"

"UM YUM — MY FAVORITE FRUIT !"

AUTHOR PHOTOS

Topsy

OUR TWO NOELL GRANDSONS, CHRIS (LEFT) AND ROBERT (RIGHT) ROMPED WITH TOPSY WHO LOVED THE KIDS. (PHOTOS BY AUTHOR)

TOPSY IN THE OLD LOG HOUSE AT THE CHIMP FARM.

OUR DAUGHTER, VELDA MAE (NOELL) DEDDO, TRYING TO COAX TOPSY INTO PUTTING THE COLLAR BACK ON.

TOMMY

TOMMY SAT ON
MY LAP FROM A
13 POUND BABY
UNTIL HE WEIGHED
300 POUNDS. Mae

THE "PLAY-BITE."
TOMMY, ABOVE,
PLAYING WITH BOB
ABOUT 1958.

BELOW, MORE
PLAY-BITE FUN, ABOUT
1963-4. PHOTOS BY
AUTHOR

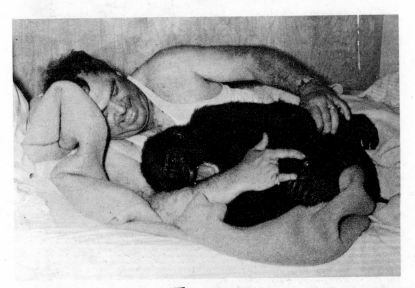

INFANT TOMMY IN BED
PLAYING WITH BOB

ADULT TOMMY + BOB
(NOTICE PICKET SHOW FENCE)
PHOTOS BY THE AUTHOR

TOMMY WEIGHED A
TINY THIRTEEN POUNDS
WHEN HE CAME TO US.
WE "WRESTLED" VERY
GENTLY WITH HIM
AND BOTH HE AND WE
WOULD "PLAY-BITE"
AT EACH OTHER.
THIS KIND OF PLAY
CARRIED OVER INTO
ADULTHOOD.

SHIRTS—WHICH WE
BOUGHT BY THE HUN-
DREDS AT GOODWILL
AND SALVATION ARMY
STORES—WERE A VERY
SPECIAL KIND OF FUN
FOR ALL OUR GORILLA
CHILDREN. THEY LOVED
TO HEAR THE CLOTH
RIP AND TO HEAR THE
AUDIENCES GASP WHEN
THEY TORE THEM.

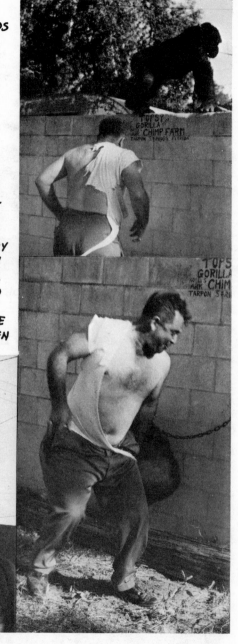

TOMMY POSING
WITH MAE IN RIDE
FOR NEWSPAPER MAN

SNEAK ATTACK ↑
"RUMP BITE"
ALL IN FUN.

← OUR SON, BOBBY
RIDES MUZZLED
TOMMY'S BACK

THE SHOULDER BITE, MORE "MOCK BATTLE" FUN

NOTICE BOB USING FLY-SWATTER FOR CONTROL!

PHOTOS BY AUTHOR

TOMMY'S
PLAYFUL
RUMP
BITE.
THIS
WAS
USUALLY
DONE
AS A
SUDDEN
"SNEAK
ATTACK"
AND
AT THE
MOST
UN-
EXPECT-
ED
MOMENT.
ALL
IN
FUN.

PHOTOS
BY
AUTHOR
ABOUT
1961
(ABOVE)
and
1965
(BELOW)

GOOD
CLEAN
WRESTLING
FUN.

TOMMY
LOVED
TO
PLAY
WITH
BOB

PHOTOS
MADE
BY
AUTHOR
ABOUT
1967

TOMMY SITTING ON MAE'S LAP INSIDE GORILLA SHOW SIDE-
WALL.   PHOTO BY NEWS-MAN DON RIGGS, 1962

BOB NOELL AND THE LAUGH GORILLA SHOW FANS LOVED
PHOTO BY THE AUTHOR

AFTER TOMMY HAD BEEN TIED OUT ALL DAY AND WAS COMING BACK TO HIS CAGE, I WOULD SIT AT A HANDY SPOT IN HIS PATH WITH A BAG OF TREATS. HE ALWAYS STOPPED TO SEE WHAT I HAD FOR HIM, I WOULD HAND-FEED ONE OR TWO ITEMS, THEN GIVE HIM THE BAG. HE WOULD THEN BE EAGER TO GET IN HIS CAGE SO HE COULD EAT HIS "GOODIES,

SNAPSHOTS
WERE MADE
BY OUR GRAND-
DAUGHTER,
DEBBIE DEDDO,
THROUGH THE
BACK WINDOW
OF OUR
TRAILER.
  TOMMY—
LIKE ALL
GORILLAS—
LIKED TO
FRIGHTEN
PEOPLE WITH
HIS PLAYFUL
CHARGES.
WHEN HE
SPIED
DEBBIE AT
THE WINDOW
HE CHARGED,
AND DEBBIE
DISCOVERED
HERSELF AT
THE OTHER
END OF THE
TRAILER
AND DIDN'T
REMEMBER
RUNNING
THERE!
TOMMY'S
FUN.

On good, warm days we tied the "Gorilla Children" under a big Pine Tree in our spacious yard, where we could play with them. Here ←Tommy shows anticipation --- Bob is bringing him a favorite treat; a half-gallon of milk.

Photographs by Norman Zeisloft

TARPIE KISSING
THE PUPPY

PHOTO BY ZEISLOFT

PHOTOS BY NORM ZEISLOFT

OUR BEAUTIFUL GIRL-RILLA - TARPIE.

BEAUTIFUL, LOVING AND PLAYFUL
TARPIE IN THE AUTHOR'S LAP.
PHOTO BY NORMAN ZEISLOFT.

OUR GRANDSON + TARPIE

THE FOLLOWING PHOTOGRAPHS OF JOEY
DEDDO PLAYING WITH TARPIE WERE
MADE BY THE AWARD-WINNING NEWS-
PAPER PHOTOGRAPHER, WHO IS ALSO A
CHERISHED FRIEND, NORMAN ZEISLOFT.

LOOKS ROUGH BUT
SHE LOVED JOEY

NORMAN ZEISLOFT PHOTOS

"TARDIE WINS THE "FIGHT"—JOEY SAYS "AUNTIE"
NORMAN ZEISLOFT - PHOTOS.

OTTO SAYS FAREWELL TO ANNE, HIS OLD BUDDY, BEFORE THE WEDDING.

PHOTOGRAPHS BY NORMAN ZEISLOFT.

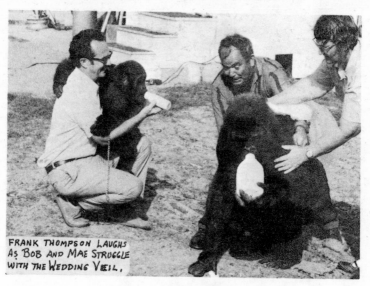

FRANK THOMPSON LAUGHS AS BOB AND MAE STRUGGLE WITH THE WEDDING VEIL.

ONCE WE GOT IT ON HER, MISS TARPIE WORE HER WEDDING VEIL PROUDLY

PHOTOS BY NORMAN ZEISLOFT

FRANK OFFICIATES AS THEY DRINK THE NUPTIAL TOAST.

THE NUPTIAL
EMBRACE — LOVE
AT FIRST SIGHT

THE TWINS ACTED
AS FLOWER GIRL
AND RING BEARER
—RELUCTANTLY

"—COME WITH ME TO THE CASBAH—"

WEDDING'S OVER AND THE HAPPY COUPLE HEADS FOR THE HILLS.

(PHOTO BY NORMAN ZEISLOFT)

WHILE WE WERE NEAR WASHINGTON D.C. WE WERE
HONORED BY A VISIT - INSIDE OUR SIDEWALK TO WATCH
BOB PLAY WITH TOMMY - WITH DR. AND MRS. WILLIAM
MANN (CENTER) AND THE MELVIN HILBRETHS. ABOUT 1956.?

ABOUT 1941 - LOUISIANA - GORILLA SHOW
CROSSING A BAYOU ON A PRIMITIVE
FERRY. HOUSE CAR, LEFT - SHOW, RIGHT

ABOUT 1939 GORILLA
SHOW CAMPING OUT AT
VIRGINIA BEACH, VA.

NOELL'S ARK

GORILLA SHOW

WINTER QUARTERS

GORILLA SHOW WINTER QUARTERS SIGN ON
FRONT WALL AT TARPON SPRINGS, FLORIDA
PAINTED BY ARTIST ⸴⸴ PHOTOGRAPH BY
O.D. ABSTON ⸴⸴ BOB WEISKOPF - 1979

B.C.

BOB AND MAE NOELL
BEFORE CHIMPS

BEFORE WE HAD CHIMPS WE LOOKED AND ACTED
LIKE EVERY OTHER YOUNG COUPLE : --
PERFECTLY NORMAL.

A.C.

BOB AND MAE
AFTER CHIMPS.

AFTER WE GOT THE CHIMPS FANCY CLOTHES WERE
"OUT." BOB GAVE UP NECKTIES FOR SAFETY'S SAKE,
AND FOR THE SAME REASON MAE GAVE UP LONG HAIR,
DRESSES AND HIGH HEELS.

WEATHER

BOB STANDING BY THE ARK MAY FIRST IN PENNA. SNOW

↑ AS OUTDOOR SHOW PEOPLE WE HAVE HAD OUR SHARE OF PROBLEMS WITH WEATHER, SNOW ON OPENING DAY IN PENNSYLVANIA ON HELLMAN'S BIG H SHOWS. WE WERE LUCKY WE SUFFERED NO DAMAGE TO THE ARK WHEN "HAZEL" ↓ STRUCK BEAM'S ATTRACTIONS AT ROXBORO, N.C. AND FALL RAINS ALMOST FLOATED THE 16 TON ARK IN S.C. ↑

WIND

RAIN